DATE DUE

CBMS

Conference Board of the Mathematical Sciences

Issues in Mathematics Education

Volume 14

Enhancing University Mathematics

Proceedings of the First KAIST International Symposium on Teaching

Ki Hyoung Ko
Deane Arganbright
Editors

American Mathematical Society
Providence, Rhode Island
in cooperation with
Mathematical Association of America
Washington, D. C.

2000 *Mathematics Subject Classification.* Primary 00A35, 97–06;
Secondary 97B40, 97D40, 97D50, 97U70.

The text from question 2 in the Appendix and the figure in question 3 in the Appendix, both on p. 14, are reprinted with permission from John Wiley & Sons, Inc.

Library of Congress Cataloging-in-Publication Data

KAIST International Symposium on Enhancing University Mathematics Teaching (1st : 2005 : Daejeon, Korea)
 Enhancing university mathematics : proceedings of the First KAIST International Symposium on Teaching / Ki Hyoung Ko, Deane Arganbright, editors.
  p. cm. — (Issues in mathematics education, ISSN 1047-398X ; v. 14)
 Includes bibliographical references and index.
 ISBN 978-0-8218-4194-5 (alk. paper)
  1. Mathematics—Study and teaching (Higher)—Congresses. 2. Electronic spreadsheets in education—Congresses. 3. Mathematics—Data processing—Congresses. 4. Microsoft Excel (Computer file)—Congresses. I. Ko, Ki Hyoung. II. Arganbright, Deane. III. Conference Board of the Mathematical Sciences. IV. Title.

QA19.C45K35   2005
510.71′1—dc22

2007060787

Contents

Preface

The First KAIST International Symposium on Enhancing University Mathematics Teaching was held in the Creative Learning Building on the Daejeon campus of the Korea Advanced Institute of Science and Technology from May 12 through May 16, 2005. There were 80 registered participants, including 20 international guests. The academic program consisted of eighteen invited presentations of 30–40 minutes, four 20-minute contributed papers, and three 90-minute workshops. The symposium speakers came from the countries of Korea, United States, Austria, Germany, Bulgaria, Turkey, Australia, Russia, and Japan. These proceedings contain 23 papers, representing all but two of the presentations. Video recordings of the presentations will help KAIST graduate students in developing their teaching abilities. In addition to the talks, Professor Erich Neuwirth of the University of Vienna gave an evening musical presentation, Tuning Musical Instruments with Mathematical Principles, as the 3rd KAIST Open Lecture on Sharing Mathematical Experiences. Other social activities included dinners, a reception on Friday, and a day at the Korean Folk Village in Suwon for the principal international speakers. Several speakers also gave presentations in other Korean universities after the symposium. We hope that the symposium will help in the development of new collaborative efforts among Korean and international universities in teaching mathematics.

University mathematicians have two primary professional foci. One is the creation of new mathematics through research and the dissemination of their discoveries through publications in research journals. A second, and equally important, focus lies in teaching a wide range of students in the classrooms. This symposium was directed toward the second focus, presenting a broad range of ways in which both new and experienced faculty can enhance and diversify their approaches to teaching. The symposium focused primarily on undergraduate teaching. While there were strong components on service teaching and the use of technology in teaching, the presentations covered a broad range of ideas. We were fortunate to have many speakers who not only excel in mathematical research, but also have devoted years to developing effective ways to enhance the teaching and presentation of mathematics. Most of the speakers have won national recognition for teaching in their home nations. This symposium was designed to be of value not only for current university mathematics educators, but also for the graduate students who will be tomorrow's university teachers. We were happy to have a significant number of graduate students participating.

As one of Korea's internationally recognized mathematics departments, the Department of Mathematics at KAIST strives to provide excellence in its teaching to complement its highly regarded research program. This symposium was a part of its effort to fulfill this commitment to teaching. Thanks to the devotion of its faculty and staff as well as its chair, the department was happy to host this symposium. We were supported substantially by the active and gracious participation of many graduate students who were essential in helping the event to run smoothly. The valuable support of the staff of the Creative Learning Building was also much appreciated. Finally, strong financial support from the KAIST Office of Public and International Relations and the KAIST Information Center for Mathematical Sciences made the event possible. The KAIST Department of Mathematics wishes to express its deep gratitude to everyone who contributed to making the symposium a successful and enjoyable experience. The editors express their deep appreciation to the Conference Board of the Mathematical Sciences for making this volume widely available to the mathematical community.

June 7, 2007
Ki Hyoung Ko
Deane Arganbright

List of Participants

Byung Hee An
anbyhee@knot.kaist.ac.kr
Korea Advanced Institute of Science
and Technology

Deane Arganbright
dearganbright@yahoo.com
Korea Advanced Institute of Science
and Technology
Currently: Martin, TN, USA

Huriye Arikan
huriye@sabanciuniv.edu
Sabanci University, Turkey

Thomas Banchoff
tfb@cs.brown.edu
Brown University, USA

Cycong-Mi Cho
gcho@dongdeo.ac.kr
Dongseo University

Young Han Choe
yhchoe@kaist.ac.kr
Korea Advanced Institute of Science
and Technology

Eun-mi Choi
emc@hannam.ac.kr
Hannam University

Solomon Friedberg
friedber@bc.edu
Boston College, USA

Jae Sun Ha
hjs83@kaist.ac.kr
Korea Advanced Institute of Science
and Technology

Deborah Hughes Hallett
dhh@math.arizona.edu
Harvard University and University of
Arizona, USA

Soon Jo Hong
lx.o.xla@kaist.ac.kr
Korea Advanced Institute of Science
and Technology

Youngsik Huh
yshuh@hanyang.ac.kr
Hanyang University

Taek-Kyu Hwang
hwangtaekkyu@kaist.ac.kr
Korea Advanced Institute of Science
and Technology

Choon Bae Jeon
jcbout@math.kaist.ac.kr
Daeduk College

Gyo Taek Jin
JinGyoTaek@kaist.ac.kr
Korea Advanced Institute of Science
and Technology

Hoyun Jung
DOSAL@kaist.ac.kr
Korea Advanced Institute of Science
and Technology

Mee Kwang Kang
mee@deu.ac.kr
Dongeui University

Seok-Jin Kang
sjkang@math.snu.ac.kr
Seoul National University

Seong Joo Kang
sjkang@duksung.ac.kr
Duksung Women's University

Dong Su Kim
dskim@math.kaist.ac.kr
Korea Advanced Institute of Science
and Technology

Hee Kyu Kim
KimHeeKyu@kaist.ac.kr
Korea Advanced Institute of Science
and Technology

Hun Kim
Hunkim@kaist.ac.kr
Korea Advanced Institute of Science
and Technology

Jee Hyoun Kim
jeehyun4@kaist.ac.kr
Korea Advanced Institute of Science
and Technology

Jin-Young Kim
Sunchon National University

Ki Chan Kim
math_chan@kaist.ac.kr
Korea Advanced Institute of Science
and Technology

Seon Hae Kim
hyperbolic@kaist.ac.kr
Korea Advanced Institute of Science
and Technology

Sung-a Kim
sakim@woosuk.ac.kr
Woosuk University

Sung Hak Kim
oraclerain@kaist.ac.kr
Korea Advanced Institute of Science
and Technology

Sung-Ock Kim
sokim@handong.edu
Handong Global University

Sung Sook Kim
sskim@pcu.ac.kr
Paichai University

Wan soon Kim
kimws@office.hoseo.ac.kr
Hoseo University

Yean Su Kim
zagal@kaist.ac.kr
Korea Advanced Institute of Science
and Technology

Ki Hyoung Ko
knot@knot.kaist.ac.kr
Korea Advanced Institute of Science
and Technology

Ulrich Kortenkamp
Ulrich.Kortenkamp@ph-gmuend.de
Technical University of Berlin,
Germany
*Currently: University of Education
Schwabisch Gmund, Germany*

Seung Woo Kuk
causyong@kaist.ac.kr
Korea Advanced Institute of Science
and Technology

Min Suk Kwak
quacks@kaist.ac.kr
Korea Advanced Institute of Science
and Technology

Oh Nam Kwon
onkwon@snu.ac.kr
Seoul National University

Byoung Soo Lee
bslee@ks.ac.kr
Kyounsung University

Gyu Bong Lee
gblee@mail.pcu.ac.kr
Paichai University

Hye-Kyung Lee
Inje University

Jae Hak Lee
jaelee@cc.knue.ac.kr
Korea National University of Education

Jang Won Lee
leejw@knot.kaist.ac.kr
Korea Advanced Institute of Science
and Technology

Kang-Sub Lee
Dongguk University

Myung Woo Lee
leemw2005@kaist.ac.kr
Korea Advanced Institute of Science
and Technology

Sang-Gu Lee
sglee@math.skku.ac.kr
Sungkyunkwan University

Chi-Kwong Li
ckli@math.wm.edu
College of William and Mary, USA

Narita Masahiro
narita@yamanashi.ac.jp
University of Yamanashi, Japan

William G. McCallum
wmc@math.arizona.edu
University of Arizona, USA

Terence Mills
T.Mills@latrobe.edu.au
La Trobe University, Australia

Erich Neuwirth
erich.neuwirth@univie.ac.at
University of Vienna, Austria

Dam Won Oh
lovecinema_zz@kaist.ac.kr
Korea Advanced Institute of Science
and Technology

Warren Page
Wxpny@aol.com
Yonkers, NY, USA

Hyo Won Park
hwowon@knot.kaist.ac.kr
Korea Advanced Institute of Science
and Technology

Seo Jung Park
micha82@hanmail.net
Korea Advanced Institute of Science
and Technology

Seonieong Park
sjeongp@kaist.ac.kr
Korea Advanced Institute of Science
and Technology

Si-Sun Ryu
Sunchon National University

James Sandefur
sandefur@georgetown.edu
Georgetown University, USA

David A.Santos
dsantos@ccp.edu
Community College of Philadelphia,
USA

Leon H. Seitelman
LSeitelman@aol.com
Glastonbury, CT, USA

Nikolay Shilov
shilov@iis.nsk.su
Korea Advanced Institute of Science
and Technology
*Currently: Institute of Informatics
Systems of Russian Academy of
Science, Russia*

Insun Shin
shinis@knue.ac.kr
Korea National University of Education

Robert S. Smith
smithrs@muohio.edu
Miami University, USA

Alexander Stanoyevitch
astanoyevitch@csudh.edu
University of Guam, USA
*Currently: California State University -
Dominquez Hills, USA*

T. Christine Stevens
stevensc@slu.edu
St. Louis University, USA

Gabriele Uchida
gabriele.uchida@univie.ac.at
University of Vienna, Austria

Elena Varbanova
elvar@tu-sofia.bg
Technical University–Sofia, Bulgaria

Seong-Deog Yang
sdyang@math.korea.ac.kr
Korea University

Jae Il Yoo
jail222@kaist.ac.kr
Korea Advanced Institute of Science
and Technology

Ji Sang Yoo
jisangy@kaist.ac.kr
Korea Advanced Institute of Science
and Technology

CBMS Issues in Mathematics Education
Volume **14**, 2007

Mathematics in General Education at KAIST

Ki Hyoung Ko

ABSTRACT. While the Mathematics Department of KAIST has a strong emphasis on producing excellent research, and it continues to be successful in maintaining high numbers of outstanding undergraduate and graduate majors, it also plays a major role in providing high-quality service courses for the entire institution. This paper provides a brief overview of this aspect, and looks at some of the issues that arise in this responsibility.

1. Introduction

1.1. About Institution. KAIST, the Korea Advanced Institute of Science and Technology, was established in Seoul 1981 as a research institute with a teaching program that consisted only of graduate-level classes. In 1989, the institution moved to the nation's new science center, Daedcok Science Town, located in Daejeon. It sits amidst numerous other world-class research institutes of science, technology, and informatics. The business magazine Asiaweek has rated KAIST several times as Asia's foremost university of science and technology [1]. In 2004, The Chronicle of Higher Education featured KAIST as one of the top three universities of Korea [2]. The impact of KAIST has been significant in developing the human resources that have brought Korea success and prosperity. For example about 10% of the Science and Engineering professors in Korean universities and about 20% of the doctor class researchers in Korean industry are alumni of KAIST.

KAIST expanded its program to include undergraduate students in 1984, and that program has developed into an increasingly vital component of the university. While the institution and its mathematics department continues to emphasize its cutting-edge research, its faculty members also strive for effective teaching in all areas, including service courses. KAIST has a faculty of approximately 400 professors in 14 departments and several interdisciplinary programs in science and engineering. It has 3,000 undergraduate and 4,500 graduate students, and supports many postdoctoral and research positions filled with both Korean and international researchers. Although most of KAIST's students come from Korea, the number of international graduate and undergraduate students is increasing steadily. The academic year starts in March, and consists of full semesters in Spring and Fall, and shorter Summer and Winter terms for more condensed courses, together with specialized workshops, camps, and conferences.

1.2. Mathematics at KAIST. The Department of Mathematics has 24 professors, 169 undergraduate majors, and 112 graduate students. After graduation, most undergraduate mathematics majors go to graduate school to pursue higher degrees, about half in areas other than mathematics. Most graduate students earning a masters degree at KAIST obtain industry jobs, while equal proportions of PhDs obtain academic, research, and industry positions. The department maintains a strong undergraduate major program producing about 20 graduates per year. Many of these pursue graduate study both at KAIST and in the leading universities of the United States and other nations.

2. Service Courses

The undergraduate student body at KAIST is a highly qualified and well-motivated group. Most have graduated from the nation's leading science high schools and have completed a substantial yearlong course in single variable calculus. This means that service courses at the institution begin at a very high level. Entering first year students do not have majors, but pursue a general curriculum that will enable them to choose a major at the end of their first year. All first year students enroll in a substantial calculus course, as most will be using calculus throughout their future studies at KAIST. The following list provides a glimpse of the primary service courses in mathematics. Each of the two calculus courses is offered in only one semester.

- Compulsuory
  - Calculus I or Honors Calculus I – Spring
  - Calculus II or Honors Calculus II – Fall
- Elective
  - Linear Algebra – Spring and Fall
  - Engineering Mathematics I – Spring
  - Engineering Mathematics II – Fall
  - Probability and Statistics – Spring

2.1. Course Overviews. While the content of the service courses is similar to that found in other universities, KAIST is distinctive in the fact that its service courses are substantial, not only in the amount of material that is included, but also in the sophistication of the courses and in the expected level of student performance. All textbooks that are used are well-regarded texts written in English. In calculus, the students will have had a year of single variable calculus in high school. Consequently, at KAIST the first semester of calculus provides both a quick review of ideas encountered previously, together with a substantial emphasis on those ideas of single variable calculus that are not covered in high school. Students also learn how to do delta-epsilon and other proofs. The current text is a version of the classical Thomas text [3]. The second semester of calculus is a substantial vector calculus course. The current text [4], takes a very sophisticated approach. Calculus provides both standard and honors sections. These use the same basic syllabus, exams, and grading. The difference between them is in the greater emphasis on theory in lectures and the more challenging problems in the honors sections. Since first-year students ultimately will choose their majors, it is vital to the department to offer good calculus classes in order to attract its majors. The paper [5] discusses further details on the calculus program. Although optional for some disciplines, linear algebra also is a major class, preparing students for their studies in a wide range of disciplines. The KAIST course covers a substantial amount of material, providing a balanced blend of computation, theory, and applications. The current text is [6]. The engineering mathematics and statistics courses have smaller enrollments. Engineering Mathematics provides students with a study of insert something here, while Statistics presents a balanced blend of computation, applications, and theory involving the fundamentals of probability and statistics. The current texts are [7] and [8].

2.2. Student Options. The department believes that it is vital to provide students with choices that are adapted to their individual learning styles. Consequently, students can select their instructor from among those teaching a given course, enroll in either a larger or smaller section, and frequently to select a section based on the language of instruction (Korean on English).

2.3. Student Services. Service courses in mathematics consist of two 75-minute lectures a week. In addition, in calculus and linear algebra students have one smaller problem session each week led by graduate teaching assistants. The department provides notes for the CAS component, and an evening help desk at which students can receive assistance. All professors schedule regular office hours, and some provide on-line information. A popular technique that some professors use is to take pictures of their classroom board presentations with digital camera, and subsequently post them on the Web.

2.4. Enrollment History. In Korea, good grades are vital for future study, employment, and general social standing. Students generally work quite hard, and are not satisfied with less than top grades. This causes large numbers of students to repeat classes. This in turn, becomes a burden on the teaching obligations of the department. We show representative data below.

Average Annual Enrollment (2002 - 2004)

	Total Enrollment	Total Repeats	Percent Repeats
Calculus I	548	163	27.9%
Honors Calculus I	172	13	7.6%
Calculus II	481	114	23.7%
Honors Calculus II	193	11	5.7%
Linear Algebra	731	209	28.6%
Engineering Mathematics I	337	79	23.4%
Engineering Mathematics I	303	59	19.5%

Except Honors Calculus the percentage of repeats is higher than 20% and is increasing every year. More than 10 independent lectures are needed to teach these repeating students. This is a large number when considering the size of mathematics faculty.

2.5. Class Sizes. While there may be some advantages to keep equal sizes of lectures, several things mitigate against this, as is discussed later in the paper. The following table provides an indication of class sizes in KAIST's service mathematics classes.

Section Sizes of Courses (2002 - 2004)

	Minimum	Median	Maximum
Calculus I	40	65	118
Honors Calculus I	78	86	94
Calculus II	38	69	142
Honors Calculus II	70	72	92
Linear Algebra	30	84	115
Engineering Mathematics I	53	84	115
Engineering Mathematics I	48	76	109

In Calculus II, the maximum class size is closed to four times of the minimum size which may represent an inefficient use of educational resource.

2.6. Instructional Languages. Because of a clear recognition of the worldwide importance of the ability to be fluent in English, Korean students have studied the language intensively since at least middle school. KAIST also recognizes this, and encourages students to become skilled in the use of English. Texts for all mathematics classes are in English, and although most classes are taught in Korean, an increasing number are offered in English. The entire faculty in the Mathematics Department earned PhDs from graduate schools at leading United States universities, where many of them also gained extensive experience in teaching in English. During each term, some service courses are presented in English, either by continuing Korean faculty, or visiting professors whose native language is English. English is the language adopted for mathematics exams, although students can respond in either language.

2.7. Technology. Service mathematics classes do not make extensive use of technology in their day-to-day operation. Graphing calculators are neither used in class not allowed on exams. Some professors do occasionally present computer demonstrations during lectures. On the other hand, in calculus students are required to learn how to use Maple, and are tested on it in exams.

2.8. Assessment. The primary assessment component for calculus and linear algebra consists of two three-hour exams - mid-term and final. Lesser amounts come from recitation section quizzes, which serve to encourage students to keep up to date. Even small components come from attendance and class participation. In the past there was a component based on homework and computer assignments. However, because of extensive much copying, these were discontinued. Because it is still important for students to obtain regular practice on current topics, the problem sessions incorporate quizzes, and exams contain computing questions. Because of selective nature, most students are well qualified and possess good work habits, so that grading uses a curve with high upper component.

3. Noticeable Trends and Issues

3.1. Excessive Repeats. As we can see from the data above, a very high percentage of students enrolled in the primary mathematics service courses are repeating the course. The primary reason for this is that students have become increasingly sensitive to the grades that they receive, as grades have become substantially more influential in obtaining good jobs and placement into the leading graduate schools. The number of repeats continues to increase noticeably. About

30% of the students taking service mathematics courses repeat them, including many who have earned respectable grades, but desire higher ones. About 10% of those repeating had a grades of at least B- in a previous semester, while at least 40% had a grade of C- or higher. The increase in the number of repeats raises the overall institutional and departmental costs.

3.2. Uneven Class Sizes. Following the introduction of extensive teaching evaluations by students, the department decided to give students the freedom to choose their own section of a course. Such things as the reputation of a professor or the convenience of certain times frequently influence their choices. This, in turn, often results in disparate sizes of the sections. The size of sections tends to become extremely uneven during the first two weeks of a semester when students can change sections, even when all sections start with roughly the same number of students. Uneven class sizes also tend to result in a waste of educational resources, and sometimes in a deterioration of educational quality.

3.3. CAS Component. Although some instructors occasionally use computer demonstrations in their lectures, the use of technology in classroom instruction is not extensive. However, the department has responded favorably to increasing requests from client departments to incorporate CAS components into the service mathematics courses, because more disciplines in science and engineering want students to be able to use CAS for mathematical modeling. However, in the past, CAS assignments tended to produce only a relatively few original solutions. Instead, many students incorporated the work of their colleagues. This made it difficult to evaluate student achievement through project assignments. This presents two dilemmas. First, the lack of a credible evaluation method tends to diminish the students' interest. Second, if the course does not incorporate the CAS component into the everyday work, then students may view assignments as being less important, or simply as a hurdle to overcome in completing the course.

4. Solutions with Limited Resources

The department has considered a number of ways to address the issues listed above when resources are limited. The department has implemented some of these, while others remain under discussion and new approaches are evaluated continually.

4.1. Excessive Repeats. One approach that is possible to use in order to discourage excessive repeats is to assign course grade by curving to only those who are taking the course for the first time. The instructors then would evaluate those repeating the course using an absolute scale. However, while it is possible that this remedy could at break the vicious cycle of repeats, it may not be as effective as other approaches. On the other hand, some of the other measures under consideration may not prove to be popular among the students. These approaches include setting a fee for repeats, applying some restriction on the number of repeats for a given course or by a given student, or apply restriction on the grade that may be earned by repeats.

4.2. Uneven Class Sizes. The current approach that the department uses to address the uneven class size situation is to organize both large and small sections simultaneously from the beginning of the semester. The quality of education that may be sacrificed by forming large classes then is compensated by creating small recitation classes and providing an evening help desk, both of which provide for more individualized assistance for students. The department's experience shows that students prefer a popular instructor in a large class to a less-popular instructor in a small class.

4.3. CAS Component. To overcome the problem of copying that occurred in the past with CAS assignments, assignments now are only for practice, and they are not collected or evaluated. The evaluation on a student's achievement in this area is carried out through questions on the regular examinations. The department's experiment in this procedure shows that the correlation between scores on these problems and the students' CAS understanding is relatively high. Moreover, students no longer have to waste time in making their copied solutions appear to be original.

5. Toward Ideal Solutions

The department could take additional steps under a more ideal setting. One can address the issue of excessive numbers of repeats through the adoption of a standardized evaluation method that allows faculty to assign course grades on an absolute basis. The difficulties arising from uneven class sizes might be lessened if it were possible to adopt a standardized classroom teaching content that ensures that a more uniform quality of the lectures, so that they are largely independent of the particular teacher. The CAS component would be enhanced by incorporating the use of CAS seamlessly into classroom teaching of the service courses, using CAS in daily assignments, by individualizing assignments, and by providing automatic grading.

We hope that we come up with better solutions by sharing ideas among world renowned experts and this is one of the reasons why we have hosted the 1st KAIST International Symposium on Enhancing University Mathematics Teaching.

References

[1] "Asia's Best Universities", Asia Week, June 30, 2000.
[2] A. Brender. "Asia's New High Tech Tiger", The Chronicle of Higher Education, Vol. 50, Issue 46, July 23, 2004.
[3] M. Weir, et al. Thomas' Calculus: Early Transcendentals, 11th ed., Pearson (2006).
[4] J. Marsden and A. Tromba, Vector Calculus, 5th ed., Freeman (2003).
[5] D. Arganbright and K. Ko, "Teaching a High-Quality Calculus Course to All First Year Students in a Research-Oriented Institute", Proceedings of ICTM3, Istanbul (2006) (to appear).
[6] H. Anton and R. Busby, Contemporary Linear Algebra, Wiley (2003)
[7] E. Kreyszig, Advanced Engineering Mathematics, 9th ed., Wiley (2005)
[8] S. Ross, Introduction to Probability and Statistics for Engineers and Scientists, 3rd ed., Elsevier (2004).

DEPARTMENT OF MATHEMATICS, KOREA ADVANCED INSTITUTE OF SCIENCE AND TECHNOLOGY, DAEJEON, 305-701, KOREA
    E-mail address: knot@knot.kaist.ac.kr

CBMS Issues in Mathematics Education
Volume **14**, 2007

Harnessing the Enthusiasm of our Best and Brightest Students for Mathematics

Deborah Hughes Hallett

ABSTRACT. Mathematics is at a critical juncture. Its role in other fields, such as biology, medicine, finance, is expanding rapidly, fueled by in part by the power of technology. Yet our courses have not changed. Enrollments in mathematics are stagnant or shrinking in many countries. How do we explain this? More importantly, what can we do about it? The solution to this problem lies in realizing that todays students are different. Unlike us, they are not willing to wait to see how mathematics is useful; they want to know now. In addition, they have different ideas about what constitutes good teaching. In this work, I will propose methods of harnessing the enthusiasm of our best and brightest students. Doing so requires raising our standards for teaching, and challenges many traditional departmental norms. Yet the health of our profession depends on our meeting these requirements successfully.

The Expanding Role of Mathematics

Over the last three decades, the role of mathematics in scientific research has exploded. The tremendous advances in biology and finance are due, in part, to their increased use of mathematics. In fields not traditionally associated with mathematics, such as public policy and international relations, new areas have been opened up by mathematics. Behind this expansion lies some new mathematics, such as stochastic differential equations, but fundamentally the advances in other fields are not driven by new mathematics, but by new uses of existing mathematics, often made possible by huge advances in computational power. The balance between different branches of mathematics has changed, and the way in which the subject is practiced has changed.

What has happened at universities? As more fields depend on mathematics, we would expect more students to take mathematics. Yet enrollments in mathematics are not growing, and in many countries, they are shrinking.

In the US, the 2000 CBMS Study [1] of Undergraduate Mathematics Programs reported that enrollments in mathematics have dropped since 1990, although total enrollments in universities had increased. Elaine Seymour and Nancy Hewitt's study *Talking about Leaving* [2] found that of 60 percent of US students who start college in mathematics switch out of mathematics or science within two years. How can this be if mathematics is so central? More importantly, what can we do about it?

The Teaching of Mathematics

Addressing this problem requires recognizing the ways in which that today's students are different than we were. Although many of us were attracted to mathematics by its beauty, our students are often not. They want to be shown its importance in their world.

Because more fields require mathematics, students now come to us with a wider range of interests and skills than previously. Some do not have the background expected by our courses, which were designed for a different population. They may also be less patient—less willing to wait and see how mathematics is used; they want to know now. Since our courses often do not reflect recent advances in the uses of mathematics, they may not make the connections students want. To continue to capture the interest and enthusiasm of our students, we have to change our courses.

In their book [2], Seymour and Hewitt report that poor teaching is one of the primary reasons that strong students leave mathematics and science. With the increased attention teaching has received both inside and outside the university, the standard of teaching expected of college faculty in the US has risen—though perhaps not as fast as students' expectations. In addition, students' ideas about what constitutes good teaching are changing. Clear lectures are no longer considered enough; students in the US want more dialog, more interaction, and some role in shaping the mathematics they learn.

Raising Standards

Seymour and Hewitt also reported that students were turned off by the "weed out" policy of many mathematics and science departments, in which a large number of students fail. Hearing this, faculty may worry that the solution will be to lower standards in our courses. I will argue that the solution is to raise standards in our teaching.

To address student concerns without lowering standards, we need to rethink our teaching philosophy. Our goal should be to make mathematics the life-blood of the natural and social sciences—providing insights that can be obtained no other way. Recent changes in the uses of mathematics give us new opportunities to alter students' perceptions of the subject, as we can now show them applications in a much wider range of contexts.

Engaging today's students puts new demands on faculty—we need to show students both the uses of mathematics and to involve them actively in the learning process.

Example of Curricular Change: Calculus. The last fifteen years have seen significant changes in the teaching of calculus in the US. Student engagement was one of the motivations for these changes, but equally important were concerns that students could not apply what they had learned in other settings. This led to a greater emphasis on conceptual understanding, often using the "Rule of Four"— that ideas be represented graphically, numerically, verbally, and symbolically. Such multiple representations more closely reflect the use of mathematics in other fields, where the reasoning may be graphical, such as in economics, or numerical, such as in analyzing experimental data. In addition, developing the ability to move flexibly between different representations contributes to understanding [3, 4].

Because computers and calculators facilitate graphical and numerical work, they play an important role in the new curriculum. However, they are also easily misused. For example, adding technology while curriculum remains unchanged can undermine thinking. Significant effort has been put into identifying topics in calculus where technology deepens understanding, such as analyzing the effect of parameters on the graph of a function, and in identifying topics which are made possible by computation, such as the use of slope fields in differential equations. Computers also enable students to use real data and analyze more realistic models than previously possible.

The emphasis on modeling in new courses has the effect that students are now exposed to a larger variety of applications. Faculty are more apt to choose an example outside mathematics, and more likely to talk to their colleagues in the sciences about mathematics at the level of calculus. Thus, although there is still much work to be done, rethinking calculus has led many mathematicians to start to build bridges to other fields. As a result, the Mathematical Association of America's recent undergraduate curriculum review requested formal input from other disciplines for the first time ever [5].

Impact of Changes in Calculus Curriculum

The changes described are now widespread in the US. They began in books that were specifically designed to incorporate them, but have now been copied by most standard texts. In addition, the Advanced Placement (AP) syllabus and exam have made many of the same changes. About a third of the US students take calculus in high school in preparation for this exam. In 2002, the National Research Council's study *Learning and Understanding* concluded that

> The AP [calculus] examinations have improved under the current syllabi. The effort to promote conceptual understanding by asking nonstandard questions and requiring verbal explanations is excellent. For example, the fact that there is now a wider variety of applications of integration (and not from a prescribed list) encourages students to think about the meaning of an integral. The inclusion of graphing problems involving a parameter focuses attention on the behavior of a family of functions [6].

However, the report felt that the AP exam needs to demand still more conceptual understanding. More multi-step problems, realistic applications, and problems that test the ability to reason theoretically were recommended.

Examples from New Calculus Curricula. Since much what students learn is shaped by problems, a good way to get a flavor of a new curriculum is by looking at the problems it asks students to solve.

Problems typical of new curricula, but largely absent on the old, include the following:

1. Let $P(t)$ be the population of the US in millions where t is the year, and let P^{-1} be the inverse function. What do the following quantities or statements represent, in terms of the US population?

(a) $P(t) + 5$ and $P(t + 100)$
(b) $P'(1990) = 2.3$
(c) $(P^{-1})'(250) = 0.5$

2. The temperature outside a house during a 24-hour period is given, for $0 \leq t \leq 24$, by

$$F(t) = 80 - 10\cos\left(\frac{\pi t}{12}\right),$$

where $F(t)$ is in degrees Fahrenheit and t is in hours.
(a) Find the average temperature, to the nearest degree Fahrenheit, between $t = 6$ and $t = 14$.
(b) An air conditioner cooled the house whenever the outside temperature was at or above 78 degrees Fahrenheit. For what values of t was the air conditioner cooling the house?
(c) The cost of cooling the house accumulates at $0.05 per hour for each degree the outside temperature exceeds the outside temperature exceeds 78 degrees Fahrenheit. What was the total cost, to the nearest cent, of cooling the house for the 24-hour period?

3. The following graph represents the number of hours of daylight in Madrid for one month.
(a) Estimate the derivative, dH/dt.
(b) What is the practical interpretation of this derivative?
(c) What month does the graph show?

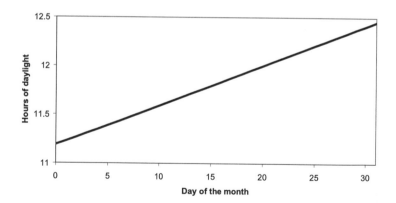

4. There is an outbreak of SARS in a nearby city. As you are working in the mayor's office, you are asked which is the most effective policy for preventing the spread to the disease to your city:
   I. Cut off contact. Shut down roads, airports, trains, busses, and other forms of direct contact with the infected region.
   II. Install a quarantine policy. Isolate anyone who has been in contact with a SARS patient or anyone who shows symptoms of SARS.
   What is the effect of each policy? Which is most effective?

The first problem focuses on the meaning of a function and its inverse, and of the derivative. Even though it involves no calculation, students find this problem difficult if they do not think of a derivative as a rate of change and are not used to using units.

The second problem, which is a slightly abbreviated version of one on the 1998 high school AP exam, required students to interpret an integral in a way that was almost certainly new to them. Fifteen year ago, such a problem would not have been considered for the AP exam.

The third problem [7] also asks for an interpretation, but the difficulty here lies in part (c), which uses the fact that in the northern hemisphere there are less than 12 hours of daylight at the start of the month of March and more than 12 hours at the end. Such problems, which require information from outside mathematics, may not be appropriate in all circumstances (for example, on exams), but they do emphasize the connection between mathematics and other fields.

The fourth problem asks students to solve a problem that is of obvious importance. The solution involves a qualitative analysis of first order differential equations using slope fields and the SIR model, where S is the number of susceptible people, and I is the number of infected people in circulation. Then

$$\frac{dS}{dt} = aSI$$
$$\frac{dI}{dt} = aSI - bI$$

Using the World Health Organization SARS data for Hong Kong, students are led to analyze the effect of the two policies. The second is vastly more effective than the first.

Theory and Conceptual Understanding

The new calculus courses also attempt to help students make a transition from the largely computational courses which precede it to the kind of understanding which is required in later mathematics courses. The first step in developing mathematical thinking is the acquisition of a clear intuitive picture of the central ideas. Historically, concepts were often understood informally before formally. For US students, this intuitive understanding of calculus needs to be built as they learn the subject. In the next course, after this foundation has been laid, students who are interested in further mathematics learn how to write rigorous arguments, and others proceed with more modeling.

US instructors are sometimes surprised that students describing the new calculus courses as "more theoretical" than the old. While not using the word "theoretical" in the usual mathematical sense, they are expressing that fact that the new courses demand more reasoning, justification, and explanation.

Example of Pedagogical Change: ConcepTests. Over the past two decades, many faculty have looked ways to improve student learning by making better, more active, use of class time. One of the most effective methods—the use of ConcepTests and peer instruction—was developed by Eric Mazur of Harvard. His pioneering work in physics has been successfully replicated in other fields, and its efficacy is clearly supported by data. Information is available under "Peer Instruction" at http://galileo.harvard.edu.

ConcepTests are now available for calculus [8]. Evaluation suggests that ConcepTests are as effective in mathematics as they are in physics.

What are ConcepTests and How are They Used?

ConcepTests are questions designed to promote the discussion and learning of mathematical concepts during a calculus class. The questions are usually conceptual, often multiple choice or true/false, with some free response questions as well. They are used as an aid in promoting student involvement in discussing mathematical concepts rather than as a method of testing students for a grade. (Some questions have more than one correct answer.) Examples of ConcepTests in calculus and statistics are in the Appendix.

Instructors usually display the ConcepTest using an overhead projector, or distribute a copy to each student. Students are given a short time (one to four minutes, depending on the question) to think about the question and then vote for the answer they think is correct. Providing almost all do not vote for the correct answer, the students are then given a few minutes to discuss the ConcepTest with adjacent students and another chance to vote on the correct answer. Students are also asked to develop reasons to support their answer. The instructor then discusses the correct answer (or answers) and has students present their reasons.

"Peer instruction" refers to the discussion that takes place between students after they have answered the question for the first time. Including the peer instruction is important to the success of the method. Giving the questions alone, without the subsequent discussion, is less effective. [1]

Because of the variety of forms of ConcepTest questions, instructors can use them in several different ways. Three of the possibilities are:

- As an introduction to a topic. This works especially well if the topic is closely tied to previous lessons or is something with which most students have some familiarity.
- After presentation of a specific topic by the teacher. Here the ConcepTest may be used to see if the students have grasped the concept, or if the topic needs more discussion or examples.
- As a review of material that has been thoroughly discussed.

Evaluation of ConcepTests

Scott Pilzer, who taught with ConcepTests in physics before writing them for calculus, gathered evaluation data for mathematics [9]. He found that at the start of the subsequent semester, students taught Calculus I using ConcepTests and peer instruction performed much better on conceptual questions than those who had been taught standard lectures, as shown in the following table:

Comparison of Grades on Common Exam Questions

	Conceptual Questions	Computational Problems
With ConcepTests	73%	63%
Standard Lecture	17%	54%

---

[1]See the evaluation discussion.

These results mirror the results found in physics: a large increase in conceptual understanding and some increase in standard computational problem solving. In his article, Scott Pilzer describes how this enthusiasm translated into more mathematics majors.

At Cornell, "Good Questions" [10] are used in the same way as ConcepTests. A comparison of the results from their use with and without peer instruction suggests that the peer instruction contributes significantly to student learning [11].

Conclusion

Revitalizing the curriculum and pedagogy of our courses enables us to provide better value to our students. If they are enthusiastic and engaged, students will bring their talent and ideas to mathematics. Consider the expanding importance of mathematics, this flow of interest will benefit not only mathematics but a huge array of other fields.

Appendix: Examples of ConcepTests and Check Your Understanding Questions

1. A population distribution is at the top left. Which of the other five graphs, A to E, could be a simulation of the sampling distribution for $n = 25$? For $n = 4$? (Adapted from ARTIST website U-Minnesota [12])

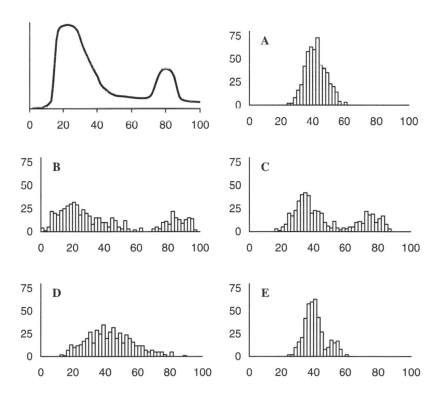

2. Which of the following would be a counterexample to the product rule? (From [**7**])
   (a) Two differentiable functions f and g satisfying $(fg)' = f'g'$.
   (b) A differentiable function f such that $(xf(x))' = xf'(x) + f(x)$.
   (c) A differentiable function f such that $(f(x)^2)' = 2f(x)$.
   (d) Two differentiable functions f and g such that $f'(a) = 0$ and $g'(a) = 0$ and fg has positive slope at $x = a$.

3. Group equal line integrals $\int_C \vec{F} \cdot d\vec{r}$ in (I)-(IV), where C is the oriented curve from P to Q and is the vector field shown. (From [**13**])

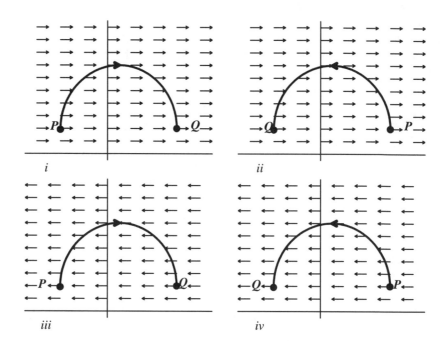

i ii

iii iv

References

[1] Conference Board of Mathematical Sciences, http://www.ams.org/cbms/cbmssurvey-ch1.pdf.
[2] Elaine Seymour, Nancy M. Hewitt, *Talking about Leaving: Why Undergraduates Leave the Sciences.* Westview Press, Boulder, CO, 1997. Reported by Robert C. Thomas, http://mtprof.msun.edu/Fall1997/THOMAS.html.
[3] R. Lesh, T. Post and M. Behr, *Representations and Translations Among Representations in Mathematics Learning and Problem Solving,* In C. Janvier, ed. *Problems in Representation in the Teaching and Learning Of Mathematics,* Hillsdale, NJ: Erlbaum, 1987.
[4] *The Role of Representation in School Mathematics,* NCTM Yearbook, 2001.
[5] *Curriculum Foundations Project: Voices of the Partner Disciplines,* http://www.maa.org/cupm/crafty/.
[6] *Report of The Content Panel For Mathematics* In Learning and Understanding:Improving Advanced Study of Mathematics and Science in U.S. High Schools, National Academy Press, 2002.
[7] D. Hughes-Hallett, A.M. Gleason, et al., *Calculus, 4th edition* New York: John Wiley, 2005.
[8] S. Pilzer, et al., *ConcepTests,* New York: John Wiley, 2005.
[9] S. Pilzer, *Peer Instruction in Physics and Mathematics* In *Primus,* XI(2) June, 2001, 185-192.
[10] M. Terrell, http://www.math.cornell.edu/~GoodQuestions/
[11] M. Terrell, http://www.math.cornell.edu/~maria/gq/handout2005.html

[12] J. Garfield, *Assessment Resource Tools for Improving Statistical Thinking*,
       http://www.gen.umn.edu/artist/
[13] W. McCallum, D. Hughes-Hallett, et al., *ConcepTests for Multivariable Calculus*, New York:
       John Wiley, 2005.

KENNEDY SCHOOL INTERNATIONAL PROGRAMS, HARVARD UNIVERSITY, CAMBRIDGE, MA 02138,
USA AND DEPARTMENT OF MATHEMATICS, THE UNIVERSITY OF ARIZONA, TUCSON, AZ 85721-
0089 USA

E-mail address: dhh@math.arizona.edu

CBMS Issues in Mathematics Education
Volume **14**, 2007

Interactive Geometry and Multivariable Calculus on the Internet

Thomas Banchoff

1. Introduction

Each of the words in the title describes several different aspects of a series of experimental Internet-based courses that we have been developing at Brown University starting in the fall of 1997. The talk upon which this article is based includes a progress report on this project supported by the National Science Foundation as we prepare for wider dissemination of our model in a variety of courses for students with a number of different backgrounds and expectations in various institutions in the US and elsewhere.

This report has three main sections after the introduction: Demonstration Software for Java Applets and Labs, Communication Software—The Tensor, and Evaluation Procedures. We will conclude with plans for future developments.

Recent Advances in Technology and Access to It. Multivariable Calculus is the first place in the undergraduate mathematics curriculum where spatial visualization becomes crucial for the interpretation of geometric objects in three dimensions. Although the hand-held graphing calculator is adequate for most situations that arise in one-variable calculus, it is necessary to have a computer with a larger screen with more resolution and more speed in order to deal with graphs of functions of two variables and with the geometry of curves on such graphs. Until recently, it was necessary to have access to a high-level workstation in order to interact with such function graphs, but it is now possible to carry out the same investigations using a personal computer or a portable "laptop" machine. These devices are coming down in price so that more and more students will have access to them in libraries and other public areas in most schools.

Until a short time ago, it was necessary to use powerful (sometimes costly) high-level programs like Mathematica or MathCad or Maple in order to work with function graphs in three-dimensional space, but now there are an increasing number of collections of special-purpose Java applets that work on most computers and that do not require expensive licenses. These applets will work on most browsers and can be operated locally on a server in each individual school. In this presentation we describe a collection of such applets developed at Brown University by the author and teams of undergraduate assistants working primarily over the past eight summers. Support for this project has come mainly from National Science Foundation grants from the Division of Undergraduate Education and the Research on Learning and Education (ROLE) program in Education and Human Resources.

Student Assistants and Program Development. It is noteworthy that the programming for the software in this project has been done almost entirely by undergraduate students. Most have been excellent students in the author's courses in multivariable calculus and geometry who have been invited to work with the author in groups of four to six for ten weeks in the summer to further the development of the software. Frequently such students will act as technical resource persons and undergraduate teaching assistants during the following academic year. Most of these students have gone on to careers in mathematics as well as computer science and physics, and many have become instructors themselves.

2. Demonstration Software – Applets and Labs

Interactive Applets for Function Graphs. We describe in some detail the first interaction that students will have with the demonstration software. The full power of the Java applets becomes apparent as students progress through a series of laboratory exercises, learning new techniques as they go along.

Almost all of the applets in our multivariable calculus laboratories feature surfaces in three-space, displayed in a three-dimensional window that can be rotated by moving a cursor controlled by a mouse. One can interact immediately with this display to show various views of a function graph. It is significant that this requires no training whatsoever. The basic principle in our project is that training time should be minimized so that it is possible to make observations of geometric phenomena in existing applets and then to make modifications to study not just one example but rather whole families of examples.

The next level of interaction is to make changes in the control panel. For the most part, the functions studied in the beginning of multivariable calculus are defined over rectangular domains, and the students can change the lower and upper limits of the variables x and y by typing in new values and remembering to hit the return key to transmit the changes which are made directly to the graph on the screen.

It may be necessary to resize the window, or to zoom in or out in order to get a better view of the graph, and this is accomplished by choosing "zoom" rather than "rotate" or "translate" in the pull-down menu in the graph window.

Next it is possible for students to modify the definition of the function being graphed, first of all by changing some of the coefficients and transmitting the changes. At this point, it is possible to introduce some conventions for multiplication by using the symbol "*" between factors and for exponentiation by using the symbol "^". Thus, for example, a quadratic polynomial can be written $f(x,y) = 2*x^2 - 3*x*y + x + 1$.

In addition to the three-dimensional window, most applets will have a two-dimen-sional window showing the domain of the function. A special feature of the applet system is a "hot spot" in the domain that can be dragged using the mouse, with the image of that point moving along the graph of the function. The spot is surrounded by a circular disc in the domain, the radius of which is controlled by another hot spot. This enables the student to see the relationship between the domain and range of the function, in particular to locate the places where the function has a maximum and minimum value over the domain of definition. As the disc moves around, the values taken on over that disc are displayed as a segment on the z-axis. The segment is large when the disc is large and arbitrarily small as the radius of the disc is shrunk, at least in the case of a polynomial function. That observation is the basis of the definition of continuity of a function, an intuition to be refined in later demonstrations.

Subsequent laboratory experiences introduce parameters that can be added to the definition of a function to give families of functions, or families of horizontal planes slicing function graphs to produce contour lines. A full range of properties of the applets is contained in a tutorial that the student can consult at any time.

One of the most significant aspects of the program is that a student can save the changes in his or her applet by copying the current state of the program into a file that can be emailed or included in an on-line homework. Anyone opening such a file will enter the program precisely where the student left off and will be able to continue the investigation based on the student's comments[1].

Demonstrations in Lectures. Frequently an instructor will want to use these applets as parts of a lecture, displaying the applets by using a projector connected with a computer attached to the Internet. This is the first level of inter-activity, between the instructor and the geometric phenomena. On the basis of such presentations, an instructor can assign homework exercises that do not require any further viewing of the applets.

The second level of interactivity occurs when students can themselves work directly with the applets, either in a workstation laboratory, or on personal computers connected to the Internet. Although we still refer to laboratory exercises, it is no longer necessary for students to go to a physical laboratory in order to interact with the geometric phenomena.

Laboratory Text and Exercises. By accessing the Laboratory software, students can read a description of an applet, in condensed or in expanded form, and can do exercises based on investigations of a series of examples. One mode of operating is to provide students with physical "laboratory pages" on which a student can record answers and hand them in. It is also possible to make these pages available electronically so students can enter responses and have them sent directly to a file server. The instructor can then make comments either on a paper copy or and can return these to the student, physically or electronically.

3. Communication Software – The Tensor

Communication software for these courses, developed by the author and teams of undergraduate student assistants, enables students to interact with instructors and with each other in new ways. We now describe the full operation of the "Tensor", a course-management arrangement with some particular interactive features, some or all of which can be used in conjunction with the applets described above.

Student Access to Tensor Software. At the beginning of each course, students who register for the course are assigned accounts for the class website, with temporary passwords that can be changed by the student. This provides access to material restricted to those registered for the course, as well as to assistants and to

---

[1]See Appendix A for two illustrations of Laboratory Demonstrations

guests designated by the instructor. Once a student enters the course website, he or she can read messages and have access to resources, such as tutorials for using the Java applets described above, for including images and links to other sites, and for scanning written work and illustrations.

Discussion, Open and Time-Dependent. A particularly important feature of the Internet-based courseware is a "threaded discussion" option, where the instructor can enter a discussion topic and specify the time when it will be open to everyone in the class. Up to that time, only the individual student and the instructor will be able to read an entry as well as the instructor comments. After the release time, everyone can read everyone else's submission and the comments, and the discussion can proceed in an open manner.

One reason for the time delay is to avoid a competition to be the first to answer a question, after which others might be discouraged from submitting their own answers. This also gives time for people to discuss a topic among themselves or with others, or to locate relevant references, on-line or in traditional resources such as textbooks and libraries. .

All entries and comments are identified by the time they are submitted, and once they are commented on, the text cannot be changed. Otherwise a comment by an instructor might become irrelevant or confusing. A student or instructor can comment on an entry directly below the last comment, rather than at the bottom of the entire discussion. Usually instructor comments are in a different color to make them easier to identify.

Discussion Example: Height versus Weight. One of the first examples of a discussion of this sort, going back to the fall of 1997, is the "warm-up" question: "Was there a time since your birth when the number of inches in your height was exactly equal to the number of pounds in your weight?" The question was posed with no further elaboration on the first day of a multivariable calculus course, and locked for the next twenty-four hours. There followed a series of responses from nearly all members of the class, some of which are reproduced in edited form in Appendix B.

Assignments and the Tensor. An instructor can set up an assignment by writing an optional introductory paragraph and then deciding on the number of problems, each of which is entered in its own dialogue box. The instructor can designate that the answers are to be unlocked, locked permanently, or locked until a specific time. The first view of the tensor shows a matrix with a row for each assignment and a column for each student in the class.

At any time an instructor can select the initials of a student in the class and see all of the responses from that student for the assignment. After the assignment has been unlocked, everyone in the class can do the same.

What makes the tensor more than a two-dimensional matrix is that it is possible to select the name of the assignment and see one row for each question in the assignment, with a square under the initials of each student indicating whether or not he or she has responded. When a response has been submitted, the square for that student is red. When the instructor has commented, that square turns green. If the student submits something further, or if another student enters a comment on the work of the first student, the square turns red again until the instructor makes a comment, which returns it to green. At any time class members can see on the original matrix whether or not a particular student has submitted something new on an assignment, and, by expanding the tensor, it is possible to see which questions have been answered and not yet commented upon.

Hints and Solution Keys. For any question on any assignment, the instructor can enter a hint and this will show up in the tensor as a green square in the first column. The second column in the tensor is a place for a Solution Key that becomes visible to all students in the class only after the assignment is unlocked. In constructing the Solution Key, the instructor can copy and paste solutions of individual students, with attribution, something especially valuable in cases where there are different ways of solving a problem.

Examinations. It is possible for an instructor to use the Assignments menu to present the questions for a take-home examination, to be answered within a particular time. The usual instructions are that books and notes and computers may be used but no one is to be consulted, electronically or otherwise, so that the submissions are the student's own work, as opposed to homework assignments where students are encouraged to work together or to make use of other resources. The security issues for an ordinary take-home test appear to be the same as for this kind of test, with the added condition that it should not be possible for anyone to see anyone else's work before the release time.

4. Evaluation of the Project

An important aspect of projects funded by the National Science Foundation is evaluation, and this is especially significant in the Research on Learning and Education (ROLE) program that supported the recent activity of our project. Starting in the summer of 2004, the dissemination phase of our project is being funded for four years by the NSF Director's Distinguished Teaching Scholar Award, which also places heavy emphasis on evaluation to determine the effectiveness of projects in enhancing teaching and learning.

The evaluation component of the current project has been designed and completed by Kathleen Marx Banchoff, principal of McCarthy Marx & Associates, a marketing research consultancy working with Fortune 100 companies since 1988. Working with the author over the past 5 years, Marx Banchoff has devised a research plan for evaluating the effectiveness of the author's use of these teaching technologies. They include:

- A standard **questionnaire** (7-9 questions formatted in an Excel spreadsheet distributed by e-mail to enrolled students in the time period between the second midterm and the final exam)
- An **analytic plan** using *content analysis* to establish
  - a standard set of **codes** for examining results across internet-based courses taught by the author (Multivariable Calculus, Linear Algebra, and Differential Geometry) and years (2001 through 2005).
  - **measures** of effectiveness and standards useful for several different applications (i.e., course evaluation across time periods, teacher evaluation across courses, use of learning technologies across courses and time periods, and suggestions for improvement in the technologies)
- A standard format for **summary tables** which allow the author to compare results, and build measures of success for these technologies and

charts of verbatim comments which allow the author to demonstrate the students' point of view on research dimensions relevant to a specific analysis.

We have been accumulating data for internet-based courses taught by the author since the start of the academic year 2001-2002: at Brown University, as well as for one course at the University of Notre Dame and one at the University of California, Los Angeles.

For this analysis, data were analyzed for Multivariable Calculus – two classes at the honors level (Fall 2003 and Fall 2004) and one at the standard level (Spring 2005). Data were collected in Excel spreadsheets, amalgamated and coded by course, and analyzed. Summary charts of the responses on two questions relevant to this analysis are included in Appendix C, along with sample verbatim comments from each of these three courses.

Summarizing the data in this way permits in-depth analysis of student reaction to features of the project, such as on-line student interaction with demonstrations and the ability of students to consult the answers of other students in the class.

5. Future Directions for Development

Planned Refinements of the Tensor. On the basis of comments made by students on their questionnaires and in response to questions from potential users of our software, we are in the process of revising some features. We are always looking for more feedback so we can make the demonstration and communication software, and the evaluation instruments, more accessible in a variety of courses at many institutions, for students with different backgrounds and expectations. We mention here two examples of work under development.

Occasionally certain students prefer to have their work remain private, accessible only to the instructor and not to other students in the class. It is always possible to handle such communications by ordinary email, but in the next version of the communication software, students and instructors will have the option of making any individual entry private. This feature will be especially valuable in cases where the instructor wants to give a grade for a particular set of questions since such grades are not meant to be public, to be viewed by other members of the class. This "grading feature" is particularly significant for tests.

Instructors and students frequently will have access to other programs, for exmple symbolic manipulation and computer algebra systems. We want to make is easier to use such programs in conjunction with the tensor, and we plan to produce tutorials that will facilitate interaction between programs.

6. Conclusion

This is an important time for developers of mathematical software as the Internet becomes more an more powerful and access to it becomes increasingly available at all colleges and universities. We appreciate the chance to take part in thie international symposium at KAIST, to share ideas with colleagues from Korea and around the world.

Appendix A. JAVA Applets and Worksheet

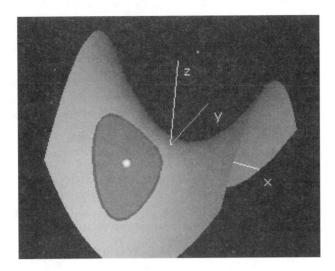

Domain and Range. This demonstration graphs a function $f(x, y)$ over a rectangular domain. By default, the domain is set to $-1 \leq x \leq 1$, $-1 \leq y \leq 1$ and the function is set to $f(x, y) = x^2 - y^2$.

In the above window, you can choose both the center and radius of a dark disc domain in the xy-plane using the white and dark hotspots respectively. The dark line segment along the z-axis in this window shows the range of $f(x, y)$ over the dark disc domain.

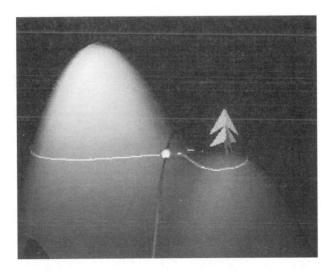

Highest Point on the Highway. The function $w(t)$ which represents the path of the highway is shown in the "Domain" window in dark gray. In the control panel there is a tapedeck that allows you to change the variable t_0 and travel along the highway. Two vectors are drawn at the point $w(t_0)$: the darker vector is the unit tangent vector to the darker curve at $w(t_0)$ while the white vector is the gradient vector of $f(x, y)$ at $w(t_0)$.

The default function $f(x, y)$ produces a graph called "Twin Peaks" which can be seen in the 3D graph window. Under $f(x, y)$, the red curve in the domain is mapped into a darker curve on the surface. This "scenic highway" has $z(t) = f(w(t))$ as its height function. With this in mind, we ask the following question. As we travel along the highway, at what point do we attain our maximum height? The question is simpler in the case of a 2D graph. To find the maximum height of the graph of a function $f(t)$, we would set $f'(t) = 0$, solve for t, and then check if the solutions were maxima or minima. This method naturally generalizes to 3D graphs as well. To find the maximum point along the highway, we set $z'(t) = 0$. By the chain rule,

$$z'(t) = f_x(x(t), y(t))x'(t) + f_y(x(t), y(t))y'(t), \text{ so}$$
$$0 = f(x(t), y(t))(x'(t), y'(t)).$$

This tells us that at the highest point $w(t_0)$ on the highway, the gradient vector at $w(t_0)$ must be perpendicular to the tangent vector at $w(t_0)$. Note that if the highway passes through a local maximum of the graph, then the gradient vector will be 0 so it will be perpendicular to the tangent vector.

Level Curves (Written by Dr. Steve Harris). To access Professor May's applets (based on work of Tom Banchoff), go to `http://www.slu.edu/classes` `/maymk/MathApplets-SLU.html` and follow the link "Level Curve" and the button "Level Curve Applet".

Spread the graphs out where you can see them all, as well as the control panel. Use the Level Cu   pplet to investigate the function:

$$f(x, y) = -x^2 y^2 + x^2 + y^2$$

- At what z-values does the contour curve change abruptly?
- What is the nature of the change?
- What is this telling you about the shape of the surface?

Appendix B. Online Interaction

HEIGHT-WEIGHT PROBLEM. *Was there ever a time in your life when your height measured in inches was equal to your weight in pounds?*

(1.1) CW at 6:02 PM on 9/3/97.

When I think back to when I was first born, I weighed very little. I weighed only 4 pounds 6 ounces. I don't remember my height, but I know I was certainly longer than 4.375 inches. Now I weigh 120 pounds and I am 66 inches tall. At some point, my weight increased and became more than my height. If I were to graph lines representing my height and weight over time, the two lines will intersect at some point and there was a time in my life when I weighed as much as my height.

Right, the crossover phenomenon is at the heart of the discussion, but you need a bit more precision in the mathematical language in order to make the argument convincing. In order to represent your height and weight over time, you will need curves rather than (straight) lines, correct? What property of these curves will guarantee that they will cross, given your initial and current conditions? -tb

(1.2) JM at 8:58 PM on 9/3/97.

There was definitely a time when my height and weight were the same.
When I was born my height was roughly 12 inches and my weight was
close to 8 pounds. At the moment I am approximately 69 inches tall
and 145 pounds heavy.
I'm making the assumption that both my height and weight can be
represented as increasing, continuous functions. Since at my birth,
the weight function was less than the height function and presently
the weight is greater than the height there must have been a time
when the two functions crossed. .....

Try to brush out a little what assumptions you need to prove,
and why. Do you need to discuss whether height is a function
that is strictly increasing? (Same for weight). You're buzzing
around a solid argument, but haven't quite hit it yet. -js

(1.4) TH at 11:52 PM on 9/3/97.

Let's assume a normal baby weighs 20 pounds and measures 15 inches
in height. .....

Your hypothetical normal baby would be, I'm afraid, pretty
abnormal-looking. At twenty pounds and fifteen inches, it would
resemble a good-sized medicine ball. Most full term babies are
somewhat longer, around twenty inches, and over ten pounds is
at the high birth weight range.

(1.5) SC at 11:55 PM on 9/3/97.

But of course.
The height and weight of one individual can both be stated as
single-valued functions of time, H(t) and W(t). (One cannot have
two different weights at one instant)
The domain of both functions is t = [9 months, 214 months],
214 months being my current age.
Both of these functions are continuous on this domain, as people
do not instantaneously grow an inch or two. At no point in the
domain is W(t) = 0, so the function F(t) = H(t)/W(t) is also
continuous. From my mother, I know that H(9) = 22 inches, and
that W(9) = 7 pounds. So, F(9) = 22/7. From my doctor, I know
that H(214) = 74, W(214) = 135. So, F(214) = 74/135. By the
statement of F(t), we know that:

$$F(t) = 1 <=> H(t) = W(t)$$

Because F(t) is continuous on [9,214], F(t) must pass through
all values in the range

$$[F(9),F(214)] = [22/7,74/135]$$

Since 22/7 > 1 > 74/135 , F(t) must equal 1 for some t-value on
[9,214], and as stated before, this implies that H(t) = W(t) for
some t on [9,214].

Excellently argued! Good work. You could also cite explicitly
the "lemma" you are using, namely that the quotient of a
continuous function by a non-zero continuous function is also
continuous. The key theorem has a name, the Intermediate Value
Theorem. And that is also good to mention. --tb

   (1.15) AL at 1:38 PM on 9/4/97.

.....However, it is interesting to note that this is an arbitrary
comparison and if other units were used the results would be
different. For example, if kilograms and centimeters were used as
units, the graphs of the functions of my height and weight would
never cross.

Very good observations, especially about the dependence of this
problem on the units employed. Using kilos and centimeters yields
weight functions below height, and if you use kilos and meters,
the weight is always above -tb

   (1.21) LC at 5:42 PM on 9/4/97.

I'm going to try the HTML thing. Hopefully this will look OK...

When I was born, I was a pretty big baby -- about 9.5 pounds. I
can't remember exactly how long/tall I was, but I think it was
in the 20 inches range. At any rate, it was almost certainly more
than 9.5 inches. I'm now 66 inches (5'6") tall, and I can tell you
that I weigh a little bit more than 66 pounds :).

Assuming that height and weight are continuous functions (e.g.
you can't go from being 40 pounds at one time to being 50 pounds
at another without being 41 pounds, 42 pounds, etc.), the graphs
of my height and weight must have crossed at some point in my life.

To prove this, let me make a few assumptions/statements:
- Let h(x) and w(x) be my height and weight, respectively, at age
  x months.
- Let h(0) = 20 and w(0) = 9.5 (my height and weight at birth)
- Let h(218) = 66 and w(218) = 140 (my height and weight at my
  current age)
- We're looking for the age a for 0 $<$ a $<$ 218 where h(a) = w(a)
  or, put differently, where h(a) / w(a) = 1. Let's define f(x) to
  be the function h(x) / w(x)
- On the interval 0 $<=$ x $<=$ 218), w(x) is never equal to 0.
  If you literally weigh nothing, you're probably not so alive.

w(x) is never equal to 0 on the specified interval, so
f(x) = h(x) / w(x) is always defined. At age x = 0,

$f(x) = h(x) / w(x) = 20 / 9.5 = $ about 2.105. At age $x = 218$,
$f(x) = h(x) / w(x) = 66 / 140 = $ about .471.

According to the Intermediate Value Theorem, if $f(x)$ is continuous
on the interval $0 <= x <= 218$ (and it is, because $h(x)$ and $w(x)$
are both continuous and $w(x)$ is never equal to 0), you can choose
any y on the interval $f(0) < y < f(218)$ and there is guaranteed
to be a solution to $f(a) = y$ for some a on the interval $0 < a < 218$.

OK. Now, this means that if we set $y = 1$, there is guaranteed to
be a solution to $f(a) = 1$ for some a on the interval. That means
that $h(a) / w(a) = 1$, or that $h(a) = w(a)$ for some a on the
interval $0 < a < 218$. This is what we were trying to prove.

As a side note, I got hold of the average height/weight data for
children ages 3 months-13 years at
http://www.babybag.com/articles/htwt_av.htm. The average
girl will have the same height in inches as weight in pounds
between 5 and 6 years of age; for boys, that point will come
between 6 and 7 years. I also put the data for girls (too lazy
to do it for boys too) into a Microsoft Excel spreadsheet and
put in trend lines for both height and weight. I used the
polynomial trend line for both; it appeared to fit the curves
best. For height, I got $h(x) = 0.2675x^{2} + 0.6438x + 15.379$
and for weight, I got $w(x) = -0.0036x^{2} + 2.4866x + 21.279$,
where x is the age measured in years.

That's a great response, LC. You give the heuristic argument,
then you go carefully through the steps, justifying each one by
appealing to the appropriate results from single-variable
calculus.

The reference to the weight and height data is a great addition
to the discussion. (How did you happen to find it by the way?)
Did you graph the two parabolas that you got for the approximations
of height and weight to see where they cross? Would using cubics or
higher order approximations give you essentially different
information? Since in the small there are daily variations in height
of an individual (shorter after a day of standing upright that upon
rising after a night of rest), it may be that a better model would
involve adding a periodic function with small amplitude. -tb

Appendix C. Course Evaluation

Q3. Online Student Interaction: Tables of Comparison.

	Math 18 Spring 2005		Math 35(*Honors*) Fall 2004		Fall 2003	
(*Base : # Respondents*)	(34)		(39)		(28)	
a. How often did you look at the work of other students?	#		#		#	
"Usually" / "Routinely"	7	21%	14	**36%**	4	14%
"Sometimes" / "occasionally"	11	32%	15	38%	17	61%
"Rarely" / "hardly ever"	13	**38%**	10	26%	3	11%
"Never"	3	9%	0	-	1	4%
No answer	0	-	0	-	3	11%
b. Did you look at the work of some students more often than others? If so, how did you decide whose work to look at?	#		#		#	
No	8	24%	9	23%	10	36%
Yes	23	68%	29	**74%**	14	50%
No answer	3	9%	1	3%	4	14%
c. How comfortable were you with having your homework available for other students to read?	#		#		#	
"Okay / no problem"	26	76%	34	**87%**	18	64%
"Some reservation *[but]* no objection"	5	15%	5	13%	7	25%
"Not comfortable"	2	6%	0	-	1	4%
No answer	1	3%	0	-	2	7%
d. How comfortable were you with having your exams available for other students to read?	#		#		#	
"Okay / no problem"	25	76%	30	77%	16	57%
"Some reservation *[but]* no objection"	3	**9%**	9	23%	6	21%
"Not comfortable"	4	12%	0	-	3	11%
No answer	2	3%	0	-	3	11%

Above columns headed: **Multivariable Calculus**

Q3. Online Student Interaction: Verbatim Comments.

Math 18 – Spring 2005

a. How often did you look at the work of other students?

> *"I looked at the work of a few other students for almost every homework. It was helpful because it helped me see what was the expectations [sic] for the course."* – jla

"Usually I looked at the work of one or two other students after I was done to see other methods of solving and, if I got the problem wrong, the 'right' way." ——ctf

"Rarely. If I was looking over a homework that I wanted to complete but didn't, I would refer to other students." –mmg

b. Did you look at the work of some students more often than others? If so, how did you decide whose work to look at?

"I was not discriminative [sic]; I generally looked at all the answers until I found one that was clear and marked correct." –msb

"Yes, but only because I had to scroll over more to get to some students. I generally started from the left and went along towards the right." – sje

c. How comfortable were you with having your **homework** available for other students to read?

"In the beginning I really did not like the system of reading other students HW. It made me feel really nervous and exposed and it made me want to leave problems blank rather than put an incorrect answer. As the semester progressed I realized what a useful tool it could be and I started reading other people's HW response more and more and fealt [sic] more comfortable with mine being read." –kmb

"It didn't really bother me that other people could look at my work. Either at the beginning or the end of the semester. Sometimes I felt bad about the quality of work that I handed in and I might have preferred that other not look at it, but it didn't concern me enough to make me want to change the system and the motivation to do a better job probably didn't hurt either." – kjm

"I felt fine having others read my homework because, frankly, I don't think anyone was using mine as a reference! On a serious note, though, I hadn't even thought of that being an issue until a friend questioned it. And Even then, I really didn't mind it. Only when I was working on the final did I personally even wonder about it." –jww

d. How comfortable were you with having your exams available for other students to read?

"On exams, I was able to put more time into refining my answer, so I didn't mind having people see that." – pbj

"See above. It didn't bother me at all until the final, and even then, it really didn't bother me." – jww

Q8/9. Demonstrations: Tables of Comparison.

(Base : # Respondents)	Multivariable Calculus					
	Math 18		Math 35(*Honors*)			
	Spring 2005		Fall 2004		Fall 2003	
	(34)		(39)		(28)	
a. Were the in-class demonstrations *useful*?	#		#		#	
No	3	9%	1	3%	1	4%
Yes	31	91%	38	97%	24	86%
no answer	0	-%	0	-%	3	**11%**
b. How *frequently* did you yourself use demonstrations in your work?	#		#		#	
Usually	6	18%	17	**44%**	6	21%
Occasionally / sometimes	15	44%	18	**46%**	12	43%
Rarely						
Never	13	**38%**	3	**8%**	2	7%
no answer	0	0	1	3%	8	29%
c. Did you create *any new demonstrations* using the software?	#		#		#	
No	31	91%	30	**77%**	10	36%
Yes	3	9%	8	**21%**	5	18%
no answer	0	-%	1	3%	13	**46%**
d. Any suggestions?	#		#		#	
No	18	**55%**	7	18%	1	**4%**
Yes	14	42%	17	44%	13	46%
no answer	1	3%	15	38%	14	50%

Q8/9. Demonstrations: Verbatim Comments.

Math 35 – Fall 2003

a. Were the in-class demonstrations *useful*?

> "The in class computer demonstrations proved very useful, and definitely helped in my understanding of the course material. I used some of the pre-made demos in my own work, and found the system was easy enough to manipulate to make it show what you wanted it to." – tlg

b. How *frequently* did you yourself use demonstrations in your work?

> "I used the demos less as the term went on because I got better at visualizing the graphs and vector analysis lent itself to a more analytical approach (as opposed to finding level sets for which it was good to have an idea what you were looking for). " – dhl

c. Did you create *any new demonstrations* using the software?

> "Being the computer illiterate that I am, I was unable to making any new demos for the use of the course"– tlg

d. Any suggestions?

> *"It would be nice if the program were made downloadable so that it could be run off a computer without having to go to the website"– yck*

DEPARTMENT OF MATHEMATICS, BROWN UNIVERSITY, PROVIDENCE, RI 02912, USA
E-mail address: `banchoff@math.brown.edu`

CBMS Issues in Mathematics Education
Volume **14**, 2007

Helping New Mathematics Faculty to Develop into Successful Teachers and Scholars

Christine Stevens

ABSTRACT. Recent changes in the way mathematics is taught at colleges and universities in North America offer special opportunities to new mathematics faculty, but they can also pose special challenges to those entering the profession. Project NExT (New Experiences in Teaching) is a professional development program for new and recent Ph.D.s in the mathematical sciences. It is run by The Mathematical Association of America, which is a professional organization devoted to collegiate mathematics, and it addresses all aspects of an academic career: improving the teaching and learning of undergraduate mathematics, maintaining research and scholarship, and participating in professional activities. During the last eleven years, Project NExT has helped almost 800 new Ph.D.s make the transition from being a graduate student to being a successful full-time faculty member. We will describe the components of Project NExT and discuss some of the factors that contribute to its success.

The excellent presentations at this symposium have described many exciting innovations in undergraduate mathematics education. We have heard, for example, about research experiences for undergraduates, creative ways to use computers to teach geometry and calculus, inquiry-based instruction, and the importance of incorporating applications into mathematics courses. These new approaches to teaching undergraduate mathematics are often especially appealing to the new recipients of Ph.D.s who join college and university faculties. Having grown up with calculators and computers, these new faculty are often eager to exploit the pedagogical potential of technology. Moreover, since they have very little experience with any method of teaching, new faculty are sometimes more willing than more established faculty to try new teaching strategies. And when they decide to implement one of these new ideas, they often have more energy than we older faculty members do.

On the other hand, pedagogical innovations can also pose special challenges for new members of the faculty. With so many good ideas available, they may have difficulty selecting a focus for their efforts, trying to do too much at once. Lacking much teaching experience, they may not be able to predict how students will react to a particular strategy, or how much of their own time it will consume. Finally, teaching is only one of their responsibilities as faculty members, and they cannot afford to neglect the other aspects of an academic career. They must establish and maintain an active research program, and they may also be expected to serve on committees and advise students.

Thus, although taking one's first job as a full-time faculty member has never been easy, the current climate of change in undergraduate mathematics education makes it especially hard for a new Ph.D. to make the transition from being a graduate student to being a full-time member of a college or university mathematics department. To ease that transition, and to promote the improvement of collegiate mathematics education, The Mathematical Association of America (MAA) in 1994 established a program called Project NExT (New Experiences in Teaching), of which I am now the director.

Project NExT is a professional development program for new and recent Ph.D.s in all of the mathematical sciences, including pure and applied mathematics, statistics, operations research, and mathematics education. It addresses all aspects of an academic career: improving the teaching and learning of undergraduate mathematics, maintaining research and scholarship, and participating in professional activities. It receives major funding from The ExxonMobil Foundation, with additional funding from other foundations, corporations, and professional organizations. In directing this project, I am fortunate to have the assistance of two outstanding co-directors Joseph Gallian (University of Minnesota Duluth) and Aparna Higgins (University of Dayton), and two excellent associate co-directors, Judith Covington (Louisiana State University Shreveport) and Gavin LaRose (University of Michigan).

The participants in Project NExT are chosen in the spring. Each year, about 70 new faculty members from colleges and universities throughout the United States and Canada are selected as Project NExT Fellows. In fact, while we are enjoying this interesting symposium, the four other members of the Project NExT "team" are busy reading this year's applications. The Fellows work at a wide range of institutions, including research universities, comprehensive regional universities, liberal arts colleges, and community colleges. What they share is an enthusiasm for teaching, a dedication to scholarly work, and an eagerness to participate in the mathematical community.

Each Project NExT Fellow participates in Project NExT sessions at three national meetings. The annual cycle begins with a workshop and the summer meeting of The Mathematical Association of America, which is the professional organization in the United States that is devoted to collegiate mathematics. It continues with special events at a large mathematics meeting in January that is jointly sponsored by several mathematics professional organizations, and it concludes at the MAA meeting the following summer. During the academic year, the Fellows are linked by a very active electronic discussion list.

Each Fellow is also matched with a more experienced member of the mathematical community, who serves as a "mentor" or "consultant" to the Fellow. In addition to establishing a personal relationship with their assigned Fellows, these consultants participate in the discussions on the Fellows' electronic discussion list, offering information and advice in response to the questions that are raised. Sometimes the roles are reversed, and the consultants seek advice from the Fellows (particularly about matters involving technology). Serendipitously, the participation of the consultants has also helped to build support for Project NExT within the mathematical community at large.

The program for the first workshop is planned by the director, co-directors, and associate co-directors. Although the program for the initial workshop has assumed a stable format, the topics and presenters are revised each year, to make sure that they reflect emerging issues in the profession, as well as our sense of the Fellows' current concerns. Last year, it included some sessions that focused on teaching specific courses, such as differential equations and geometry, and others devoted to general teaching strategies, such as using writing to teach mathematics. There were also a plenary address on the mathematical preparation of elementary and secondary school teachers, a panel on different techniques for assessing student learning, and a four-hour session on writing research papers and grant proposals. A copy of the program for the 2004 workshop at Brown University is included as an appendix.

The programs for the second two meetings are planned by the Fellows themselves, with guidance from the project directors. This arrangement permits the Fellows to tailor the topics to their interests, and it also gives them valuable experience in organizing sessions for professional meetings. At the Joint Mathematics Meetings this past January, the 2004-05 Fellows organized sessions on such topics as keeping current in research (especially if you are at a small institution), mentoring undergraduates, developing interdisciplinary courses, using technology appropriately in teaching, and dealing with departmental politics. At the upcoming workshop in August, 2005, they will be sharing ideas about how to teach calculus, discussing how to grade writing assignments in mathematics and how to incorporate the history of mathematics into their teaching, exploring collaborative learning, and discussing senior theses and senior "capstone" courses (courses that provide mathematics majors with an opportunity to integrate what they have learned).

Thus, from one perspective, Project NExT might be viewed as a giant human database of information about teaching, research, and service. Such a description would miss, however, one of the most essential features of Project NExT – the sense of community that it develops among the Fellows. Indeed, in preparation for this symposium, I asked some of the Fellows to identify those aspects of Project NExT that would be appropriate for mathematics faculty in other countries, where the educational system might be very different. Their immediate reply was "networking." Although the Fellows spend a significant amount of time at the workshops listening to presentations, the time that they spend in formal and informal discussions with each other and with the presenters is even more important. Having met and grown to trust one another at the initial workshop, they are able to use the Project NExT electronic discussion list to share their experiences, insights, successes, and even their failures.

Here's how one Fellow described the value of the electronic discussion list: "Project NExT gave me the confidence to try out new techniques, blending them with my own style. I could e-mail the group when something wasn't working, and fix it that way. I wasn't going it alone." By providing this kind of on-going support, Project NExT helps the Fellows to overcome one of the most common obstacles to implementing new teaching strategies, which is the temptation to give up if the new strategy does not work perfectly the very first time. With the help of the Project NExT electronic discussion list, the Fellows are able to refine their teaching techniques until they reached their intended pedagogical goal.

Project NExT also helps new faculty to overcome the isolation that they feel if they work in small departments or in departments where they lack colleagues who share their teaching and research interests. As one Fellow put it: "Project NExT has absolutely changed my life. Without it, I would have worked in virtual isolation at a small school, exposed to very little." The Fellows appreciate the fact that "at any time, day or night, there are dozens of people eager to serve as sounding boards or provide information." One Fellow summed up the value of the Project NExT electronic discussion list by likening it to "joining the biggest and most active mathematics department in the world." This sense of belonging simultaneously to a group of supportive peers and to an active mathematical community enables the Fellows to continue their growth as teachers and scholars, long after their formal participation in Project NExT has ended.

As Project NExT enters its twelfth year, we are beginning to see the long-term effects of this professional development program on the individual participants themselves, on their departments, and on the profession as a whole. Looking first at the numbers, we note that a total of 766 new mathematics faculty have participated in Project NExT, and the 2005-06 Fellows, who will be selected later this month, will bring that figure up to about 835. They work in about 500 different colleges and universities, and in most cases the entire department has benefited from the Fellows' participation in Project NExT. Indeed, many institutions support their Fellows' participation in Project NExT precisely because they anticipate that the Fellow will play a major role in revising curriculum and pedagogy. Fellows have, for example, been given responsibility for revising and revitalizing specific courses, such as pre-calculus, differential equations, or mathematics for future elementary teachers. They have introduced technology into the curriculum and implemented cooperative learning. They have created distance learning courses and developed new graduate programs in mathematics education.

Project NExT has also gotten the Fellows involved in the mathematical community. When I go to a mathematics meeting in the United States, I am always impressed by the large number of young mathematicians who are participating. They are presenting papers and organizing sessions at meetings; publishing expository, pedagogical, and research papers; winning grants for research and education; and serving on the committees and even the governing boards of mathematics professional organizations.

Project NExT seeks to engage the Fellows, at the outset of their careers, in a stimulating discussion of important issues in teaching and learning, to introduce them to a professional community in which those issues can be discussed in a sustained way, and to supply them with tools that will enable them to address these issues in their own classes and their own institutions. It also seeks to develop a broad understanding of their responsibilities as faculty, so that they can integrate their roles as teachers, scholars, and advisers.

These goals are relevant to mathematical communities throughout the world, and so it is natural to ask what the example of Project NExT might offer to mathematicians in other countries who want to establish professional development programs for new faculty. Perhaps the best way to answer that question is to identify several issues that play a critical role in the design and operation of Project NExT:

Do new mathematics faculty already have teaching experience, either as graduate students or before attending graduate school? In the United States, most mathematics graduate students have already taught several different courses by the time they receive their doctorates. As a result, they already know some of the "basics" of teaching. Although each individual's experiences are fairly narrow, collectively the Fellows have taught many different courses in many different ways. By sharing those experiences, they can learn quite a lot from each other. For topics with which they have no personal experience, however, such as teaching theoretical or advanced courses, they very much appreciate the advice of experts, and they find it frustrating if they are asked to discuss these topics on their own.

What do institutions expect from new faculty? Almost all institutions of higher education in the United States expect their faculty to be effective teachers, to engage in scholarly activities, and to provide service to the institution and to the profession. The relative importance of these components varies from institution to institution, however, as does the definition of "scholarly activities." Some institutions expect new faculty to publish mathematical research papers, while others value papers and presentations about pedagogy. A professional development program for new faculty should help them to figure out what their institution expects and give them guidance in meeting those expectations.

How much freedom do new mathematics faculty have in deciding how and what to teach? We have found that the Fellows want ideas that they can use right away – or, at least, very soon – in their classes. If a professional development program is going to emphasize innovations in mathematics curriculum and pedagogy, then it is important for them to have the freedom to implement these new ideas, at least to some extent. Even if new faculty do not choose the textbook or write the syllabus, they may be able to introduce changes in the kinds of assignments that they give to students or in the way that they use class time. In order to assure that the Fellows have the necessary freedom to try new ideas, we require that each application to Project NExT include a letter of support from the department chair that describes how the applicant's participation in Project NExT would contribute to the department's goals.

What is the role of new faculty in the mathematics department? In large mathematics departments in the United States, most curricular decisions are made on a department-wide basis, and there may be little opportunity for new faculty to influence those decisions. In smaller departments, however, we often find that the Fellows are expected to take a leadership role in implementing change. The letters written by the applicants' department chairs, for example, often identify major changes for which they want the Fellows to take primary responsibility. These changes include such innovations as introducing technology into the curriculum, developing distance learning courses, and completely revising the mathematics courses taken by future elementary and secondary school teachers.

How does the mathematical community welcome new members of the profession? In Project NExT, we were surprised to discover how timidly new faculty approached the profession and how little they felt welcomed into it. By making a deliberate effort to involve new faculty in their activities, the mathematics professional organizations in the United States have not only contributed to the professional development of these new faculty, but have also enhanced their own vitality.

How can one build a sense of community among the participants? For several reasons, this may be the most important question to ask. New faculty have many questions about their new responsibilities, and they need a forum in which they can seek candid advice from trusted friends and counselors outside their institutions, without fear of professional reprisal. That same sense of community prompts others to contribute their replies to those questions. Moreover, if a professional development program can succeed in establishing a community that continues beyond the official Fellowship year, then it will greatly enhance the long-term impact of the program.

In describing Project NExT, I have focused on what new faculty learn from it. But it is also a professional development program for the more experienced mathematicians who run it and participate in it. Through Project NExT, I have learned about teaching strategies that I use in my own classes, and Project NExT gave me an insight into the perspective of new faculty that helped me to be a better department chair. So I am grateful to Project NExT for what it had done for me, and also to my co-directors and associate co-directors, Joseph Gallian, Aparna Higgins, Judith Covington, and Gavin LaRose. Finally, I express my thanks to Deane Arganbright and KAIST for inviting me to this outstanding conference.

For more information about Project NExT, consult our website at `http://archives.math.utk.edu/projnext/`

Project NExT: New Jobs, New Responsibilities, New Ideas
Program for the Workshop in Providence, Rhode Island
August 9 - 11, 2004

The Project NExT registration area is in the lobby of Barus & Holley on the Brown University campus.

MONDAY, AUGUST 9

11 am - 1:15 pm	Arrival and registration
1:30 - 1:45 pm	Welcome and opening remarks
	T. Christine Stevens, Project NExT director
2:00 - 2:45 pm	Small group discussions
2:55 - 3:45 pm	*The Freedom of Choice*
	Janet Andersen, Hope College
3:50 - 4:20 pm	BREAK
4:30 - 5:15 pm	Small group discussions
5:30 - 7:00 pm	DINNER
7:30 - 9:00 pm	*Conversation with the Leadership*

Carl Cowen, Indiana University Purdue University, Indianapolis President-elect, The Mathematical Association of America

Martha Sicgcl, Towson University Secretary, The Mathematical Association of America

John Ewing, Executive Director, American Mathematical Society

Gilbert Strang, Massachusetts Institute of Technology Former President, Society for Industrial and Applied Mathematics

TUESDAY, AUGUST 10

7:00 - 8:15 am	BREAKFAST
8:30 - 9:45 am	*Selected topics in teaching undergraduate mathematics I* (Five simultaneous sessions)

Getting Your Students to Read Their Calculus Text
– Thomas Ratliff, Wheaton College, MA

Adding the Words: Using Writing to Teach Mathematics
– John Meier, Lafayette College

Discrete Math, Arthur Benjamin, Harvey Mudd College

Group Projects in Upper Division Courses such as Abstract Algebra and Real Analysis – Cheryl Chute-Miller, State University of New York, Potsdam

So You're an Advisor – Now What?
– Sandra Paur, North Carolina State University, Raleigh

9:55 - 10:25 am	BREAK
10:25 - 11:40 am	Panel: *Using class time well*
	sarah-marie belcastro, Xavier University, Ohio

	Thomas Garrity, Williams College

Thomas Garrity, Williams College
Richard Jardine, Keene State College

11:45 am - 1:15 pm   LUNCH

1:15 - 2:30 pm   Repeat of morning breakout sessions

2:40 - 3:40 pm   *A Mathematician's Role in the Mathematical Education of Teachers*
W. James Lewis, University of Nebraska, Lincoln

3:40 - 4:10 pm   BREAK

4:10 - 5:25 pm   Panel: *The faculty member as teacher and scholar*
David Carothers, James Madison University
Megan Kerr, Wellesley College
Bozenna Pasik-Duncan, University of Kansas
Brian Winkel, United States Military Academy

5:30 - 7:00 pm   DINNER

8:00 - 10:00 pm   Social Event for all Project NExT Fellows and invited guests

WEDNESDAY, AUGUST 11

7:00 - 8:00 am   BREAKFAST

8:15 - 9:30 am   *Selected topics in teaching undergraduate mathematics II*
(Five simultaneous sessions)
Alternative Approaches to Geometry
– Colm Mulcahy, Spelman College
The Pleasure of Teaching Linear Algebra
– Gilbert Strang, Massachusetts Institute of Technology
Teaching Students to Write Proofs
– Carol Schumacher, Kenyon College
Effectively Using Applied Writing Projects in Calculus
– P. Gavin LaRose, University of Michigan
Teaching Differential Equations – Michael Moody, Olin College

9:35 - 10:05 am   BREAK

10:10 - 11:25 am   Panel: *Finding out what your students have learned*
Thomas Banchoff, Brown University
Olympia Nicodemi, State University of New York, Geneseo
Catherine Roberts, College of the Holy Cross

11:25 - 11:40 am   Planning session for January Meetings in Atlanta

11:45 - 12:30 pm   Small Group Discussions with other Project NExT Fellows
(organized by research area)

12:30 - 1:45 pm   LUNCH

2:00 - 3:15 pm   Repeat of morning breakout sessions

3:15 - 3:50 pm   BREAK

3:55 - 5:45 pm   *Closing Session*
Recognition of 2003-04 Fellows
Presentation: *Finding Your Niche in the Profession*
Joseph Gallian, University of Minnesota, Duluth

7:30 – 9:30 pm   Mathfest Opening Banquet
Master of Ceremonies: Annalisa Crannell,
Franklin & Marshall College
Presentation: *Captivating Stories for Mathematics Students*
Dan Kalman, American University

Project NExT Courses During the Mathfest: Four-hour courses meeting on Thursday and Friday, August 12 and 13.

- A. *Math Modeling in the Curriculum* – Catherine Roberts, College of the Holy Cross, 1:00 - 3:00 p.m.
- B. *Preparing to Teach Mathematics for Prospective Teachers* – Judith Covington, Louisiana State University, Shreveport, 1:00 - 3:00 p.m.
- C. *Introductory Statistics* – Jeff Witmer, Oberlin College, 1:00 - 3:00 p.m.
- D. *Getting Your Research off to a Good Start/ Proposal Preparation for Projects in Undergraduate Mathematical Sciences*– Joseph Gallian, University of Minnesota, Duluth, and Calvin Williams, National Science Foundation, 3:15 - 5:15 p.m.
- E. *Undergraduate Research – How to Make It Work* – Aparna Higgins, University of Dayton, 3:15 - 5:15 p.m.

Mathematics and Computer Science Department, St. Louis University, St. Louis, MO , 63103, USA

E-mail address: stevensc@slu.edu

CBMS Issues in Mathematics Education
Volume **14**, 2007

Computer Algebra and Human Algebra

William G. McCallum

ABSTRACT. The existence of computer algebra systems, whether or not we use them in our classroom, requires us to think more carefully about the problems we give our students. In particular, in trying to separate out the purely computational aspects of student work, the parts that could be done by a computer, we can see more clearly the parts that require mathematical understanding. I will illustrate this distinction with some examples of problems and projects that make use of computer algebra systems.

1. Computer Algebra

About ten years ago, I found a final exam from the calculus course at a prestigious United States university, and gave it to the symbolic manipulation program Mathematica. Here is the exam:

(1) Evaluate $\int \dfrac{x^2}{x^2 - 3x + 2}\, dx$.

(2) Evaluate $\int \dfrac{dx}{(9 - x^2)^{3/2}}$.

(3) State whether the following integrals converge or diverge, and give your reasons:

   (a) $\int_2^\infty \dfrac{x^2 + 4x + 4}{(\sqrt{x} - 1)^3 \sqrt{x^3 - 1}}\, dx$.

   (b) $\int_0^1 (1 - x)^{-2/3}\, dx$.

   (c) $\int_0^{\pi/2} \tan x\, dx$.

(4) State whether the following series converge or diverge and justify your answers.

   (a) $\sum_{n=4}^\infty \dfrac{1}{n(\ln n)(\ln(\ln n))^2}$.

   (b) $\sum_{n=1}^\infty \dfrac{5\sqrt{n} + 100}{2n^2\sqrt{n} + 9\sqrt{n}}$.

   (c) $\sum_{n=1}^\infty \dfrac{(-1)^{n-1}}{\sqrt{n}}$.

(5)   (a) Find the Taylor series at $x = 0$ (McLaurin series) of $f(x) = x\cos\sqrt{x}$.

(b) Find the radius of convergence of $\displaystyle\sum_{n=0}^{\infty} \frac{n^2}{5^n} x^n$.

(6) Write all solutions of $z^3 = 8i$ in polar and Cartesian form, simplified as much as possible.

(7) (a) Find $\displaystyle\lim_{x \to 0} \frac{\cos(x^3) - 1}{\sin(x^2) - x^2}$.

   (b) Evaluate $\displaystyle\sum_{n=0}^{\infty} \frac{\sin n\theta}{n!}$.

(8) Find all real solutions of the following:
   (a) $y'' - 2y' + 5y = 0$.
   (b) $y'' - 2y' + 5y = \cos x$.

(9) The region between $y = x^{1/3}$, the x axis, and the line $x = 1$ is revolved around (a) the x axis, (b) the y axis. Find the volume in each case.

(10) Find the arc length of $y = \cosh x$ (i.e., of $y = \dfrac{e^x + e^{-x}}{2}$) from $x = 0$ to $x = 1$.

Notice that all the problems on this exam are requests to perform a computation, something computers are quite good at. Mathematica did indeed do well on the exam, although it only gave the answers and did not show any work, and it had to resort to numerical approximation in some cases; for example, it did not appear to try any convergence tests on the series. Nonetheless, the fact that it can do essentially the entire exam is quite shocking, and has an effect on attitudes both of instructors and students.

There is, however, an important difference between the reaction of instructors and the reaction of students when they encounter this fact. Instructors tend to react by forming attitudes to the technology. Some want to ban the technology from the classroom, so that students will learn to carry out the procedures by hand. Others look for more interesting ways to use technology in their teaching. Either way, there is a focus on the technology: how to use it, or how to get rid of it.

Students, however, are more inclined to experience a change in attitude to the mathematics itself when they discover that it can be done by computer. They are likely to wonder why they must learn to do it by hand, and are going to need different justifications from the ones that might have worked in previous times. The sorts of questions exhibited here are likely to seem quite pointless to them. Maybe not ten years ago, when Mathematica was an exotic program to most students. But these days there are much more friendly "homework helpers" available on the web, which will not only give you the answers, but show the work necessary to achieve the answers as well. For now such things are not easily accessible in exam rooms. But soon we will have to start confiscating mobile phones as students enter the exam if we don't want such access.

Sooner or later, we must face the effect of technology on student attitudes to mathematics. It is worth spending some time now thinking about how human algebra and computer algebra might co-exist. In order to do this, I suggest that we enter a frame of mind where it is not the technology that is foremost, either as an eagerly welcomed tool or as a despised abomination, but rather one where the mathematics is foremost, and we imagine what it might be like to explore mathematical ideas in an environment where symbolic computational power is available at our fingertips. What questions would we like to ask our students in such an environment?

2. Using the Power of the CAS

It seems pretty clear that purely computational questions are not appropriate for CAS. Good CAS questions need an extra element, in addition to computation. One possibility is to take advantage of the CAS to pose questions which would normally have been too intensely computational. Here is an example.

> A population, P, in a restricted environment may grow with
> time, t, according to the *logistic function*

$$(1) \qquad P = \frac{L}{1 + Ce^{-kt}}$$

> where L is called the carrying capacity and L, C and k are
> positive constants.
> (1) Find $\lim\limits_{t\to\infty} P$. Explain why L is called the carrying capacity.
> (2) Using a computer algebra system, show that the graph of
> P has an inflection point at $P = L/2$.

One might imagine that students will do the first part by hand, and use a CAS for the second part. Using a CAS, we find

$$(2) \qquad \frac{d^2 P}{dt^2} = -\frac{LCk^2 e^{-kt}(1 - Ce^{-kt})}{(1 + Ce^{-kt})^3}.$$

Thus, $d^2 P/dt^2 = 0$ when

$$1 - Ce^{-kt} = 0$$

and there is an inflection point at $t = \ln(1/C)/k$, yielding

$$P = \frac{L}{1 + Ce^{\ln(1/C)}} = \frac{L}{1 + C(1/C)} = \frac{L}{2}.$$

Notice that there is a more elegant way to see this, suggested by the close proximity of equations (1) and (2): the second derivative is zero when $1 - Ce^{-kt} = 0$, which implies that $1 + Ce^{-kt} = 2$. A hand computation would have separated the function from its second derivative by a considerable number of lines and a considerable amount of student exhaustion, but the CAS, by juxtaposing the two, opens up the possibility for this kind of insight.

In this sort of problem, computers are viewed as tools that enable us to give more interesting and difficult questions. This is certainly a possibility. But it seems unlikely that students will make such a neat division between simple computations, which they do by hand, and more complicated ones, which they do by computer. If computers do all the algebra, what is left for humans? Quite a lot, it turns out.

3. Approaching Simple Questions Differently

Consider the problem of computing

$$\int_a^b \sin(cx)\, dx.$$

One might give this problem just after teaching the Fundamental Theorem of Calculus, expecting students to find an antiderivative for $\sin(cx)$ and use it. But what if a student uses a CAS to get

$$\int_a^b \sin(cx)\,dx = \frac{\cos(ac)}{c} - \frac{\cos(bc)}{c}.$$

Is there any way we can profit from the situation mathematically? We might ask the student to compare

$$\int_a^b \sin(cx)\,dx = F(b) - F(a)$$

with the answer from the CAS, which suggests that

$$F(x) = -\frac{\cos(cx)}{c},$$

a conjecture that is confirmed by taking the antiderivative. The Fundamental Theorem of Calculus appears in this line of reasoning, but rather as a vehicle for reflection than a computational tool. Nonetheless, it seems reasonable to expect that this sort of problem can be useful in teaching students to find antiderivatives.

4. Exploration and Conjecture

Another sort of CAS problem asks students to use the CAS as a probe in the mathematical world.

(1) Use a computer algebra system to differentiate $(x+1)^x$ and $(\sin x)^x$.
(2) Conjecture a rule for differentiating $(f(x))^x$, where f is any differentiable function.
(3) Prove your conjecture by rewriting $(f(x))^x$ in the form $e^{h(x)}$.

Answers from different computer algebra systems may be in different forms. One form is:

$$\frac{d}{dx}(x+1)^x = x(x+1)^{x-1} + (x+1)^x \ln(x+1)$$

$$\frac{d}{dx}(\sin x)^x = x\cos x(\sin x)^{x-1} + (\sin x)^x \ln(\sin x)$$

Both answers follow the general rule

$$\frac{d}{dx}f(x)^x = xf'(x)\,(f(x))^{x-1} + (f(x))^x \ln(f(x)),$$

which the student can then verify. This problem calls on skills of pattern recognition that are not required when students are asked to compute derivatives by hand. Indeed, the skill of logarithmic differentiation is often learned in a purely mechanical way by students, so that although they can carry it out, they do not always see the regularity and structure in the answers it produces. The CAS reverses the process of learning by asking students first to see the regularity and structure, and then to learn the procedure.

5. Puzzles

If you play around with a CAS for a while, you are bound to come across problems like the following, which are best described as mathematical puzzles.

(1) Use a computer algebra system to find $P_{10}(x)$ and $Q_{10}(x)$, the Taylor polynomials of degree 10 about $x = 0$ for $\sin^2 x$ and $\cos^2 x$.

(2) What similarities do you observe between the two polynomials? Explain your observation in terms of properties of sine and cosine.

The Taylor polynomials of degree 10 are

For $\sin^2 x$, $P_{10}(x) = x^2 - \dfrac{x^4}{3} + \dfrac{2x^6}{45} - \dfrac{x^8}{315} + \dfrac{2x^{10}}{14175}$

For $\cos^2 x$, $Q_{10}(x) = 1 - x^2 + \dfrac{x^4}{3} - \dfrac{2x^6}{45} + \dfrac{x^8}{315} - \dfrac{2x^{10}}{14175}$

The coefficients in $P_{10}(x)$ are the opposites of the corresponding coefficients of $Q_{10}(x)$. The constant term of $P_{10}(x)$ is 0 and the constant term of $Q_{10}(x)$ is 1. Thus, $P_{10}(x)$ and $Q_{10}(x)$ satisfy

$$Q_{10}(x) = 1 - P_{10}(x).$$

This makes sense because $\cos^2 x$ and $\sin^2 x$ satisfy the identity

$$\cos^2 x = 1 - \sin^2 x.$$

In this problem the puzzle is to explain a surprising pattern in the coefficients, and a simple identity is the key to unlocking the puzzle. This puzzle is not only enjoyable, but reinforces the connection between the Taylor polynomial and the corresponding function.

Let me conclude with one more extended puzzle.

For positive a, consider the family of functions

$$y = \arctan\left(\frac{\sqrt{x} + \sqrt{a}}{1 - \sqrt{ax}}\right), \qquad x > 0.$$

(1) Graph several curves in the family and describe how the graph changes as a varies.

(2) Use a computer algebra system to find dy/dx, and graph the derivative for several values of a. What do you notice?

(3) Do your observations in part (b) agree with the answer to part (a)? Explain.

The graph has a jump discontinuity whose position depends on a. The function is increasing, and the slope at a given x-value seems to be the same for all values of a.

Most computer algebra systems will give a fairly complicated answer for the derivative. Here is one example; others may be different.

$$\frac{dy}{dx} = \frac{\sqrt{x} + \sqrt{a}\sqrt{ax}}{2x\left(1 + a + 2\sqrt{a}\sqrt{x} + x + ax - 2\sqrt{ax}\right)}.$$

When we graph the derivative, it appears that we get the same graph for all values of a.

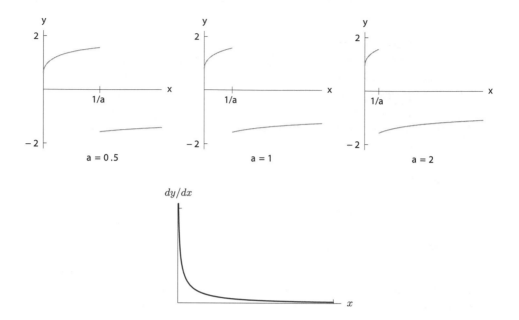

How do we explain what is going on here? Since a and x are positive, we have $\sqrt{ax} = \sqrt{a}\sqrt{x}$ (a CAS usually needs to be told this fact, since it can't be assumed in general). We can use this to simplify the expression we found for the derivative:

$$\frac{dy}{dx} = \frac{\sqrt{x} + \sqrt{a}\sqrt{ax}}{2x\left(1 + a + 2\sqrt{a}\sqrt{x} + x + ax - 2\sqrt{ax}\right)}$$

$$= \frac{\sqrt{x} + \sqrt{a}\sqrt{a}\sqrt{x}}{2x\left(1 + a + 2\sqrt{a}\sqrt{x} + x + ax - 2\sqrt{a}\sqrt{x}\right)}$$

$$= \frac{\sqrt{x} + a\sqrt{x}}{2x\left(1 + a + x + ax\right)} = \frac{(1+a)\sqrt{x}}{2x(1+a)(1+x)} = \frac{\sqrt{x}}{2x(1+x)}$$

Thus the derivative is independent of a. This explains why all the graphs look the same in part (b). (In fact, of course, they are not exactly the same, because $f'(x)$ is undefined where $f(x)$ has its jump discontinuity.)

6. Conclusion

There is a common thread to all these problems: they reverse the normal order of things. Whereas a paper-and-pencil problem ends with the answer, or at least with the result of a computation, a CAS problem starts with that result. In each case, there is a chance to contemplate the answer given by a CAS and see structure in it. This has the effect that the work the problem demands is more about reflecting on or interpreting a symbolic form, rather than in producing it. This is a radical change in the cognitive demand of algebra problems. Although we might in retrospect wish that we had all along been asking students to reflect on their answers, this piece is usually lost, and students in general do not think of algebraic expressions as objects for interpretation. Rather they think of them as grist for the computational mill; things to which something—anything—must be done. The CAS, by pulling the carpet out from under the skill of doing things, brings to the fore the fact that algebra is a subject with meaning as well as actions.

In the computer age, human algebra is more a matter of reflection, interpretation, and pattern recognition, and less a matter of computation.

DEPARTMENT OF MATHEMATICS, THE UNIVERSITY OF ARIZONA, TUCSON, AZ 85721-0089, USA

E-mail address: wmc@math.arizona.edu

CBMS Issues in Mathematics Education
Volume **14**, 2007

Teaching Mathematics Graduate Students to Teach: An International Perspective

Solomon Friedberg

ABSTRACT. We discuss a new method for the development of university teaching skills: case studies. Case studies are accounts of classroom interactions that pose a set of difficulties or crises to be analyzed. When groups of graduate students and faculty analyze these cases, sometimes from different points of view, they are led to think deeply about what makes high-quality mathematics teaching.

High-quality teaching of mathematics at the university level is important to every country. Almost all of the best jobs in the global economy require fluency in mathematics, and a great many require advanced technical knowledge. High-quality university math instruction contributes to high student achievement in the quantitative disciplines and prepares students for good jobs. Moreover, university faculty in most countries teach the students who will themselves become the next generation of pre-collegiate math teachers. If these teachers are to succeed with their own students they must have, along with teaching skills, detailed mathematical knowledge, understanding, and skills. So it is important that these teachers-to-be attend well-taught mathematics classes at the university. Thus every nation should be vitally interested in high-quality mathematics teaching at the university level.

Such considerations suggest that faculty development as regards teaching might be useful. Though this is certainly true, it is also true that math faculty find themselves with a wide range of responsibilities and time constraints and might not be receptive to such development. Instead, it may be more practical to focus on future math faculty.

Mathematics graduate students go on to become the next generation of university faculty. I wish to argue here that it is possible to develop programs for such graduate students that equip them to do an excellent job as future university teachers. Moreover, it is possible to do so without unduly impacting their mathematics studies. The implementation of such a program—one whose goal is to prepare its graduates to teach a class independently and excellently upon graduation—can thus be a high-reward, low-cost opportunity.

A case studies workshop as described in this paper was presented by the author at the 1st KAIST International Symposium on Enhancing University Mathematics Teaching. The author wishes to thank the organizers sincerely for the invitation to do so. The author's research during the preparation of this article was supported by NSF grant DMS-0353964.

The question of what to do to achieve this goal, then, is the concern here. Certainly, students in such a program should practice giving mathematical explanations. One can bring graduate students to the blackboard to explain some problem or concept, and then give them critical feedback. In addition, one should talk about technical aspects of teaching, such as how to plan a course, how to write a syllabus, how to write and fairly grade a test, and how to assign course grades. To go beyond this, one might read advice about how to teach well, such as the book by Krantz [4], and students might then practice the teaching of a specific mathematical topic, balancing examples, heuristics, theorems, explanations or proofs, and problems that extend the topic. One might also wish to discuss things specific to one's institution, such as university rules as regards registration and grading, accommodations for students with disabilities, privacy of student records, and cheating. All university mathematics faculty must be aware of such matters.

Though such steps are valuable, one can rightly ask if they are sufficient to promote excellence in teaching. They do not prepare novice teachers, for example, for crises in the classroom, for student responses that were not expected, for students who are not motivated to learn mathematics or who have difficulty in learning mathematics, for classrooms with a range of student abilities, interests, and knowledge levels, for what to do when the students do not understand what has been taught. In the rest of this article, I will discuss an approach to developing excellent teaching that seeks to go beyond the steps outlined in the preceding paragraph but that functions well in concert with them, that takes full account of the need for individuals to develop their own styles of excellent teaching, and that addresses teaching crises and issues such as the ones mentioned above.

The approach is based on *case studies*. Case studies are written (possibly fictionalized) depictions of university student-TA (Teaching Assistant) interactions in undergraduate mathematics instruction. Each case presents a teaching difficulty or a key moment of decision in the classroom—in short, a teaching crisis—together with a context for understanding or examining the crisis. Typically a number of issues are intertwined, sometimes subtly. The cases are to be read and analyzed by a group consisting of the teaching assistants and a faculty facilitator. The goal of such a discussion is to consider different approaches and to invite different judgments concerning the teaching crisis. In doing so, the participants are led to think deeply about teaching and to learn from the collective experiences and judgments of the full group of participants.

It is important to emphasize that the case studies method is open to different approaches to teaching excellence. Indeed, just as not all first-rate mathematics researchers have the same style in their approach to research, there is more than one way to be an excellent teacher. Choices, governed by personal style, mathematical taste, and individuals' understandings of the goals of their teaching (among other factors), play a role. Such choices often appear in the case discussion, and participants will understand that there are a range of well-thought-out decisions that could be appropriate to a given situation.

As an example, here is a brief outline of one case study. A graduate student runs a problem session for Calculus students. He is concerned that students are interested only in obtaining the answers to the homework at the problem session. He wants to promote their understanding without undercutting the principle that they should do the homework themselves. What should he do? (The full case is approximately 10 pages long and describes the TA's interactions with his students during a specific class meeting in detail. It raises not just one but a number of pedagogical issues.)

The key point of the case studies method is that the group analyzes the case events. They need not agree but should be able to support their ideas. The case discussion is a variation on the Socratic method[1]. What is behind such a method? It is this. Beyond the fundamental requirement of subject matter knowledge, and beyond technical skills such as the ability to write clearly, *good teaching requires good judgment*. A good teacher must decide how to blend examples and theorems to maximize understanding of the result and its applications, how to balance the needs of students of different levels and abilities, how to assign homework that will get students to work to the maximum of their abilities, what to say when a student is in difficulty. Good judgment enters fundamentally into the classroom choices that make the difference between excellent and mediocre teaching.

Can good judgment in the context of teaching be taught? There is a great deal of evidence that, surprising, it can be, using the case study method described above. Case studies originated in US business and law schools, professions where good judgment is a key to success. In those disciplines, students read written depictions of key decisions in commerce and legal proceedings and analyze them, typically in a group discussion format. The persistence of this method attests to its usefulness. The case studies method has been applied to university-level teaching since the 1960s, much of this work originating with Prof. C. Roland Christensen of the Harvard Business School [1]. Once again, the goal is to develop good judgment by the group analysis of cases, this time concerning teaching. However, the issues and situations that appear in Christensen's cases are far from the ones of concern to most mathematics graduate students.

This author led a large-scale project to develop case studies that were directed at mathematics graduate students in US universities[2]. This work has been published in the book [3] (available in both faculty and graduate student editions) and it is now being used in a wide range of US universities. The cases in [3] give mathematics graduate students the chance to analyze complicated realistic teaching situations, to think in advance about how to handle teaching crises so that they can deal with them when they arise in real life, to formulate their own approach to teaching, and to view teaching as non-trivial and a worthy subject of serious discussion.

The cases we produced were evaluated for effectiveness. Among the conclusions was that the cases were effective in promoting thought and dialogue about teaching, and that they were also effective at communicating to foreign graduate students many aspects of university culture in the United States that impact teaching. We did find that beginning graduate students, many of whom have not thought about how to teach mathematics, did not all possess the experience base to use the cases

---

[1]Socratic method: "A pedagogical technique in which a teacher does not give information directly but instead asks a series of questions, with the result that the student comes either to the desired knowledge by answering the questions or to a deeper awareness of the limits of knowledge."—American Heritage Dictionary of the English Language, Fourth Edition, Houghton Mifflin Company.

[2]Development team members: Avner Ash, Elizabeth Brown, Solomon Friedberg, Deborah Hughes Hallett, Reva Kasman, Margaret Kenney, Lisa A. Mantini, William McCallum, Jeremy Teitelbaum, and Lee Zia.

effectively, but also that it was possible to address this by including a more experienced TA in the discussion group. Lastly, we found that leading a case discussion requires the faculty leader to use very different skills—the skills of a discussion leader—than come in to play in most mathematics teaching.

To address this last point, the author, Dr. Diane Herrmann of the University of Chicago, and the American Mathematical Society have teamed up to offer a series of workshops for faculty who work with TAs on teaching. The latest of these was at the 2005 joint math meetings, the annual conference sponsored by all the major American mathematical societies. Attendees included 4 faculty from non-English-speaking countries.

This brings us to the topic of applying these methods internationally. There are two separate reasons to do so. The first is to prepare individuals to go to the United States for graduate school or to hold postdoctoral or other faculty positions. These individuals are more likely to be successful if they are able to teach US students well (for graduate students, for example, good teaching is critical to receiving and retaining financial support). Doing so requires language ability in English, knowledge of the culture and expectations of United States universities, and skill in the teaching of mathematics. The case studies in [3] contribute to all of these. Besides contributing to the development of mathematics teaching skills, they serve as a catalyst to reflect on how the culture of US universities will affect the way that someone from another culture teaches in the US. They also contribute to language ability if the discussion takes place in English, particularly if participants are asked to directly model or role-play their proposed response to a classroom situation. So it would be valuable to implement a TA-development program using the case studies in [3] for this reason.

The second reason to apply the case study method internationally is to improve the teaching of mathematics graduate students worldwide. As we have argued above, this method has the potential to be highly effective when used with mathematics graduate students, and implementing such a program can be of value to every country. However, it seems likely that some additional, country-specific, work with the cases will be necessary to achieve the full potential of the method. The first question is to how to produce high quality relevant case studies for other, non-English speaking, countries. A starting point would be to to translate the materials we have produced into other languages. Some of the cases could be translated with minimal changes. Others might reflect aspects of university culture in the United States that are not relevant elsewhere; for example, issues related to teacher-student interactions that are different in different cultures. An alternative approach would be to generate a set of case studies specific to another country's university teaching. The cases in [3] were developed through an extensive process of writing, feedback from graduate students and faculty, and rewriting. This process is described in detail in [3]. It might be possible to shortcut the process described there somewhat, but the following guiding principles are important: (i) the cases (though possibly fictional) must be completely true-to-life; (ii) the cases must raise non-trivial questions in teaching; (iii) the cases must not be one-sided, but rather raise questions about which it is possible for intelligent people to disagree. Feedback from graduate students is crucial in evaluating draft cases.

Another issue for applying the case study method internationally concerns how to lead a discussion. Faculty must create an environment in which graduate students are willing to express their opinions candidly, and they must learn to facilitate discussions that truly promote good judgment in making teaching decisions. Doing so requires a range of skills related to discussion-leading. There are several ways to develop such skills. One is to learn the method from someone who is skilled in using it with mathematics graduate students. The number of such individuals is increasing, but most are based in the United States. A second is to seek out those who have discussion-leading skills in one's own country. For example, discussions are a common feature in the humanities, and many US universities provide workshops for faculty on how to lead discussions. If such opportunities are available elsewhere it might be valuable to take advantage of them. A third method is to learn about discussion-leading by reading about it, and then to experiment. To learn the method by reading, one might consult the faculty edition of our book [3], which contains extensive information on how to use case studies (as well as detailed teaching notes on each of our cases), or Christensen's classic text [1]. The volume [2] contains additional information about discussion leadership and the potential impact of discussions.

In conclusion, it is time for the mathematics profession to articulate the goal that each new Ph.D. in mathematics be an excellent mathematics teacher upon completion of their doctoral studies. Case studies for mathematics graduate students can contribute to achieving this goal. It would be of great interest to implement this method in a variety of cultures and countries.

References

[1] L. B. Barnes, C. R. Christensen, and A. J. Hansen, *Teaching and the Case Method*, Third Edition, Harvard Business School Press, Boston, MA, 1994.

[2] C. R. Christensen, D. A. Garvin and A. Sweet (eds.), *Education for Judgment: The Artistry of Discussion Leadership*, Harvard Business School Press, Boston, MA, 1991.

[3] S. Friedberg and the BCCase Development Team, *Teaching Mathematics in Colleges and Universities: Case Studies for Today's Classroom*, Issues in Mathematics Education Volume 10, (available in faculty and graduate student editions), American Mathematical Society, Providence, RI, 2001.

[4] S. Krantz, *How to Teach Mathematics*, Second Edition, American Mathematical Society Providence, RI, 1999

DEPARTMENT OF MATHEMATICS, BOSTON COLLEGE, CHESTNUT HILL, MA 02467-3806, USA
E-mail address: friedber@bc.edu

CBMS Issues in Mathematics Education
Volume **14**, 2007

Computers Supporting Mathematical Insight-
Two Case Studies

Erich Neuwirth

ABSTRACT. Quite often computers are seen as tools to implement mathematical methods after they have been completely understood (and the theorems setting the ground have been proved). We set out to show - with two examples - how computers can help with understanding mathematical concepts, and how mathematics teach ing possibly can be enhanced by integrating facilities to develop concepts and to experiment with methods into the curriculum. The first example uses only very simple mathematics, the second one, on the other hand, tries to illustrate some important concepts in combinatorics with computer support.

1. Preliminaries

Quite often computers are seen as tools to implement mathematical methods after they have been completely understood (and the theorems setting the ground have been proved). We set out to show - with two examples - how computers can help with understanding mathematical concepts, and how mathematics teaching possibly can be enhanced by integrating facilities to develop concepts and to experiment with methods into the curriculum. The first example uses only very simple mathematics, the second one, on the other hand, tries to illustrate some important concepts in combinatorics with computer support.

2. Geometry, Caricatures, and Spreadsheets

Compare the two faces in Figure 1. The face is easily recognized. It is Arnold Schwarzenegger. For many people the second face is more easily recognized than the first one, it looks "more like Arnold". The first picture, however, is a digitized photo of Arnold's face. The second one is derived from the first one by mathematical means. To be able to do this, we need another face in Figure 2.

Before we discuss this face, we need to know that faces are represented as sets of open polygons. Each line is a polygon with up to 15 vertices. A whole face is described by 186 points. The third face is an average face in a very literal sense, it was constructed by averaging a few hundred faces, both male and female. Then, we connect corresponding points by line segments, as illustrated in the next image. The original data can be found in [**1**] and [**2**].

FIGURE 1

FIGURE 2

Now we divide each of these line segments by a fixed ratio (say 0.5) and connect all these "generalized midpoints". Figure 3 shows the base face (the average face), the reference face (Arnold's face), and the face produced by connecting the midpoints. It also shows the connecting lines.

Changing the division ratio allows us to construct a face very similar to Arnold, or a face very similar to an average face. Instead of constructing points between the two faces, we can also extend the line segments beyond Arnold's face. The second picture above was constructed by extending the connection lines by a factor of 0.25. This method computes the difference between a face (Arnold's face in our case) and the average face, and then exaggerates the difference. This concept is also used for drawing caricatures. Therefore, our algorithm is a mathematical way of creating caricatures. This method also can be used to construct somebody's opposite by taking the difference from the average and inverting. Put more formally, a face is a set of 186 points (and therefore can be considered a point in $\mathbb{R}^{392}$). Given two faces F_0 and F_1 we can create a parameterized family of faces $F(\alpha) = \alpha F_0 + (1 - \alpha)F_1$. We have $F(0) = F_0$ and $F(1) = F_1$. $F(1.25)$ for many faces works quite well as a caricature. $F(-1)$ is the opposite.

This example can be used to illustrate the concept of convex and affine linear combinations. It can easily be implemented with a spreadsheet program. If the

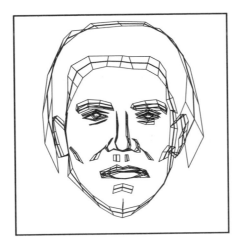

FIGURE 3

spreadsheet program also allows the use of sliders (described in) to control cell values, it is possible to create an animated graph with the user changing α, the caricature factor, to their wishes. Using such an easy to use animation tool (described in [**3**]) opens new ways of understanding concepts like parameterized families of curves and also shows surprising applications of important mathematical concepts.

In TV, movies quite often use the effect of morphing, meaning to transform one object smoothly into another one. Our example helps students understand that the underlying technique is rather simple mathematics, namely convex combinations. Therefore, just a little linear algebra and analytic geometry can be used to create surprising visual effects. Making such effects accessible to students and showing them that this may be implemented without any special software, but with easily available programs like spreadsheet programs, can help our students to enjoy mathematics while learning abstract concepts.

3. Some combinatorics, mainly recursive

Let us start with a simple question: Among all the one million numbers with 6 digits, how many can be written using exactly one digit (like 222222), exactly 2 digits (like 344343), and so on?

Of course, mathematicians will try to solve a more general problem. Given n positions and k different digits, how many numbers can be written using k digits in the n positions. 344343 in this sense is a 6-position 2-digit number. We want to find an expression for $F(n, k)$ for any possible value of n and k. We also can rephrase the problem and state that we would like to fill the table

	1	2	3	4	5	6
1	F(1,1)	F(1,2)	F(1,3)	F(1,4)	F(1,5)	F(1,6)
2	F(2,1)	F(2,2)	F(2,3)	F(2,4)	F(2,5)	F(2,6)
3	F(3,1)	F(3,2)	F(3,3)	F(3,4)	F(3,5)	F(3,6)
4	F(4,1)	F(4,2)	F(4,3)	F(4,4)	F(4,5)	F(4,6)
5	F(5,1)	F(5,2)	F(5,3)	F(5,4)	F(5,5)	F(5,6)
6	F(6,1)	F(6,2)	F(6,3)	F(6,4)	F(6,5)	F(6,6)

In each cell of the table, we count the corresponding number of numbers with a given number of positions and a given number of digits in use. If only one digit is available, it always is possible to write exacly 10 numbers. The 3-position 1-digit numbers are 111, 222, 333, ... It is also clear that no number can be written if the number of digits is larger than the number of positions. Therefore, we can fill some places in our table:

F(n,k)	1	2	3	4	5	6
1	10	0	0	0	0	0
2	10		0	0	0	0
3	10			0	0	0
4	10				0	0
5	10					0
6	10					

For 2-position 2-digit numbers, we have free choice for the first number, giving us 10 possibilities, and 9 choices (since we are not allowed to use the same digit again) for the second digit. So in total, we have 90 2-position 2-digit numbers.

F(n,k)	1	2	3	4	5	6
1	10	0	0	0	0	0
2	10	90	0	0	0	0
3	10			0	0	0
4	10				0	0
5	10					0
6	10					

We could extend this argument for all n-position n-digit numbers, but the remaining cells in our table cannot be filled by this argument. Therefore, we need to find a new way of solving the problem. We may notice that each 3-position number produces 10 successors, namely 4-position numbers which have the initial 3 digits equal to the original 3-position number. If the original number has 2 different digits, the successors can only have 2 or 3 digits. Therefore, each n-position k-digit number produces 10 successors. k of these successors have k digits, and $(10 - k)$ successors have $k + 1$ digits. This is best illustrated by the following diagram:

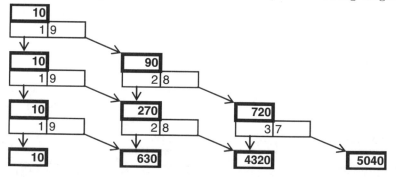

Each number in a cell migrates down in the row below twice. When migrating vertically it is multiplied by the column number. When migrating down diagonally, it is multiplied by 10 - column number *of the source column*. It is important that we describe the structure in terms of a number being split. This helps us understand the counting mechanism. If we want to know how many n-position k-digit number there are, we need to find the the number of the n-1-position k-1-digit numbers and the number of the n-1-position k-digit numbers. Translating what we know we get $F(n,k) = kF(n-1,k) + (10 - (k-1))F(n-1,k-1)$, or $F(n,k) = kF(n-1,k) + (11-k))F(n-1,k-1)$. Only our way of looking at the successor relation makes it clear how 11 gets into this formula. Our flow diagram also makes it clear how the relationship produces the computational result. It also makes very clear what the marginal cases are. In short, we get visual insight in the structure of the problem much better than of the recursion equation were stated without any visual considerations.

Additionally, the flow diagram also makes it clear that recursive definitions are not extremely difficult to understand. If in a table each number can be computed from some numbers in the row above and to the left, it is quite obvious that the table is well defined. Of course, without computers computing F(300,125) in this way would be rather tedious, but nevertheless quite possible. This illustrates that computers can turn recursive definition from theoretical objects to practical tools.

We also observe that the geometric relation of the input objects in the recursion equation to the result is always the same: only the element above and above and to the left are used. This is exactly the kind of relation that spreadsheet formulas handle extremely well. In spreadsheet language this kind of reference is called relative reference. Therefore, we also see that software which is available on almost every desktop PC in any workplace can be used to study mathematical ideas of rather abstract nature. This might help demonstrating that the power of mathematics is not tied to specialists and specialized software like computer algebra programs, but also can help to solve problems with everyday tools.

It turns out that this basic point of allows to derive rather deep and surprising results even in such a well established field as combinatorics (see [4]).

4. Summary

Out two examples tried to demonstrate that the use of computers in somewhat nontraditional ways can help to make mathematics more enjoyable. In some cases as illustrated in our first example – mathematical concepts can be used to create pleasing but surprising applications.

Relatively simple software like spreadsheet programs can also help students understand mathematical structures and gain new insights by creating new metaphors going beyond visualization of functions. Therefore, mathematics educators should look even more seriously into using computers as conceptual notepads, and not just as tools for creating illustrations for already well understood problems.

References

[1] Susan E. Brennan, Caricature Generator: The Dynamic Exaggeration of Faces by Computer. *Leonardo*, Vol.18 no.3, 1985, pp. 170-178.
[2] A. K. Dewdney, Computer Recreations. *Scientific American*, Oct. 1986. Reprinted in Dewdney, *The Armchair Universe* (1988)
[3] E. Neuwirth, D. Arganbright *The Active Modeler - Mathematical Modeling with Microsoft Excel*, Brooks-Cole (2004)
[4] E. Neuwirth, Recursively defined combinatorial functions: extending Galton's board. *Discrete Math.* **239** (2001), 33-51.

FACULTY OF COMPUTER SCIENCE, UNIVERSITY OF VIENNA, VIENNA, AUSTRIA
E-mail address: erich.neuwirth@univie.ac.at

CBMS Issues in Mathematics Education
Volume **14**, 2007

Mathematics—at your service

T.M. Mills and Peter Sullivan

ABSTRACT. The aim of this paper is to discuss mathematics service teaching. We discuss the roles of the mathematics professor, the student, the Head of the Department of Mathematics, the Dean of the Faculty, and the President on the University in successful service teaching.

1. Introduction

The aim of this paper is to discuss mathematics service teaching in a university.

We use the term *mathematics* to refer to the mathematical sciences in general and hence we include pure mathematics, applied mathematics, statistics, and operations research.

The term *service teaching* covers two types of mathematics teaching found in universities.

(1) The first type involves teaching mathematics to a group of students from a particular discipline. For example, one might teach a subject *Pharmacy Mathematics* which is, as the name suggests, a mathematics subject designed specifically for students in a Pharmacy degree. We can assume that such a class of students ought to have homogeneous academic and professional interests which are often not particularly mathematical.

(2) The second type of service teaching involves presenting a mathematics subject to students from a variety of disciplines other than mathematics. Many courses on calculus or elementary statistics are of this type. A standard calculus course may be attended by students from engineering, arts and sciences, and business. And we cannot assume even that students in these subgroups have homogeneous interests; some science students may have strong preference for the life sciences while others much prefer the physical sciences. Often, in subjects of this type, the class size is large.

This paper is concerned with both these types of mathematics service teaching. Thus, teaching topology to advanced undergraduate students who are majoring in mathematics is not regarded as service teaching.

We assume that this service teaching takes part in the following environment. The mathematics subject is presented by a professor in the Department of Mathematics; the department is led by a Head of Department; the department is part of the Faculty of Science led by a Dean; the Faculty of Science is a faculty in the university led by a President.

In this paper we consider the roles of different players in service teaching. The role of the mathematics professor is considered in the next section; then we consider the role of the student, the role of the Head of Department of Mathematics, the role of the Dean, and finally the role of the President. The role of the student has been placed near the centre of the paper to reflect the central place of the student in the learning process.

The findings in this paper are based on the research literature and the authors' academic experience which has been gained, for the most part, in Australia.

The paper concludes with a list of ideas for further research.

2. Professor

Teaching service subjects in mathematics presents major challenges.

The professor has to explain difficult, technical concepts to students who may not be well trained in mathematics. For example, to convey the meaning of *the line of best fit in the least squares sense* to students in a business statistics course, is more demanding than explaining the concept to students in a mathematical statistics course. The challenge for the professor is to convey this idea in a manner that is clear, accurate, understandable, and interesting.

Another challenge for the professor is to provide some motivation for these students in a class where, as mentioned in §1, the students may have either diverse interests or interests aligned with a specific profession.

These challenges also provide opportunities to foster desirable graduate attributes, and to incorporate research findings into the teaching process. In this section we discuss these two avenues.

2.1. Graduate attributes. Professional bodies, universities, and even governments are now interested in developing lists of attributes that are deemed to be important for today's university graduate. The professor can use these attributes to motivate students, to develop course materials, to suggest new approaches to assessment.

For example, *The Institution of Engineers Australia* defines clearly the attributes it expects to see in a graduate engineer. We quote from [13, p. 5].

> "Graduates from an accredited program should have the following attributes:
> - ability to apply knowledge of basic science and engineering fundamentals;
> - ability to communicate effectively, not only with engineers but also with the community at large;
> - in-depth technical competence in at least one engineering discipline;
> - ability to undertake problem identification, formulation and solution;
> - ability to utilise a systems approach to design and operational performance;

- ability to function effectively as an individual and in multi-disciplinary and multi-cultural teams, with the capacity to be a leader or manager as well as an effective team member;
- understanding of the social, cultural, global and environmental responsibilities of the professional engineer, and the need for sustainable development;
- understanding of the principles of sustainable design and development;
- understanding of professional and ethical responsibilities and commitment to them; and
- expectation of the need to undertake lifelong learning, and capacity to do so."

It is clear that engineering students can develop some of these attributes through their mathematical studies e.g. the "ability to apply knowledge of basic science and engineering fundamentals". It is not so clear how they can develop "professional and ethical responsibilities" through mathematics. But it is worthwhile considering how this can be done because such consideration may lead to interesting developments in how we teach engineering mathematics.

We emphasise that using relevant professional examples need not detract from the rigor of the discipline, nor from the generalisability of the principles underlying the examples.

Once the mathematics professor is aware of these professional requirements, they can be built into the teaching. Then the engineers-in-training also become aware of both the expectations of their profession, and the role of their mathematical studies in their professional training. Furthermore, when the degree program is being accredited by the professional body, it is helpful to the accreditation process if the professor has deliberately built these considerations into the teaching.

Some universities set their own expectations for graduate attributes. For example, the University of New England in Australia expects that UNE graduates will display the following eight attributes: knowledge of a discipline, communication skills, global perspective, information literacy, life-long learning, problem solving, social responsibility, and, team work. (These are developed in more detail in [29].) The mathematics professor at UNE will be able to demonstrate how a student could develop most of these attributes through studying mathematics.

While it is not necessary for the student to develop all these attributes in every subject, again it is an interesting exercise to consider how studying mathematics can contribute to developing a "global perspective" or "social responsibility".

As an aside, at least some of the attributes can be fostered simply by considering the format in which a question is posed. For example, in teaching students about correlation, one might ask students to calculate the sample coefficient of correlation from some bivariate data. On the other hand, if students are asked to construct a sample of bivariate data in which the sample coefficient of correlation is 0.5, then they have a deeper learning experience in problem solving. Not only do they get a richer sense of the concept, but the task is suitable for team work. Further, the teams will find that there are many possible solutions and pathways to those solutions. A useful resource about asking questions in mathematics and statistics in university courses is Hubbard [12].

By utilising the sheer variety of graduate attributes listed above, the professor will ensure that more students in a service subject will be able to see how studying mathematics contributes to their general education. And reflecting on these attributes may bring new perspectives to how the professor presents the subject. Reflecting on these attributes does help to give the subject more cohesion and alignment [3].

2.2. Teaching informed by research. Since the main functions of universities are teaching and research, it is important that undergraduate students get a taste of both throughout their training. Then they will graduate with a full appreciation of the role of universities in our society. Hence, at La Trobe University, we strive to provide "teaching and learning that is both student-focussed and is informed by research, scholarship and professional practice." [16]

Now it is easy to see how research work could have an impact on the presentation of mathematics subjects for advanced students. It is also easy to see how the research literature in the relevant profession could be linked to the presentation of targetted service subjects such as *Numerical Methods for Civil Engineering*, or *Statistics for Zoology*.

However, it is more difficult to see how the results of academic research can be used to inform the presentation of general service subjects such as *Calculus 1*. Here are some suggestions.

- The research underpinning presentations in these proceedings can be utilised: peer support, case studies, undergraduates learning through research, using technology effectively all have potential for improving service teaching.
- The research findings in education generally, and mathematics education in particular, can be applied or adapted to our own university teaching. Ramsden [23] discusses "deep learning" as distinct from "surface learning" among university students; Biggs' [3] thesis is that objectives, teaching activites, and assessment in a subject ought to aligned to provide coherence in the subject. Prosser and Trigwell [22] is excellent summary of the research on what we know about how university students learn.

  The professor's task is to *apply* this knowledge to teaching mathematics in universities.
- Suggestions for specific research projects are offered at the end of this paper.
- In [20], the role that professional practice can play in service teaching and course development is explored.
- Mathematical service courses are often large first classes. Practical suggestions for teaching in such situations can be found in [11], [12], [24], [26]. Work on popularizing mathematics as outlined in [9] can be adapted to making service teaching more interesting for professors and students alike.
- McInnis *et al.* [18] report on a study of the first year experience of Australian undergraduate students across a range of degree programs, backgrounds, and universities. Part of the study involved the analysis of 4028 responses to a questionnaire. One item on the questionnaire asked first year students to react to the statement:

Staff are enthusiastic about the subjects that they teach.

According to the report, 14% strongly agreed, 39% agreed, 34% neither agreed nor disagreed, 10% disagreed, and 3% strongly disagreed [18, Table 6.1, p. 57].

Thus, 47% of respondents could not bring themselves to agree that the teaching staff are enthusiastic about the subjects they teach. On the other hand, research tells us that a feature of good teaching is a "desire to share your love of the subject with students" [23, p. 86].

University professors who are involved in teaching first year students (and mathematics service teaching is often at first year level) ought to be aware of these research findings.

In this section we have discussed how the professor can use graduate attributes and published research findings to enhance service teaching in mathematics.

3. Student

In discussing service teaching, Jones [14, p. 147] issues the following challenge.

"The essential point is to present a sufficient variety of approaches that each student can find something appropriate to his interests and abilities."

Thus we come to considering the needs of *each* student.

3.1. What is relevant to the student? The student in a service subject may not regard mathematics as a "first love". Here we examine two common, broad generalisations and see that the situation is more complicated than such generalizations suggest.

1: Students in service courses like to see applications of mathematics to their primary discipline. A first year student in an engineering degree may be interested in ideas associated with engineering and regard mathematics as a useful tool for solving real engineering problems. However, usually the student knows more about mathematics than engineering! After all, the first year student has been studying mathematics for many years but has been studying engineering for only a few months. Thus, trying to sell mathematical ideas in terms of engineering problems may introduce more confusion than clarity.

It is not unusual to encounter engineering students who do not like chemistry or even physics; they may even prefer mathematics to physics or chemistry. Hence, trying to explain mathematical ideas in terms of the physical sciences may not be illuminating to such students.

2: Students in service courses do not enjoy mathematics for its own sake. In some service courses, especially—but not only—those with a strong mathematical flavour such as engineering or computer science, students may really enjoy mathematics for its own sake even though they do not see their vocation in mathematics. "Mathematics is a subject, not an occupation" [10, p. 4]. However, an enjoyable, successful experience in a mathematics class may influence them to change their views on this matter. Just one particular lecture, or one special assignment, or even an encouraging remark from the professor can have disproportionate benefits.

So it is difficult for the professor to decide what is relevant to each student in a service course.

3.2. Ask the student. In service subjects, students often ask "How is this relevant to me?". Clearly the professor has some responsibility to answer this question. However, the student also has some responsibility in this regard.

Just think about how you, as a professional mathematician, attend a seminar. When you sit in a seminar, you try to follow the speaker's argument; in your mind, you try to find connections between what the speaker is saying and your own experience; you try to find examples and counter-examples to the ideas being put forward. This active listening is how we develop awareness of the subject.

The undergraduate student needs to develop a similar level of awareness and responsibility. So, when teaching regression to pharmacy students, the professor may well turn the tables and ask the student:

What is the use of regression in pharmacy? (Hint: Go to a search engine; enter the terms "regression" and "pharmacy" and discuss two examples.)

The Australian Vice-Chancellors' Committee puts it plainly in a national policy statement:

> "Learning is the outcome of a collaborative partnership between teachers and students. Over time students should take increasing responsibility for their own learning."[1, p. 9, para 26]

We suggest that students should begin the process of shouldering this responsibility in their first year—and service courses in mathematics have an important place in this process. In listening to lectures, reading their texts, and studying mathematics, students should heed the advice from Buddha:

> "Monks and scholars must not accept my words out of respect, but must analyze them the way a goldsmith analyzes gold—by cutting, scraping, rubbing, melting." [19, p. 18]

4. Head of Department

In Australian universities, the income of an academic departments is a function of many variables, the most important of which is the number of students being taught by the department. Thus, teaching more students leads to a greater income for the department. It is not unusual for a Department of Mathematics in an Australian university to rely heavily on service teaching income for its survivial. Hence the role of the Head of Department is important in managing service teaching. For a thorough discussion of the role of Head of Department, see Tucker [27].

In this section, we discuss two particular aspects of the role of the Head of Department of Mathematics in promoting service teaching.

4.1. Inter-departmental relations. In a business-like manner, we will use the word *customer*. From the point of view of the Head of Department, there are two types of customers to consider: the students in the service subject, and the departments with which these students are associated. Thus, for example, in teaching *Statistics for Zoology*, the Head of Department of Mathematics must be aware of the needs and aspirations of the Department of Zoology as well as those of the students. It is sensible for the two departments to be engaged in discussions about the subject on a regular basis. Indeed, the Department of Mathematics may wish to appoint a mathematician to take special responsibility for liaising with the the Department of Zoology.

Thus, some of the most important tasks of the Head of Department are to ensure that relations with other academics departments are running smoothly, and that the Department of Mathematics is well regarded in the university.

Relationships with other departments can be enhanced through research activities also. Collaborative research projects, and seminars of mutual interest, can be useful tools for building strong links with colleagues. While these links may be developed for the purpose of research, they can be valuable when considering teaching issues.

However, in spite of efforts to build good relations between departments, things may change. Here are two examples.

First, the Department of Zoology may decide that it will no longer insist that its students take *Statistics for Zoology* as a separate subject. Instead, statistical ideas will be incorporated into a bigger subject called *Research Methods for Zoologists* which will deal with ethics, research planning, writing a literature review, using research software, and statistical analysis.

As a second example, a new zoologist, who is also a very capable statistician, is hired. This newly appointed professor will be able to incorporate statistical ideas in the context of contemporary zoology research. So the Department of Zoology decides that it can teach *Statistics for Zoology* quite well without assistance from the Department of Mathematics.

In situations as depicted in these two examples, there is little that the Department of Mathematics can do to change matters. Indeed, if we focus on the education of students in these examples, perhaps the Department of Mathematics ought not resist such developments. However, the good relationships that have been nurtured in the past between the two departments will enable both groups to deal with these changes in a professional and amicable manner.

We have seen in this section that successful service teaching requires mutual respect and trust between departments. The Head of Department carries a key responsibility in these matters.

4.2. Assigning teaching responsibilities. Another major task of the Head of Department to allocate teaching responsibilites. Many years ago in Australian universities, lectures to large first year classes were often presented by the most senior professors.

This is no longer as common. Muller and Hidgson mention that the faculty members who are teaching large service subjects may be "sometimes less than enthusiastic" [21, p. 152]— a view endorsed by first year students in the study by McInnis *et al.* [18]. The Head of Department needs to be sensitive to this possibility and encourage the department to create an environment that values this work. To this end, it is instructive to consider whether the income generated by a particular class is commensurate with the associated expenditure on teaching for that class. One may draw up a table like Table 1.

This simple exercise encourages us to value those large first year classes with students from many disciplines. Although some cross-subsidisation from larger classes to smaller classes is inevitable, it is only fair to the students, and faculty, involved in those large classes that they receive a commitment from the department which is in accordance with the contribution of that class to the department's income. In any case, it is useful for all members of the department to be aware of these data.

Subject	Calculus for Engineers	Statistics for Zoology	...	Total
Class size	n_1	n_2	...	$\sum n_i = N$
% Department load	$100n_1/N$	$100n_2/N$	...	100%
Teaching hours	c_1	c_2	...	$\sum c_i = C$
% Department effort	$100c_1/C$	$100c_2/C$	...	100%

TABLE 1. Income & expenditure

5. Dean

Just as it is important for the professor to understand the students' perspective in service teaching, so too is it important that the professor and Head of Department understand the Dean's perspective.

In general, in addition to similar concerns to the Head of Department related to financial viability, deans are interested in the reputation of the faculty. They are delighted when professors engage in high profile, peer recognised, research and publication. They also rejoice in courses that attract high quality students and produce satisfied, employable professionals with an orientation to life-long learning and perhaps further study, preferably within the faculty.

These days, there is considerable potential for mathematics service teaching across faculty boundaries. The Department of Mathematics may be located in the Faculty of Science. But there is considerable scope for the mathematical sciences in business, health science, social sciences, IT, education. Here the Deans play a key role in facilitating service teaching across faculties. It is possible that two or more deans have interest in mathematics service teaching and hence it is necessary that there be good relationships between the faculties in order to maximise the potential for mathematics teaching in the university. Thus, it is important that each Dean endeavours to build cooperative links with other Deans.

For a general discussion of the role of the Dean, see [28]. Being aware of the academic research on the role of a dean would be helpful to a dean's professional development.

6. President

Neither author of this paper has been a university president. However, this does not prevent us from having some views of the role of the President in the successful delivery of service teaching. Bargh *et al.* [2] provide a thorough analysis of the role of a President in a contemporary university. We make three suggestions that have some bearing on teaching in general, and service teaching in particular, in the university.

First, the President should set the tone by emphasising the importance of teaching in the university. Teaching is central to the university's mission and its importance should be reflected in many policies and procedures. Dartmouth College in USA has long had a reputation for excellence in teaching. When asked what are the reasons behind this success by one of the authors in 1984, John Kemeny [15] wrote:

"In my opinion, the most important factor is the institution's reward system.... At Dartmouth the tenure review places equal emphasis on research and teaching".

In writing about how universities can develop life-long learning in undergraduate teaching, Candy *et al.* [**4**, p. xiii] write:

"there must be congruence between institutional rhetoric and the reality, and this applies not only to students' experiences, but also to valuing and rewarding of academic staff for their needs to emphasise and develop lifelong learning competence".

Thus, the university's systems for appointment, tenure, and promotion play a key role in how teaching is regarded in the university by the faculty. Furthermore, the special difficulties associated with service teaching should be recognised in such systems.

Many academic disciplines are now becoming far more quantitative. We see the mathemaical sciences playing an important role in social sciences, business, health sciences, education, as well as traditional areas such as science and engineering. Thus, there is considerable scope for mathematics service teaching across faculty lines. Thus, the President needs to ensure that there are appropriate policies and practices in place that facilitate cooperation between the deans of the various faculties. This spirit of cooperation is essential to the success of cross-faculty teaching.

Third, on the national front, the President needs to ensure that there is appropriate input from the university into national debates that are relevant to university teaching [**1**], [**7**]. Related to this, the President needs to make the university community aware of these national issues [**2**, p. 109].

Note that the President may realise these goals by delegating the responsibility to another senior person (e.g. Vice President for Academic Affairs).

7. Conclusions

Jones [**14**] argues that the classifying of a university mathematics subjects as either a subject for the mathematician or a subject for the non-mathematician is too simplistic. He suggests that a balance of theory and applications ought to be present in all subjects although the balance will vary from subject to subject.

We would agree with Jones' suggestion about balance. However, the size of the class and the backgrounds of the students in many service subjects means that these subjects often present special challenges that face all those involved. Service teaching is important, requires hard work, and should be a team effort across the university.

In this paper we have discussed the roles that various people play in successful service teaching of mathematics in a university. We summarise our suggestions in Table 2. The bibliography contains resources that contain many useful suggestions and ideas.

Evidence based practice is emphasised particularly in clinical health sciences: we believe that the same regard for evidence based practice ought to apply to teaching—especially in a university. Thus, for each of the faculty members involved, we have emphasised the importance of being aware of research findings in our roles as professor, head of department, dean of faculty, or president.

We conclude with a selection of suggested research topics that require further investigation.

Player	Role with respect to service teaching
Professor	Provide motivation for students to learn Understand students' perspectives Be aware of research on university teaching [3], [22], [23]
Student	Take increased responsibility for learning Be aware of the subject structure —objectives, teaching methods, assessment
Head of Department	Promote the importance of teaching in the Department Allocate teaching assignments and appropriate resources Develop good relations with other departments Be aware of research on chairing the department [27]
Dean	Promote the importance of teaching in the Faculty Facilitate cooperation between departments Be aware of research on role of Dean [28]
President	Promote the importance of teaching in the University —especially in policies on appointment, tenure, promotion Facilitate cooperation between faculties Contribute to national debate on university teaching Be aware of research on role of President [2]

TABLE 2. Roles of key players in successful service teaching

(1) **How do students learn mathematics?** This is a very broad—but fundamental—question. We need to explore the vast amount of knowledge about how university students learn in general ([22], [23]) in the specific context of learning mathematics. The paper by Cope and Prosser [6] is an excellent example of how one applies this general knowledge to learning about information systems in particular. The results of investigating such issues for mathematics service teaching to some discipline could vary from with the discipline.

(2) **How do students read mathematics?** (This is a specific instance of the preceeding general question.) Reading mathematics is a difficult task when compared with reading texts from other disciplines. The language of mathematics is concise, precise, and laced with symbols. How do our students read the text books — especially in service courses? (This question was motivated by a famous study on how students in education read their texts, [17, pp. 16 *et seq.*].)

(3) **How do we present mathematics using IT?** The role of symbols in mathematics offers challenges to those involved in presenting mathematics via on-line teaching, video-conferencing and other forms of IT. As such courses will often be *service courses*, these challenges are relevant to this paper.

(4) **How do we organize service teaching?** In §1, we assume that mathematics service subject is presented by a professor in the Department of Mathematics. There are other ways in which mathematics service teaching could be provided to students. A research project could be designed around comparing various administrative structures in which mathematics could be offered in a university. This study may involve a survey of universities around the world to examine different arrangements.

(5) **What does industry want?** A professor who is involved in teaching statistics to accounting students could investigate the needs of professional accountants for statistical training. Such a study would involve talking to professional accountants in a range of careers, examining job descriptions for accounting positions, discussions with key people in professional bodies, and assessing the role of statistics in the professional literature. Other professors involved in teaching statistics to accountants or designing accounting programs would be interested in reading the results of such a research project.

Similar studies could be developed for ascertaining the mathematical needs of other industries or professions. Furthermore, the results may vary with time and country.

(6) **Is service teaching in graduate courses different?** According to F. Simons [**25**, pp. 35–43]:

> "Service teaching to undergraduates has its own particular problems, both with respect to mathematical contents and to didactics."

Indeed, the literature concentrates on service teaching to undergraduate students. This raises the following research question. Is the situation different when we offer mathematical service courses in graduate courses in areas such as management, engineering, health sciences, social sciences? Given the necessity of understanding how students learn in planning for effective teaching, it is important to understand how graduate students in non-mathematical areas approach mathematical ideas that they will encounter in their course work programs.

(7) **Graduate attributes for mathematics graduates.** Reflecting on how mathematics contributes to the attributes of graduates in other disciplines leads one to ask the question: *What do we expect of graduates in mathematical sciences?* This question could be investigated at a national level.

Acknowledgement

We are grateful to Dr Johwan Ahn (Biotechnology Research Centre, La Trobe University) for assistance with preparing the overheads for the presentation of this paper at the symposium.

References

[1] Australian Vice-Chancellors' Committee, *Universities and their Students: Principles of the Provision of Education by Australian Universities*, Canberra: AV-CC, 2002.

[2] C. Bargh, J. Bocock, P. Scott, and D. Smith, *University Leadership: The Role of the Chief Executive*, Buckingham: SRHE and Open University Press, 2000.

[3] J. Biggs, *Teaching for Quality Learning at University*, Second ed., Buckingham: SRHE and Open University Press, 2003.

[4] P.C. Candy, G. Crebert, and J. O'Leary, *Developing Lifelong Learners through Undergraduate Education*. Canberra: Commonwealth of Australia, 1984.

[5] R.R. Clements, P. Lauginie, and E. de Turckheim (eds.), *Selected Papers on the Teaching of Mathematics as a Service Subject*. Wien: Springer-Verlag, 1988.

[6] C.J. Cope and M. Prosser, Identifying didactic knowledge: An empirical study of the educationally critical aspects of learning about information systems. *Higher Education*, **49** (3) (2005), 345–372.

[7] Department of Education Science & Training, *Striving for Quality: Learning, Teaching and Scholarship*. Canberra: Commonwealth of Australia, 2002.

[8] A.G. Howson, J.-P. Kahane, P. Lauginie, and E. de Turckheim (eds.), *Mathematics as a Service Subject*. Cambridge, Cambridge University Press, 1988.

[9] A.G. Howson and J.-P. Kahane (eds), *The Popularization of Mathematics*. Cambridge, Cambridge University Press, 1990.

[10] A.G. Howson and J.-P. Kahane, A study overview. In [**9**, pp. 2–37].

[11] R. Hubbard, *53 Interesting Ways to Teach Mathematics*. Bristol: Technical and Educational Services Ltd, 1990.

[12] R. Hubbard, *53 Ways to Ask Questions in Mathematics and Statistics*. Bristol: Technical and Educational Services Ltd, 1995.

[13] The Institution of Engineers, Australia, *Manual for accreditation of professional engineering programs* Canberra: Inst. Eng. Aust., 7 October 1999.

[14] G.A. Jones, Teaching mathematics to mathematicians and non-mathematicians. In [**5**, pp. 136–147]

[15] J.G. Kemeny, personal communication to T.M. Mills, 1984.

[16] La Trobe University, *Learning and Teaching at La Trobe University 2005–2008*. Bundoora: La Trobe University, 2005.
     Available at URL: http://www.latrobe.edu.au/teaching/

[17] F. Marton and S. Booth, *Learning and Awareness*. Mahwah NJ: Lawrence Erlbaum Assoc., 1997.

[18] C. McInnis, R. James, and C. McNaught, *First Year on Campus: Diversity in the Initial Experiences of Australian Undergraduates*. Canberra: Australian Government Publishing Service, 1995.

[19] A. de Mello, *Awareness*, New York: Doubleday, 1992.

[20] T.M. Mills, A mathematician goes to hospital. *Australian Mathematical Society Gazette*, **31** (5) (2004), 320-327.
     Available at URL: http://www.austms.org.au/Publ/Gazette/2004/Nov04/

[21] E.R. Muller and B.R. Hidgson, The mathematics service course environment. In [**5**, pp. 149–156]

[22] M. Prosser and K. Trigwell, *Understanding Teaching and Learning: The Experience in Higher Education*. Buckingham: SRHE and Open University Press, 1999.

[23] P. Ramsden, *Learning to Teach in Higher Education*. Second ed., London: RoutledgeFalmer, 2003.

[24] C. Sandison (née McPhail), Teaching large first year maths classes. School of Mathematics and Applied Statistics, University of Woolongong NSW 2522, Australia.

[25] F. Simons, Teaching first-year students. In [**8**, pp. 35–43]

[26] E.R. Sowey, Teaching statistics: making it memorable. *Journal of Statistical Education*, **3** (2) (1995).
     Available at URL: http://www.amstat.org/publications/jse/v3n2/sowey.html

[27] A. Tucker, *Chairing the Academic Department: Leadership among Peers*. New York: American Council on Education/Macmillan, 1984.

[28] A. Tucker and R. Bryan, *The Academic Dean: Dove, Dragon, and Diplomat*. New York: American Council on Education/Macmillan, 1988.

[29] University of New England, Attributes of a UNE Graduate. Armidale: UNE, 2004.

Department of Mathematical and Statistical Sciences, La Trobe University, Bendigo, Victoria 3552, Australia
   E-mail address: t.mills@latrobe.edu.au

Faculty of Education, Monash University, Clayton, Vic. 3800, Australia
   E-mail address: Peter.Sullivan@Education.monash.edu.ac

CBMS Issues in Mathematics Education
Volume **14**, 2007

A Leverage in Learning

Huriye Arikan

ABSTRACT. The basic challenge in teaching, including the teaching of mathematics, is to teach so that learning takes place. There are further challenges in meeting the student's needs that call for the development of methods to facilitate learning as well as teaching. Sustaining the learning environment is important. The 'Learning Center' project that facilitates the establishment of a healthy learning environment is an integral part of the student support system at Sabanci University (www.sabanciuniv.edu). The project, in comparison to classical student support models, is based primarily on peer support, offers intervening activities and has a self-sustaining structure. Inspired by 'Peer Instruction' and active learning techniques, the model adopts several in-class teaching methods. The essence of achievement and the dynamics of the program rely upon student involvement at each organizational level and at every stage of program activity, as well as the transmission of acquired study skills among students. The scope is not restricted to learning mathematics, but also includes other fundamental disciplines. However, the cognition of mathematical concepts and problem solving skills form the core and develop good learning habits. Qualitative and quantitative assessments reveal affirmative results in terms of individual student accomplishment and the development of a learning community.

1. Introduction

Mathematics is a Greek word meaning 'learning', and as a discipline mathematics is in a rather funny position, not really being an art and not being immediately useful enough to be a science. Mathematics is generally viewed as being hard to understand, counterintuitive some of the time and enemy number one among all of the academic disciplines. Mathematicians, educators, curricula developers and administrators struggle to enhance the teaching of mathematics and the appreciation of the subject. A lot of effort is put into figuring out new teaching methods, writing effective textbooks, developing and creating tools and in sharing experiences, all to make the subject more clear and comprehensible. The success rates and cognition levels of students are affected by their beliefs and prejudiced perceptions of mathematics prior to their enrollment in university. Socioeconomic conditioning and the community's reaction toward mathematics play a role in the comprehension of the subject, and learning itself is a complex practice of the human mind affected by many personal and circumstantial factors.

Effective teaching methods, technology supported teaching and other learning tools are common interests of mathematics instructors. To make our teaching more effective, most of us have faced challenges in using technology, teaching tools and teaching methods at many levels. The enthusiasm of students for learning mathematics or any subject in relation to their future objectives affects the process of teaching. The common dream of mathematics instructors is to have a class full of enthusiastic students, learning mathematical concepts at a high level of cognition with joy and admiration.

In large classes, addressing students with diverse educational backgrounds and interests makes the teaching of mathematics more difficult. Even in homogeneous classes of interested students, individual learning aptitudes and differences in the learning paces and habits of the students add complexity to the task and make the teaching process difficult.

2. Some Comments On Teaching And Learning

The first duty of any teacher is to be well prepared before each class, give lucid explanations of the concepts enriched by examples, explain the subject in several ways, repeat the important topics emphasizing the key ideas and make sure that the majority of the class understands clearly. No matter how well we are prepared and support our lectures with teaching tools, the students will learn in line with their learning habits at their own pace. The average student will grasp the subject by spending additional time studying later, and the good student will master it by practicing and solving problems. Making concepts clear and accessible to all the students is a tough problem that becomes more difficult if the class is large, if students have diverse backgrounds, and if they have different objectives. In large classes the most common practice is to lecture. Lectures are supported by problem solving sessions for smaller groups of students and support systems.

Even in classes of students with homogeneous background knowledge and with common interests, building new and advanced mathematical concepts is still not an easy task. In any circumstance, while effective teaching is the instructors' responsibility, learning is the students' task.

How we learn is a research subject based mainly on neurobiology and cognitive psychology. It is not at all simple, as it is influenced by circumstantial and cultural factors, so it is important to set up a learning environment inside and outside the classroom. As mentioned before, a majority of the students learn by studying outside the classroom at their own pace. They examine, replicate and study what was offered to them previously by their instructors. Some students have good learning and study habits, while others need to acquire them.

Do we really know why students cannot understand the mathematical concepts and have had poor exam grades? The reason of their failure may not always be our teaching, the methods used, and the design of the course or supporting tools. If we had studied with each student, going through questions and problems step-by-step, would they have been more successful? Surely results would be better. That is the reason most of us set up discussions and problem solving sessions.

Since learning is something that we continually do, and as mathematicians something that we practice as a life style, we have the tendency to believe that we know what learning mathematics is about. Mathematics is called the lonely man's job with good reasons, and most of us advise our students to sit down and study, to practice and - most importantly - to think over the assertions to grasp the concepts. This advice is sound, but learning processes take place collectively and cooperatively as well. Mathematics is not easy to understand for many people, otherwise the phenomenon of math-phobia would not exist.

Besides learning from our teachers, we also learn from our peers. If we recall our childhood, we learned how to cycle or to use a skateboard from our friends, and we also learned in the playground about reproduction. The information obtained was neither perfect nor the ultimate, but it triggered our curiosity and encouraged us to learn from experience. We chose some peers as role models, and expanded our abilities with our friends' encouragement. Examples can also be given from sports activities, team effort, and the spirit of being in a team. There are various reasons for teams to be successful, and bonds keep the members together. Teams provide examples of cooperative and collaborative learning. It is useful to involve students as mentors in support systems, as teaching assistants in courses, to facilitate student success. Results show that the peer support, coupled with active and cooperative learning methods, improves the student learning processes.

To understand, one needs to conceptualize teaching and learning. These are strongly related, but learning takes place mainly outside the classroom. Fostering learning facilitators can improve our discourse. Likewise, transmitting some aspects of our teaching outside the classroom and backing students up through support systems considerably improves academic achievement. Many universities and schools nowadays have student support units to facilitate the learning processes.

Student Involvement In Teaching And More. The 'Peer Instruction' method introduced by Eric Mazur (see [1]) is one of the most effective ways of teaching. The method offers solutions to three very important problems that may occur in addressing large numbers of students. The method facilitates the formation of effective interaction between students and the instructor. It makes the lecturer aware of the clarity of the subject during the discourse and provides the instructor with the opportunity to stop and try another approach. In simple terms, to stop at an appropriate time of the lecture and pose a conceptual question, let the students discuss for a few minutes and ask the question again. If the class has the right answer, it is fine to proceed. If not, the instructor is aware that another explanation is necessary. By letting the students interact and explain the concept to each other with their own, and maybe more understandable, terms, not only can large classes enjoy having interaction, but also the efficiency of the instruction can be amplified considerably.

Ever since I first encountered the 'Peer Instruction' method, I have become an admirer of the approach and have practiced several versions of it in a range of classes. The Peer Instruction method, and in particular the use of concept tests (see [2]) that is derived from this, have produced positive results toward the effectiveness of teaching. These methods have several more features underlining their achievement and important practical advantages.

There are some other important benefits to the involvement of the peers in instruction beside its effectiveness in conceptual understanding. Firstly, peers can be more effective in the transmission of information and act as role models. After all, a lecturer is a lecturer, but a peer can be more sympathetic, can figure out what is wrong, and can provide emotional support to get to understanding. I put this observation in practice when we founded the Academic Support Program Project at Sabanci University. The main principle is to get the students to work together. This is easy to write, but it is not that easy to achieve.

Conducting large classes is not desirable, because of the difficulty of communicating complex ideas to students. No matter which method we use, there is always the risk of not communicating with students possessing weak background knowledge and not keeping the fast learners interested. However, splitting courses into smaller classes and labeling the students according to their educational backgrounds or their compatibility levels makes the whole issue worse, not better. This problem is not restricted to mathematics, and affects many disciplines. There are even books written for assorted versions of a course: Calculus Made Simple, Calculus for Engineers, Calculus for Biology, Physics for Engineers and Scientists, Physics for Poets, etc. Apart from generating course inflation by an endless creation of new courses from the subdivisions of a course, there also are other drawbacks. The practice shows a tendency among weaker students to compete less, and for good students to burn out as well as to perform. What is desirable is being able to access the majority of the students without lowering course standards. One solution is leveraging the weaker students to the desired compatibility by backing them up with an academic support program to fill their knowledge gaps.

At this point it is worthwhile to discuss the systems supporting learning along with innovative and efficient teaching/learning methods. In general, the success of student support systems depends on how accessible they are and how the students use them. In relation to that, the rest of this article will be about the Sabanci University Learning Center Project. This project successfully combines teaching practices with peer support.

3. The Learning Center Project

The Learning Center Project is an integral part of the Academic Support Program at Sabanci University. The center is specially designed to support students in meeting the particular needs of the academic programs of the University. All students go through a common program in the first year of their education that will equip them with an interdisciplinary training so as to assist them to conceive the disciplines as a whole. As a result, students are required to take the same courses independent of their objectives to be engineers, natural scientists, political scientists, economists, historians, art historians or artists, etc. Calculus and the social and natural sciences are the basis of the first year undergraduate programs. These courses are structured around lectures given to three hundred students. There are problem solving sessions and discussions in small groups. WebCT support is also integrated into these courses.

Freshmen, with diverse backgrounds and interests, are treated equally, and their performances are assessed together in calculus, and the natural and social sciences. Quite naturally, there are a number of competitive students with a wide range of knowledge and abilities, and there are some who lack motivation and need extra assistance. The Academic Support program, including a Learning Center Project, is designed to provide the necessary support to the students.

The Academic Support program is formed of three main components.

- **The Learning Center**
  - Help Desk
  - Individual Tutorials

 — Peer Study Groups and Peer Discussion Sessions
 — Workshops
- **Seminars and Workshops**
  - General Seminars
  - Scholarly Seminars
  - Science and Culture Festival
  - Developing Individual Skills
- **Remedial and Adjunct Courses**
  - Pre-Calculus
  - Basic Mathematical Concepts for Physics
  - Basic Mathematical Concepts for Chemistry and Biology
  — ...

The core of the support programs is the Learning Center. The aim of the unit is to sustain learning and create a learning environment. The Center's motto is 'Learning to Learn'.

The scope of the center is not restricted to the learning of mathematics, but also includes other fundamental disciplines, mainly physics, chemistry and biology. However, cognition of mathematical concepts and problem solving skills form the essence of the development of learning habits. The main principle of the Learning Center is 'interactive learning'. The central activity is the individual tutorials, offering individual guidance in accordance with specific student needs. The type of guidance may range from teaching to practicing study skills. Students attend peer discussions or study groups where they are encouraged to share their academic knowledge and experience and to study in a friendly atmosphere. A freshman or a sophomore moderates the groups and acts as a mentor. The workshops are for larger groups of students where the group has the chance to study a specific subject intensively. There are also workshops set up that are based on information fed back from tutorials, instructors, moderators, mentors and students.

To participate in the program, students can drop in to the Center during the work hours or can schedule individual appointments. For immediate help and guidance, the Help Desk is open twelve hours a day including Sundays and some holidays. Students coordinate the program activities for each course, and help the formation of study groups in line with students' needs and requests. All of the activities aim to improve academic performance as well as to assist them in acquiring skills related to course subjects and general learning. The services include calculus, physics, chemistry and biology.

The Learning Center involves students actively at an organizational level. The administrative components of the Academic Support Program are the student bodies: Program Coordinators, Executive Board, Human Resources, Documentation Group and Public Relations. Currently fifteen freshmen, two sophomores, ten juniors and three seniors are working for the program. Needless to say, the training of the students who work for the center is integrated into the support program. Although the supervision and the training are coordinated and done by myself, there is still a lot of student involvement.

There are various services and programs offered by the Academic Support unit other than the Learning Center. These are set up to challenge the students who work for the program by keeping them motivated. The human resources unit also awards the successful mentors with the title of peer-assistant. Motivating is a vital aspect of working well, and it has to do with how committed people are to doing their work and achieving their goals. The program activities are planned to create a highly motivated staff and sustain their momentum.

The Science and Culture Festival is a big event involving high schools and other university units. Peer-assistants raise money for the Center by finding sponsors. This fosters team spirit and creates a challenge because this sponsorship is the main income of the Center.

Scholarly seminars are built around a student project and involve the contribution of the faculty, aim to introduce freshmen to the contemporary research areas, and to promote the inquisitiveness, critical thinking, and enthusiasm of the students in doing research. They are designed to have an interactive nature giving the students a chance to see the undergraduate programs and possible research areas through the eyes of their peers and to encourage them to learn through their experiences.

Panels and forums are arranged around discussion topics involving all of the university and serve as public relation tools. The topics are chosen from contemporary subjects, contributing to the formation and maintenance of a healthy academic campus climate.

Remedial and adjunct courses are offered as a part of a course or conducted separately depending on the course contents. For example, the 'Basic Mathematics Concepts for Physics' course is conducted just before the academic term starts and provides the mathematical background for a physics course. The course requires registration and has a place on the academic calendar. These courses help the training of peer-assistants and endow them with teaching experience.

The main factors underlying the effectiveness of the system are the extensive use of peer support, the active involvement of students, and the sense of belonging to the unit and to the university. Feeling to be a part of a respected learning community affects the learning processes and academic achievement of the students positively.

The Learning Center In Practice. Students, mentors and the moderators often use analogies to explain mathematical concepts and relate the new concepts to some others that are well known. Unlike the experts, students do not care to choose their examples from a 'real case' or make their explanations 'mathematically correct'. Instead they tend to give an idea or produce a mental picture to explain a mathematical concept. On the other hand, having a tool and a way of thinking about mathematics is a common denominator of many subjects and facilitates peer interaction.

The contents of the physics and calculus courses are not synchronized. At the time when kinematics (motion), Newton's laws, force, work, kinetic energy, potential energy, conservation of energy and gravitation have been summarized, the formal introductions of the derivative and integral are yet to be done. Hence, a number of tutorials are organized for the students who feel less confident about their backgrounds either in physics or in mathematics.

For example, in study groups peer assistants tend to explain dt as a time interval that is even smaller than any attainable time and dx is explained to be a distance that is smaller than any possible distance traveled. Furthermore, the distance traveled is explained to be roughly the summation of the distances traveled in a time interval Δt. Thus, the formula $x_2 = x_1 - \int_{t_2}^{t_1} v(t)dt$ where x_i are the position vectors at times t_i, $i = 1, 2$ and $v(t)$ is the velocity of the particle, has been sufficient to give an idea about the definite integral.

The product rule, chain rule and integration are practiced through the work-kinetic energy theorem as: $F_{net} dx = d(\frac{1}{2} mv^2)$, where a constant net force of magnitude F_{net} acts on an object of mass m. The trigonometric functions and uniform circular motion are covered simultaneously. Projectile motion is used to explain several concepts including the geometric meaning of the derivative. It is observed that peer tutorials of this sort have not only made students feel confident in physics, but have also helped them later to understand the mathematical concepts in calculus.

The book (Calculus, Hughes-Hallett, Gleason, McCallum, et al. [3]) that is used for the calculus course focuses on conceptual understanding, and presents the topics geometrically, numerically, analytically and verbally. This approach not only helps the students to improve their problem solving skills and to master mathematical concepts, but also has helped them to carry out discussions. For instance, a discussion at a peer study session on chemistry about the covalent bonding and organic compounds has revealed that for most of the students it has been difficult to visualize the molecules in 3-dimensions. To solve this problem, a workshop is designed and 3-dimensional illustrations are used to explain the subject. This workshop has helped the students to grasp the matter thoroughly and to develop themselves further. During the workshop students have discussed among themselves the bond angles of the molecules. They not only have discovered that the bond angles in a tetrahedral molecule are the same and are equal to $109.5°$, but also ended up providing a geometric proof of this fact, although this was not the aim of the workshop.

The discussions and the peer study group are good in reflecting analytic thinking approaches and learning habits, and the dynamic structure of the center makes the transmission of acquired study skills possible.

The following points summarize the benefits of the peer study and discussion groups:

- Transmission of healthy learning habits, among the students
- Promote study skills
- Facilitate peer interaction among classmates
- Help diagnosing the background knowledge of the students
- Provide immediate feedback about the level of understanding
- Supply arguments for discussion and explanations
- Address the reasons for poor performance
- Eliminate negative attitudes
- Help understanding the individual needs
- Motivate
- Use students as an extra force supporting the instruction process
- Help figuring out the roots of student mistakes
- Time and energy saver for the instructor
- Help the formation of a learning community

Some of these points are similar to those that can be observed in a class conducted by interactive teaching methods. However, in this case students have the opportunity to learn according to their own pace and improve their study skills.

Some Assessment Results. The Learning Center activities are subject to evaluation, and the academic development of the program participants is followed. The mentors as well as the moderators provide written reports with detailed information. The reports include the duration of the sessions, the names of the participants and the subjects studied, as well as remarks about the effectiveness of the sessions and the progress of each participant. The results of these reports are taken into consideration for the development of the program and are used as future references. The reports have given us reasons to believe that the peer discussion sessions, are natural platforms for the inquisitive young minds where they can question each other's interests and learn from different perspectives.

For illustration the recent comparative results showing achievements of the participants are provided.

Graph 1: Distribution of Cumulative Grade Point Average

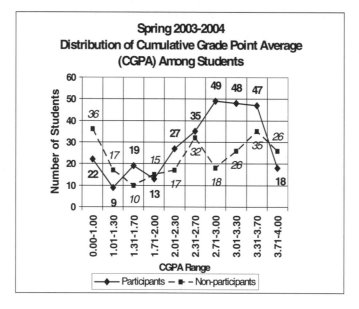

Graph 2: The Calculus Letter Grade Distributions among the Learning Center Participants and Non-Participants

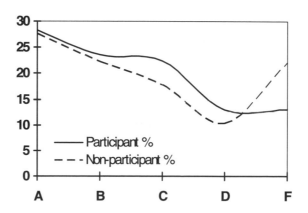

Graph 3: The Physics Letter Grade Distributions among the Learning Center Participants and Non-Participants

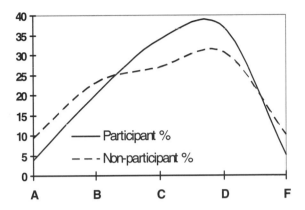

During this academic term, around 600 sessions have been organized and 40% of the 632 freshmen enrolled in Calculus and 37% of the 633 freshmen enrolled in Physics have benefitted from the Learning Center.

The Learning Center activities not only promote academic and individual student development, but also encourage teamwork, collaboration, cooperation and interaction among peers. Since the students are strong in different subject matters, interaction among peers has had a role in building up mutual respect among the students and also has had a positive effect upon maintaining a learning environment.

4. Conclusion

The program is subject to systematic evaluation, and statistical results have revealed the significance of the program activities as well as its role in the building up a learning environment and a healthy academic campus climate.

Letting freshmen act as mentors gives them the opportunity to monitor classroom activities and to move along with the lectures. It seems courageous to employ freshmen as peer-assistants, but doing so keeps the program attached to the courses continuously. This feature differentiates the Learning Center significantly from other student support systems.

Besides its advantages, the program has a number of drawbacks. The tutorials and workshops may discourage students from attending classes, and students may become reluctant to share what they know in addition to plagiarizing homework. The utmost effort has been put into raising awareness about plagiarism. Supplementing lectures and classes in the Learning Center may create a conflict of interest with the lecturer and this should be avoided.

Although the program is very popular among the students and is quite successful, the underlying reasons for its achievement are attributed to the design and content of the academic programs of the Sabanci University. Furthermore, the program does not aim to organize tutorials for sophomores, juniors or seniors. A university is a culture where creativity blooms and students need to grow up on their own in order to research, discover and create.

References

[1] Masur, Eric, 1997, *Peer Instruction A User's Manual*
[2] Hughes-Hallett, Gleason, McCallum, et al, 2003, *ConcepTest*
[3] Hughes-Hallett, Gleason, McCallum, et al, 1998, *Calculus Single and Multivariable*

CENTER FOR INDIVIDUAL AND ACADEMIC DEVELOPMENT, SABANCI UNIVERSITY, ISTANBUL, 34956, TURKEY
E-mail address: huriye@sabanciuniv.edu

CBMS Issues in Mathematics Education
Volume **14**, 2007

Towards Inquiry-Oriented Mathematics Instruction in the University

Kwon, Oh Nam

ABSTRACT. Research on the relationship between different teaching methods and students' understanding of mathematics at the university level is essential for cumulative improvement in mathematics. However, some researchers have reported that there is a gap between what is taught and what is learned in mathematics in traditional modes of teaching. This presentation explores more effective teaching methods at the university level. Examples of inquiry-oriented mathematics teaching at the university are discussed and illustrate how to enhance students' authentic understanding in a differential equations course.

1. Introduction. If teaching and student learning are to improve, faculty must recognize the characteristics of effective teaching. The research literature contains many examples of successful standards and practices for effective teaching that are based on evidence of enhanced student learning. However, many faculty were never introduced to this knowledge base during their graduate or postdoctoral years and have not acquired this perspective. These instructors may struggle through teaching assignments, often redeveloping techniques and approaches that others already have tested and disseminated. The aims of this presentation are to share an innovative approach called "inquiry-oriented" instruction and to point out some constructive ideas on learning and teaching mathematics at the university level.

2. Evidence of the gap between teaching and learning. In mathematics classrooms which use a traditional, textbook-dominated approach, effective participation involves students in listening to and watching the teacher demonstrate mathematical procedures, and then practicing what was demonstrated by completing textbook exercises. This prevalent phenomenon of the traditional approach to instruction is linked with some general existing 'myths' and practices in the teaching of mathematics at the undergraduate level (Alsina, 2002):

- The researchers-always-make-good-teachers myth. Good researchers are always good teachers. Therefore the key criteria for selection and promotion must be high quality research.
- The self-made-teacher tradition. This myth is based on the claim that excellence in university teaching does not require any specific training - it

is just a matter of accumulated experience, clear presentation skills and a sound knowledge of the subject.

- Reduction organization. Topics are presented linearly; definitions-theorem-proofs are sequentially stated in their most general form. The top-down approach. Learning is a bottom-up process, so teaching top-down is not an effective way of helping learners.

- The perfect-theory presentation. Students become convinced that mathematics is almost complete; that theorem proving is just a deductive game; that errors, false trials, and zigzag arguments, which play such a crucial role in human life, have no place in the mathematical world. This style of presentation steals the 'human nature' aspect of mathematical discoveries. This perfect-theory presentation turns a living discipline into a dead garden.

In the last two decades, there has been a growth in educational research on undergraduate mathematics courses. The research began by investigating students' learning and understanding of specific mathematical concepts. The results obtained gave statistical evidence of the limitations of traditional teaching practices. The evidence of the gap between what is taught and what is learned was noted by several researchers:

- Students having significant difficulty in conceptualizing the limit processes underlying the notions of derivative and integral (Orton, 1980)

- Discrepancy between the formal definitions students were able to quote and the criteria they used in order to check properties such as functions, continuity, derivative (Tall & Vinner, 1981)

- Students' difficulties with logical reasoning and proofs (Alibert & Thomas, 1991; Schoenfeld, 1985; Selden & Selden, 1995)

- Students' difficulties in connecting graphs with physical concepts and the real world (McDermott, Rosenquist, & van Zee, 1987; Svec, 1995)

- Students' difficulties in learning the basic notions of linear algebra (Harel, 1989).

To bridge the gap between teaching and learning, there is a need to take positive steps towards another way of teaching.

3. Conceptualizing inquiry-oriented instruction. Recent reports suggest that some gaps stated in the previous section can be overcome by emphasizing inquiry-oriented instruction (eg., Ebert-May et al., 1997; Kwon, Rasmussen, & Karen, 2005; Rasmussen, C., Kwon, O. N., Allen, K., Marrongelle, K., & Burtch, M., 2004). There are several definitions regarding inquiry or inquiry-oriented teaching and learning. National Science Education Standards defines them in the following way:

- Inquiry is a multifaceted activity that involves making observations; posing questions; examining books and other sources of information to see what is already known; planning investigations; reviewing what is known in light of experimental evidence; using tools to gather, analyze and interpret data; proposing answers, explanations, and predictions; and communicating the results. Inquiry requires identification of assumptions, use of

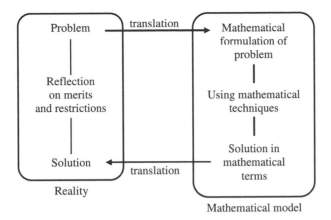

Adapted from Wubbles, Korthagen, & Broekman (1997)

FIGURE 1. A model for the mathematical inquiry process

critical and logical thinking, and consideration of alternative explanations (NRC, 1996, p.23).

By the same token, inquiry-oriented instruction can be defined as teacher practices that foster student use of personal experience and schooled knowledge for generating new information, new problem-solving approaches, or new solutions that were not heretofore a part of the learning environment (Rowe, 1973). We can expect that students in classrooms are engaged to propose and defend mathematical ideas and conjectures and to respond thoughtfully to the mathematical argument of their peers. Thus, the practice and beliefs developed within inquiry-oriented classrooms frame learning as participation in a community of practice characterized by inquiry mathematics, where students learn to speak and act mathematically by participating in mathematical discussions and solving new or unfamiliar problems (Richards, 1991).

A model for the mathematical inquiry process. The inquiry process is characterized by consecutive steps of translating a real world problem into a mathematical problem, the analysis and structuring of such a problem, the creation of a mathematical solution, the translation of this solution to the real world and the reflection on the merits and restrictions of the problem, which can be followed by the next cycle in which the translation of the problem is refined, generalized or otherwise changed.

Roles of instructor and students in a community of inquiry. A model suggesting the articulation of the roles of teacher and students in the community appears in this figure. In this model, the ovals represent critical elements of a community of inquiry based on the literature, while the rectangles represent the key players in this community of inquiry: the instructor and the students.

Using the Inquiry-oriented Differential Equations (IO-DE) project as a classroom-based model, the instructor selected realistic tasks that focused the inquiry on

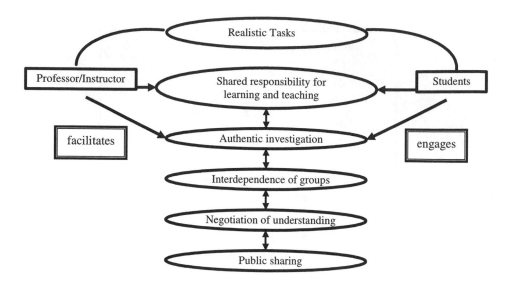

FIGURE 2. Roles of instructor and students in a community of inquiry

important mathematics concepts. Working in small groups students selected a possible solution to investigate, and then engaged in investigations to answer student-generated questions. Group discussions centered on negotiating understanding concepts. Over time, groups developed interdependency and began to rely on group members instead of only the teacher. Often students would share newly discovered information with the instructor, or with other members of the class, and share responsibility for learning and teaching. Public sharing involved groups presenting findings in a formal presentation. In the learning environment of the IO-DE project, the emphasis on reasons did not have the effect of bringing closure to the discussions, but of creating opportunities to advance the mathematical agenda.

The model highlights instructor and student roles that differ from the traditional teacher as knowledge-giver and student as knowledge-receiver. Thus students in an inquiry-oriented learning environment are active participants in the construction of mathematical knowledge.

4. An example of inquiry-oriented instruction: IO-DE project. The innovative approach, referred to as the IO-DE project, capitalizes on advances within the discipline of mathematics and on advances within the discipline of mathematics education, both at the K-12 and tertiary levels. Given the integrated leveraging of developments within both mathematics and mathematics education, the IO-DE project is paradigmatic of an approach to innovation in undergraduate mathematics, potentially serving as a model for other undergraduate course reforms.

Background theory. From the Discipline of Mathematics. Drawing on a dynamical systems point of view (Blanchard, Devaney, & Hall, 1998; Kallaher, 1999; West, 1994), the IO-DE project treats differential equations as mechanisms that describe how functions evolve and change over time. Interpreting and characterizing the behavior and structure of these solution functions are important goals, with central ideas including the long-term behavior of solutions, the number and nature of equilibrium solutions, and the effect of varying parameters on the solution space.

Addressing these central ideas draws on graphical, numerical, and analytical techniques, made viable with the use of technology (Kallaher, 1999). These techniques utilize a variety of different graphical representations, such as slope fields for first order differential equations and vector fields for systems of differential equations, as well as numerical algorithms such as Euler's method for producing approximate solutions.

From the Discipline of Mathematics Education. At the outset of the IO-DE project we conjectured that theoretical advances originating from K-12 classroom based research could be useful for informing and guiding the learning and teaching of undergraduate mathematics. There are two complementary lines of K-12 research from which we draw: the instructional design theory of Realistic Mathematics Education (RME) (Freudenthal, 1991; Gravemeijer, 1999) and the social neogotiation of meaning (Cobb & Bauersfeld, 1995).

Central to RME is the design of instructional sequences that challenge learners to organize key subject matter at one level to produce new understanding at a higher level. In this process, referred to as mathematizing, symbols, algorithms, and definitions can be better understood when students build them from the bottom up through a process of suitably guided reinvention (for elaboration see Kwon, 2002; Kwon, 2003; Rasmussen & King, 2000, Rasmussen, Marrongelle & Keynes, 2003, Rasmussen, Zandieh, King, & Teppo, 2005). As researchers working within an RME approach emphasize, a coherent sequence of learning tasks does not guarantee that students will learn mathematics with understanding (Treffers, 1987). In addition to theoretically informed design with extensive classroom testing where learning tasks are continually refined and revised, the IO-DE project works from the premise that the way in which instructional tasks are constituted is as important as the material itself, and it is toward this aspect that we now turn.

An explicit intention of IO-DE project classrooms is to create a learning environment where students routinely offer explanations of and justifications for their reasoning. Following Richards (1991), Cobb, Wood, Yackel, and McNeal (1992) define such learning environments as "inquiry oriented." As described by Cobb et al (1992), "students who participate in an inquiry mathematics tradition typically experience understanding when they can create and manipulate mathematical objects in ways that they can explain and, when necessary, justify" (p. 598). Because of the strong emphasis on argumentation, we conjectured that the theoretical constructs arising from research in inquiry-oriented elementary school classrooms would be useful for learning advanced mathematics, such as differential equations. After all, mathematicians engage in similar forms of argumentation when creating new mathematics (Richards, 1991).

Research focusing on student conceptions in differential equations also pointed to a number of relevant issues for instructional design and teacher planning. For example, in one case study of a differential equations class that treated contemporary topics in dynamical systems, Rasmussen (2001) found that rather than building relational understandings (Skemp, 1976), students were learning analytical, graphical, and numerical methods in a compartmentalized manner. An important lesson from this research is that working with multiple modalities does not guarantee that students will build a coherent network of ideas. It is also important to have a long-term, coherent sequence of tasks, and our adaptation of RME was useful for this purpose.

Other informative research on student cognition in differential equations highlights students' concept images of Euler's method and students' informal or intuitive notions underlying equilibrium solutions, asymptotical behavior, and stability (Artigue, 1992; Rasmussen, 2001; Zandieh & McDonald, 1999). Knowledge of such informal or intuitive images was useful for the IO-DE project because it suggested task situations and instructional interventions that could engage and help reorganize students' informal and intuitive conceptions.

Assessment of student learning with and without inquiry-oriented instruction. The evaluation study (Rasmussen, Kwon, Allen, Marrongelle, & Burtch, 2004), which took place at the end of the course, compared students' understandings of central ideas and analytic methods for solving differential equations between students in inquiry-oriented and traditionally taught classes at four undergraduate institutions in Korea and the United States. During the Fall semester, 2002, data on IO-DE project and comparison students' skills, and understandings in differential equations were collected. Comparison classes at all sites typically followed a lecture-style format whereas IO-DE project classes at all sites typically followed an inquiry-oriented format in which students routinely offered explanations and justifications for their ideas as they cycled between small group work and whole class discussion. Course materials for the IO-DE project grew out of several semester long classroom teaching experiments and represent an innovation adaptation of RME to the undergraduate level.

The routine assessment consisted of five problems of an analytic nature, one numerical problem to compute two steps of Euler's method, one phase plane graph sketching problem, and one modeling problem. The conceptual assessment was aimed at evaluating students' relational understandings of important ideas and concepts. Two problems focused on the meaning or relationship between exact and approximate solutions, two problems focused on aspects related to modeling, and four problems dealt with the behavior or structure of solutions and/or the solution space. As shown in Figure 3, however, there was no significant difference between the two groups on routine problems, even though this was not a primary instructional focus. However the IO-DE group did score significantly higher than the comparison group on conceptual problems.

Thus, our main results were that students in the reform-oriented classrooms scored significantly higher on the conceptually oriented items. There was no significant difference on student performance on the procedurally oriented items, despite the fact that analytic solutions were the main focus of the traditional classes.

The follow-up study examined retention of knowledge one year after instruction for a subset of the students from the comparison study (Kwon, Rasmussen, & Karen, 2005). Specifically, we examined the retention of conceptual and procedural knowledge in the context of differential equations one year after instruction. Students' retention of knowledge is compared across a traditional and an inquiry-oriented instructional approach. For the purpose of this analysis, procedurally oriented items are defined as those questions that were readily solved via analytic/symbolic techniques. Conceptually oriented items were defined into two

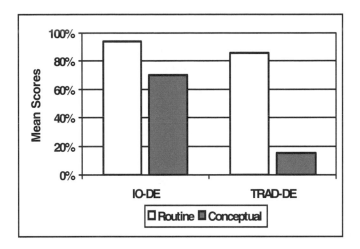

FIGURE 3. Mean Scores of IO-DE and Comparison Groups on Routine and Conceptual tests

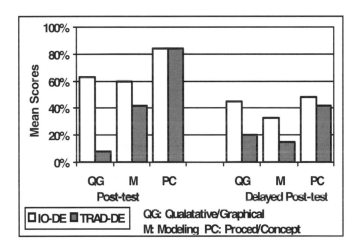

FIGURE 4. Students' retention of mathematical knowledge and skills in differential equation

categories, modeling tasks and qualitative/graphical tasks, each of which represent important and conceptually demanding thinking in mathematics, in general, and in differential equations, in particular. The two modeling tasks posed involved determining an appropriate differential equation to fit a given real-world situation. The qualitative/graphical tasks involved predicting and structuring the space of solutions. Figure 4 shows that posttest and delayed posttest scores of IO-DE and TRAD-DE groups on procedurally and conceptually oriented items.

An analysis of covariance (ANCOVA) was conducted on the delayed posttest scores using the posttest score as a covariate, testing for the effects of the group. The analysis indicates that there was no significant difference in retention between the two groups on the procedurally oriented items. IO-DE project students were equal in proficiency to the TRAD-DE class on the procedurally oriented items, even though such items were not a primary instructional focus of the inquiry-oriented instructional materials. The IO-DE group scored significantly higher than did the TRAD-DE group on the concepturally oriented tasks according an ANCOVA analysis.

This study shows that long-term retention of conceptual knowledge after students' participation in the IO-DE project as seen in student responses to modeling and qualitative/graphical problems was positive compared to retention by students in its traditional counterpart. At the same time, there was no difference between IO-DE and TRAD-DE students' retention of procedural understanding.

5. Conclusion. The implications of the inquiry-oriented differential equations are twofold. First, based on the preliminary results of the post-test and the delayed post-test (Kwon et al., 2005; Rasmussen et al. 2004), all IO-DE students from each of the four institutions, regardless of academic backgrounds and gender differences, outperformed TRAD-DE students on the post-test. Therefore, if the delayed post-test were given to all IO-DE students at the different sites, students may again similarly outperform TRAD-DE students. This result demonstrates that this instructional approach can be applicable to university mathematics regardless of academic preparations and gender differences. Secondly and more importantly, the instructional methods and curriculum design approach guided by RME are applicable to promoting student learning in all mathematics classrooms. Indeed, RME has its origins and broadest use in K-12 instructional settings. Yet, regardless of grade level or student differences, this inquiry-oriented instructional design could enhance long-term mathematics retention for all students.

Thus, the IO-DE may be an example of an inquiry-oriented instruction at the undergraduate level which can help the type of conceptual understanding that can make mathematics meaningful to students and develop students' mathematical reasoning ability. The innovative approach to teaching differential equations suggested in this paper may give a possible arena for exploring the prospects and possibilities of improving undergraduate mathematics education.

References

[1] Alibert, D., & Thomas, M. (1991). Research on mathematical proof. In D. Tall (Ed.), *Advanced mathematical thinking* (pp. 215-230). Dordrecht, The Netherlands: Kluwer Academic Publishers.

[2] Alsina, C. (2002). Why the professor must be a stimulating teacher. In Derek Holton (Ed.), *The teaching and learning of mathematics at University level: An ICMI study, 3-12*. Dordrecht, The Netherlands: Kluwer Academic Publishers.

[3] Artigue, M. (1992). Cognitive difficulties and teaching practices. In G. Harel, & E. Dubinsky (Eds.), *The concept of function: Aspects of epistemology and pedagogy* (pp. 109-132). Washington, DC: The Mathematical Association of America.

[4] Blanchard, P., Devaney, R., & Hall, R. (1998). *Differential equations*. Pacific Grove, CA: Brooks/Cole.

[5] Cobb, P., Wood, T., Yackel, E., & McNeal, B. (1992). Characteristics of classroom mathematics traditions: An interactional analysis. *American Educational Research Journal, 29*, 573-604.

[6] Cobb, P., & Bauersfeld, H. (1995). *The emergence of mathematical meaning*. Hillsdale, NJ: Lawrence Erlbaum Associates.

[7] Ebert-May, D, C. Brewer and S. Allred. (1997). Innovation in large lectures-teaching for active learning. *BioScience, 47*(9), 601-607.

[8] Freudenthal, H. (1991). *Revisiting mathematics education: The China lectures*. Dordrecht, The Netherlands: Kluwer Academic Publishers.

[9] Gravemeijer, K. (1999). How emergent models may foster the constitution of formal mathematics. *Mathematical Thinking and Learning, 2*, 155-177.

[10] Harel, G. (1989). Learning and teaching linear algebra: difficulties and an alternative approach to visualizing concepts and processes. *Focus on Learning Problems in Mathematics, 11*, 139-148.

[11] Kallaher, M. J. (Ed.) (1999). *Revolutions in differential equations: Exploring ODEs with modern technology*. Washington, DC: The Mathematical Association of America.

[12] Kwon, O. N. (2003). Guided reinvention of Euler algorithm: An analysis of progressive mathematization in RME-based differential equations course. *J. Korea Soc. Math. Ed. Ser. A: The Mathematical Education, 42*(3), 387-402.

[13] Kwon, O. N., Rasmussen, C., & Allen, K. (2005) Students' Retention of Mathematical Knowledge and Skills in Differential Equations. *School Science and Mathematics, 105*(5), 1-13.

[14] McDermott, L. C., Rosenquist, M. L., & van Zee, E. H. (1987). Student difficulties is connecting graphs and physics: Examples from kinetics. *American Journal of Physics, 55*(6), 503-513.

[15] National Research Council (1996). *National science education standards* Washington, DC: National Academy Press.

[16] Orton, A. (1980). *A cross-sectional study of the understanding of elementary calculus in adolescents and young adults*. Unpublished doctoral dissertation, University of Leeds, England.

[17] Rasmussen, C. (2001). New directions in differential equations: A frame work for interpreting students' understandings and difficulties. *Journal of Mathematical Behavior, 20*, 55-87.

[18] Rasmussen, C. & King, K. (2000). Locating starting points in differential equations: A realistic mathematics approach. *International Journal of Mathematical Education in Science and Technology, 31*, 161-172.

[19] Rasmussen, C., Kwon, O. N., Allen, K., Marrongelle, K., & Burtch, M. (2004). *Capitalizing on advances in K-12 mathematics education in undergraduate mathematics: An example from differential equations*. Manuscript submitted for publication.

[20] Rasmussen, C., Zandieh, M., King, K., & Teppo, A. (2005). Advancing mathematical activity: A view of advanced mathematical thinking. *Mathematical Thinking and Learning, 7*, 51-73.

[21] Richards, J. (1991). Mathematical discussions. In E. von Glasersfeld(Ed.), *Radical constructivism in mathematics education* (pp. 13-51). Dordrecht, The Netherlands: Kluwer Academic Publishers

[22] Rowe, M. B. (1973). *Teaching Science as Continuous Inquiry*. New York : McGraw-Hill.

[23] Schoenfeld, H. (1985). *Mathematical Problem Solving*. Orlando: Academic Press.

[24] Selden, A. and Selden, J. (1995). Unpacking the logic of mathematical statements. *Educational Studies in Mathematics, 29*, 123-151.

[25] Skemp, R. (1987). *The psychology of learning mathematics*. Hillsdale, NJ: Lawrence Erlbaum Associates.

[26] Svec, M. T. (1995). Effect of micro-computer based laboratory on graphing interpretation, skills and understanding of motion. Paper presented at the 1995 *annual meeting of the National Association for Research in Science Teaching*.

[27] Tall, D. and Vinner, S. (1981). Concept image and concept definition in mathematics with particular reference to limits and continuity. *Educational Studies in Mathematics, 12*, 151-169.

[28] Treffers, A. (1987). *Three dimensions. A model of goal and theory description in mathematics education: The Wiskobas project*. Dordrecht, The Netherlands: Kluwer Academic Publishers.

[29] West, B. (Ed.) (1994). Special issue on differential equations [Special issue] *The College Mathematics Journal, 25*(5).

[30] Wubbels, T., Kortthagen F., & Broekman, H. (1997). Preparing teachers for realistic mathematics education, *Educational Studies in Mathematics, 32*, 1-28.

[31] Zandieh, M. & McDonald, M. (1999). Student understanding of equilibrium solution in differential equations. In F. Hitt & M. Santos (Eds.), *Proceedings of the 21st Annual Meeting of the North American Chapter of the International Group for the Psychology of Mathematics Education* (pp. 253-258). Columbus, OH: ERIC.

DEPARTMENT OF MATHEMATICS EDUCATION, SEOUL NATIONAL UNIVERSITY, SEOUL, 151-742, KOREA

E-mail address: onkwon@snu.ac.kr

CBMS Issues in Mathematics Education
Volume **14**, 2007

The Influence of Technology on Mathematics Instruction: Concerns and Challenges [1]

Warren Page

ABSTRACT. Given the increasing uses in education of rapidly evolving technologies, some of which include animation and many of which have embedded computer algebra systems, we examine how technology can or will influence the ways mathematics is taught, learned, used, and created. This focus on technology provides an important context for addressing critical issues that lie at the heart of mathematics instruction.

"Computer Algebra Systems: Issues and Inquiries" [1] illustrates how computer algebra systems (CASs) can enable students to comprehend rich structures, visualize complicated relationships, breathe life into static representations, pursue limiting cases, and make intuitive leaps. It also includes examples that show a variety of ways that CASs can constrain, misdirect, or in other ways influence how students think and learn mathematics. A major theme of the article was Page's concern that

"CASs can vitiate conceptual understanding if they are permitted to foster an immediacy towards, or overdependence on, computation. CASs can also preclude or thwart creative thinking if we allow them to anesthetize our impulses to consider other representations, to seek new relationships lurking in representations, and to be innovative in how we process information."

In a response to Page's paper, David Smith writes [2],

"... The possible evils he sees in the use (or abuse) of CAS technology are already evils in our educational system, even without technology.... Whether we are discussing blackboards or computers, it is not the tools that create these distortions of education. The real threat posed by the availability of more powerful tools is that they will enable the educational establishment to scale new heights in its lemming-like drive to replace education with training ... "

Given the increasing uses in education of rapidly evolving technologies, some of which use animation and many of which have embedded CAS capabilities, we here re-examine some earlier issues and consider further how technology can or will influence the ways mathematics is taught, learned, used, and created at all levels. This focus on technology provides a context for addressing critical issues that lie at the heart of mathematics instruction.

---

[1]Part of the material in this article was published in "Computer Algebra Systems: Issues and Inquiries", W. Page, *Computers and Mathematics with Applications* **19**:6 (1990), pp. 51–69, © 1990 Elsevier.

1. Fundamental assumptions.

Everything in this paper is predicated on the belief that the two most critical factors in teaching mathematics concern "what" one conveys and "how" we do so. Both factors are intimately intertwined with information-processing and learning; each has affective as well as cognitive dimensions.

What we communicate in mathematics transcends the elucidation of mathematical concepts: we also convey (consciously and unconsciously) a great deal to students about the intrinsic nature and value of the discipline itself.

How we teach mathematics also goes beyond the exchange of ideas and information. Our actions and instructional demands on students imprint them with long lasting psycho-social values on what it means to do mathematics and who should do it.

The remarks and simple examples in this paper illustrate and exemplify what is succinctly articulated by Davis and Anderson [3].

"Mathematics has elements that are spatial, kinesthetic, elements that are arithmetic or algebraic, elements that are verbal, programmatic. It has elements that are logical, didactic, and elements that are intuitive or even counterintuitive. ... These may be compared to different modes of consciousness. To place undue emphasis on one element or groups of elements upsets a balance. It results in an impoverishment of the science and represents an unfulfilled potential."

Today, it is well known that there exists major differentiation of functions between the brain's left and right hemispheres. In the most simplistic terms, left-hemispheric thinking resembles the discrete, sequential processing of a digital calculator whereas right-hemispheric thinking simulates the concurrent, relational activity of an analog computer. Compare, for example, the proof by induction with Gauss's relational proof (Figure 1) that $1 + 2 + \cdots + n = \frac{n(n+1)}{2}$. (Would Gauss have thought of "pairings" if he had been weaned on a numeric calculator?) If the dots on the right triangle's hypotenuse in Figure 2 are labeled a and all the other dots are labeled d, we obtain the (right-hemispheric) representation [4] that the sum of the first n terms of an arithmetic progression plus n^2 times the difference equals the sum of the next n terms of the progression.

$$\sum_{k=1}^{n} a_k + n^2 = \sum_{k=n+1}^{2n} k$$

$$S = 1 + 2 + 3 + \ldots + (n-2) + (n-1) + n$$
$$= (n/2) \text{ pairs of } (n+1)$$
$$= n(n+1)/2$$

FIGURE 1   FIGURE 2

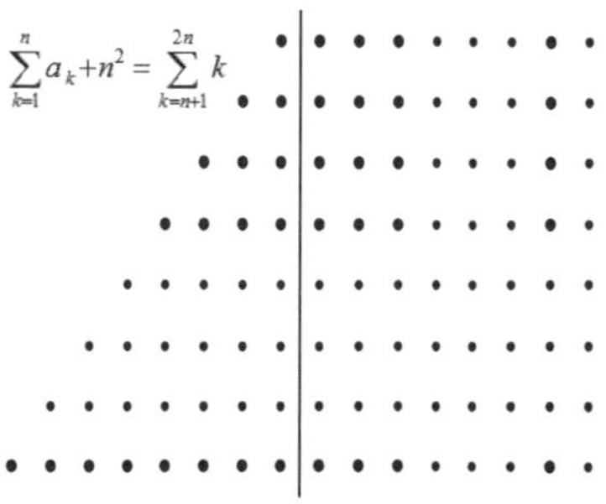

Students with diverse career objectives (science, engineering, statistics, computers, liberal arts, etc.) have differing predispositions toward learning and using mathematics. Thus, because there are different modes of cognitive functioning, mathematics instruction is more effective when several modes of thinking are used.

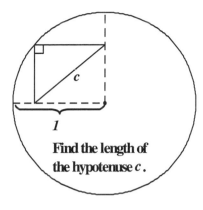

For which value of α does

$$\left\{ \begin{array}{c} x^2 - y^2 = 0 \\ (x-\alpha)^2 + y^2 = 1 \end{array} \right\}$$

Have 0,1,2,3, or 4 solutions?

FIGURE 3   FIGURE 4

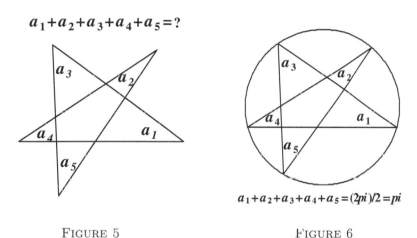

FIGURE 5   FIGURE 6

We are much more explicit in enunciating principles than in when and how they are applied. Formulas and theorems, for example, do not always carry internal information about contexts or situations that should evoke their use. Students usually adopt the representation of a problem from the language of the statement rather than search for a more efficient representation of the problem. For example, consider the following.

In Figure 3, how many students would relate "hypotenuse c" to the rectangle's other diagonal (the circle's radius)? Although one could get the answers in Figure 4 by a (left-hemispheric) solution of the simultaneous equations, moving the unit circle's center along the x-axis would be a quicker (right-hemispheric) way to see where the circle intersects the lines $y = \pm x$. [It will be interesting to see if the increased instructional uses of computer animations will increase student's inclinations to use more dynamic representations and ways of thinking.] Figure 6 depicts a student's solution based on the assumption that the result for the inscribed star was true for every 5-pointed star. The author's solution (Figure 7) was obtained by rotating a paper arrow (vector).

It should be clear that a higher order-awareness is needed to be able to recognize and apply concepts in different relational contexts. Thus, instructors need to help and encourage students to develop their skills in reformulating and restructuring problem representations.

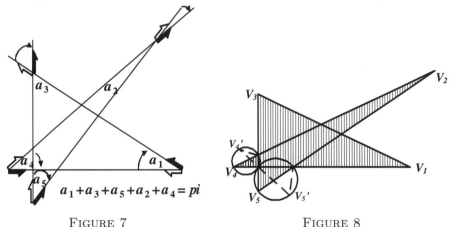

$$a_1 + a_3 + a_5 + a_2 + a_4 = pi$$

FIGURE 7   FIGURE 8

Figures 7 and 8 are from "Summing the Vertex Angles of Stars", W. Page, *International Journal of Mathematics Educatin in Science and Technology* **22** : 5 (1991), pp. 759–768; http://www.informaworld.com, © 1991 Taylor & Francis.

For another exploration (Figure 8), the author imagined the triangle's sides were rigid extensible rods pinned at the vertices or at the "elbows" (points where the sides intersect). By a sequence of vertex movements, none of which changed the star's vertex sum, it was possible to transform one five-pointed star to another with the same vertex sum. The interesting combinatorics-topological results discovered are described in [5]. Students may also learn and discover interesting things by playful hands-on exploration. Although technology today can quickly display such results (say, envelopes of curves), students may enjoy and prefer the related hands-on activities (paper-folding methods) for producing them. As Page writes in [1]:

"Neither CASs, nor any other prescribed representational medium, can be (or should be attempted to be) the sole means to accommodate the rich and diverse ways we process information, formulate conjectures, and attempt to solve problems." He argues for the creation of mathematics laboratories that make use of a wide variety of physical objects and computational processes through which students can discover mathematical principles and build intuitions that CASs can further enhance and develop in meaningful ways.

2. Misperceptions and misconceptions.

As Figures 3 and 4 illustrate, students do not always see or interpret what is obvious to, or intended by, instructors. This should not be surprising give that what we perceive depends on our experiences and cognitive structures. Even the simplest of computer-displayed graphs can be misperceived by students. For instance, as Schoenfeld [6] shows, the vertically translated graphs in Figure 9 appear to get closer as x increases. After explaining and dispelling this illusion (by measuring vertical segments joining the two curves), he concludes, "We can't assume that students will see what we want them to see, even if it's accurately represented on the screen."

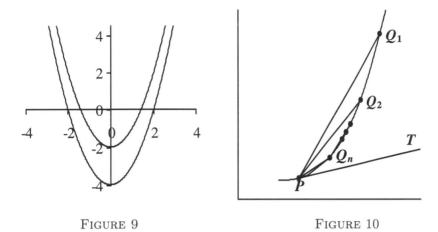

FIGURE 9   FIGURE 10

Orton [7] asked 110 calculus students what happens to the secants PQ on a sketched curve (Figure 10) as the point Q_n tends toward P. Forty-three students could not answer this even after being prompted to see the result. Typical responses were "The line gets shorter" and "It becomes a point." Students apparently focused on the wording "secants PQ." Would the responses have been better responses if the secant lines are extended, or if a dynamic representation was presented?

In Visual Thinking [8], Arnheim questions what learners see in a textbook diagram or film.

"Have we the right to take for granted that a picture shows what it represents, regardless of what it is like and who is looking?" ... "Careful investigation of what the persons for whom these images are made see in them is indispensable."

Good advice! To improve and enhance our instructional visualizations and created animations, we should nominate our students to be beta testers who describe what they perceive and understand.

Computing carries with it the potential for various types of misperceptions. These can be sources of confusion for students or opportunities for instructors to enrich mathematical thinking.

Example 1. (a) Because of roundoff error, the graphical and numerical depictions of $\sum_1^n \frac{1}{k}$ as n increases will corroborate that the harmonic series converges. After explaining this misperception, here is the chance for an instructor to illustrate another way of thinking – as, for example, the following analogical proof that the harmonic series diverges.

If $S = \sum_1^\infty \frac{1}{k}$ for some real number S, then $S = \sum_1^\infty \left(\frac{1}{2k-1} + \frac{1}{2k} \right) > \sum_1^\infty \frac{1}{k} = S$ yields the contradiction $S > S$. (Would Euclid equipped with a CAS have thought of his analogical proof of the infinitude of the primes?)

(b) Students who use implicit differentiation to compute $y' = -x/y$ for $x^2 + 1 + y^2 = 0$ can easily confirm that their answer is the same as $y = \frac{-x}{\sqrt{-1-x^2}}$ displayed by a CAS. Since the equation $x^2 + 1 + y^2 = 0$ does not define a real-values function $y = f(x)$, the derivative does not exist. (Although the CAS is interpreting $y = \frac{-x}{\sqrt{-1-x^2}}$ and its derivative as complex-valued functions, this is not accessible to students who have no knowledge of complex function theory.) Here, however, is an example instructors can use to emphasize to students their need to establish before calculating a function's derivative that the function is differentiable.

(c) A more serious misperception of doing mathematics is students' uses of a computer to solve a problem by examining all possible test cases – as, for example, the response to "Determine the highest power of 5 that divides 50!, where $n! = n \cdot (n-1) \cdot (n-2) \cdots 2 \cdot 1$."

Solution: "Enter the expression $50!/5^m$, then substitute several guesses for m using the $\cdots$ command. You will know that you have the right answer when your quotient is an integer and yet any larger power yields a fractional part." (It would be interesting to speculate what that student would have written based on the hint "What power of 5 divides each number from 1 to 50?")

The following example illustrates the extent to which computing enables students to apply that which is not well understood.

Example 2. For a data set $\{(x_i, y_i)\}$ that has large x-values, students are often told to use the $\{(X_i, y_i) = (x_i - a, y_i)\}$ data to model and make predictions about the $\{(x_i, y_i)\}$ data. If regression produces the function $y(x)$ that models the $\{(x_i, y_i)\}$data and the same type regression yields the function $Y(X)$ for the $\{(X_i, y_i)\}$ data, does $Y(x_i - a) = y(x_i)$ for each x_i? The answer, of course, depends on the type of regression used. However, many student activities and explorations that involve regression do not mention this, nor do they (or their teachers) explain to students why they may observe ERROR, OVERFLOW, or other unexpected messages.

Since the scatter plot of the $\{(X_i, y_i) = (x_i - a, y_i)\}$ data is the scatter plot of the $\{(x_i, y_i)\}$ data horizontally translated a units, both scatter plots have the same spatial configuration. Therefore (Figure 11), for linear and polynomial regression, $Y(x_i - a) = A(x_i - a) + C = y(x_i)$ for each x_i. This is also true for exponential regression via linear regression of the $(x_i, \ln y_i)$ data, which can be seen by relabeling $Y(X)$ and $y(x)$ as $\ln Y(x)$ and $\ln y(x)$. Since $\ln Y(X_i) = \ln y(x_i)$, we have $Y(X_i) = y(x_i) = e^B (e^A)^{x_i}$ for each x_i. For data involving large x-values, $(e^A)^X$ is very large (and may cause overflow) when $A > 0$, and $(e^A)^X$ is very small (and roundoff to zero may produce an error message) when $A < 0$.

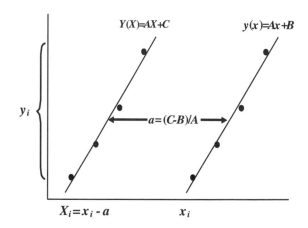

FIGURE 11

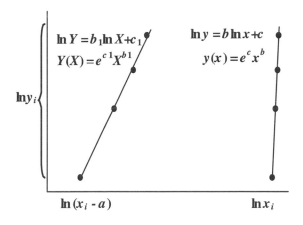

$$\ln Y = b_1 \ln X + c_1$$
$$Y(X) = e^{c_1} X^{b_1}$$

$$\ln y = b \ln x + c$$
$$y(x) = e^c x^b$$

$\ln y_i$

$\ln(x_i - a)$ $\ln x_i$

FIGURE 12

Figure 12 shows why power regression on shifted $\{(x_i - a, y_i)\}$ data depends on the choice of a. Since the logarithm compresses large values much more than it does small values, the $(\ln x_i, \ln y_i)$ scatter plot will be horizontally compressed more than the $(\ln(x_i - a), \ln y_i)$ scatter plot. And, since both scatter plots have the same $\ln y_i$ values, the slope b of the best linear fit for the $(\ln x_i, \ln y_i)$ data is greater than the slope b_1 of the best linear fit for the $(\ln(x_i - a), \ln y_i)$ data. Therefore, the power function $y(x)$ that models the $\{(x_i, y_i)\}$ data has a larger exponent than the power function $Y(X)$ that models the $(\ln(x_i - a), \ln y_i)$ data, and so $Y(x_i - a) \neq y(x_i)$ for every x_i. For very large x-values, the best fit line $y = b(\ln x) + c$ may look almost vertical – in which case $b \ln x$ is very large and c is a very small negative number. Because of this, a utility may display an overflow message for x^b, and display 0 or an error message due to e^c.

The explanations above should be accessible to students who are asked to perform regression. Following this discourse, students can be asked to show, or explain why, logarithmic regression is not translation invariant, and in a related exploration [9], students are guided to discover what can be said about regression on scaled $\{(x_i/b, y_i)\}$ data for $b > 1$. As this example demonstrates, we must help students understand what they are computing and why before asking them to do so.

In [10] Paul Zorn laments:

"Compared with exact or closed-form methods, approximate, numerical, iterative, and recursive techniques get too little attention. ... Because closed-form methods fail with so many innocuous-looking problems, exercises and applications are carefully contrived, and they show it. Arc-length integral problems are especially ludicrous; they can almost never be computed in a closed form. An excellent opportunity to use numerical integration where it is needed is wasted."

Of course Zorn is correct. But wait! As in Example 2, we must be sure that students understand what they are computing before they are asked to do so.

Example 3. Although students may use numerical integration to compute $L = \int_a^b \sqrt{1 + \{f'(x)\}^2}\, dx$, there is no reason to claim that L is the actual arc length of $y = f(x)$ from $x = a$ to $x = b$. Briefly, for every natural number n, the length L_n of the inscribed piecewise linear path with n segments is bounded above by the arc length $\mathcal{L}$ to be computed. Therefore, $\mathcal{L}$ is an upper bound for the sequence

$\{L_n\}$ of approximating paths' lengths. Since $\{L_n\}$ is monotonically non-decreasing as n increases, the value L is the least upper bound for $\{L_n\}$. But how do we know that this least upper bound L really is the arc length $\mathcal{L}$? The increasing physical proximity to a curve of approximating paths (as n increases and the partition's mesh tends to zero) does not necessarily imply better numerical approximations to the curve's true length. (For instance, the curve $y = x$ from $x = 0$ to $x = 1$ has arc length $\sqrt{2}$, but every inscribed polygonal path consisting of horizontal and vertical segments has length 2 no matter how close such an inscribed polygonal path is to this linear segment.) This logical gap in the development of the formula for arc length appears to have eluded a sizable proportion of the mathematics community. This same incompleteness exists in other applications of the definite integral. For instance, there is no justification in most texts that the definite integrals for surface area in three dimensions do indeed actually measure the actual surface area. In [11], Page shows how these logical gaps can be eliminated.

3. Influences of technology on reasoning and problem solving.

Mathematical reasoning predicated on knowledge of a solution's existence may be quite different from reasoning that does not presuppose existence. Compare, for example, Leibniz's proof (Figure 13) that the geometric series converges for $0 < r < 1$ with the proof (Figure 14) based on the fact that the sum of the series is a real number, S.

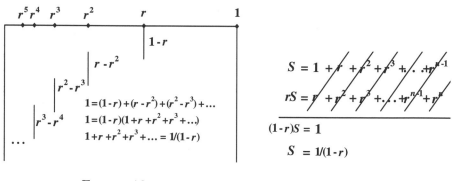

FIGURE 13   FIGURE 14

The following example illustrates how computer processing can influence students' reasoning and attempts to solve problems.

Example 4. For $x > 0$, what is the number $\sqrt{\cdots\sqrt{\sqrt{\sqrt{x}}}}$? In the rush to compute, students using test cases etc., may too readily conclude that the repeated

x	$\sqrt{x}$	$\sqrt{\sqrt{x}}$	$\sqrt{\sqrt{\sqrt{x}}}$	$\sqrt{\sqrt{\sqrt{\sqrt{x}}}}$	$\cdots$	?
2.36	1.53623	1.23945	1.11330	1.05513	$\cdots$	1.00000
0.84	0.91652	0.95753	0.97844	0.98916	$\cdots$	1.00000

square roots of a positive number eventually yields the number 1. No thinking is required, and no insights result. Using the fact that $\sqrt{\ldots\sqrt{\sqrt{\sqrt{x}}}}$ is a real number – say, y, one might write $y^2 = y$ and obtain $y = 1$. Thus, observing the existence of a solution (limit) enables one to determine its value. Instructors can provide more insight to the problem by showing, or leading students to observe, that

$$\sqrt{x} = x^{1/2}, \quad \sqrt{\sqrt{x}} = x^{1/4}, \ldots, \sqrt{\ldots\sqrt{\sqrt{\sqrt{x}}}} = x^{1/2^n} \to x^0 = 1$$

as n increases. Here also is an opportunity to display a cobweb diagram that shows how the iterates of $f(x) = \sqrt{x}$ converge to f's fixed point $x = 1$. Curious students who display the successive graphs of

$$f_1(x) = \sqrt{x}, \quad f_2(x) = \sqrt{x + f_1(x)}, \quad f_3(x) = \sqrt{x + f_2(x)},$$

and so on, will observe that the graphs converge to the graph of some function $F(x)$ for $x > 0$. As above, they can use (or be led to use) this observation to obtain $F(x) = \left(1 + \sqrt{1 + 4x}\right)/2$. What additional insight can instructors impart? How might instructors respond to students who plot the data $\{(x, f_9(x)) : x = 1, 2, \ldots, 8\}$ and use quadratic regression to claim that "$F(x)$ is closely approximated by the function $y = -0.01517x^2 + 0.38132x + 1.27562$"?

In [**12**], Hosack argues that "numerical integration can be developed as the 'norm' or 'standard' with closed form integration being considered as a special case." Although this may have merit for those oriented toward analysis, one must naturally wonder how this emphasis might affect students' propensities to discover patterns, interrelate concepts, and engage in creative explorations.

Example 5. Given the new norm of numerical integration, how many students who compute

$$\int_0^{\frac{\pi}{2}} \sin^2 x \, dx \approx 0.785398164$$

would be motivated to compute $\int_0^{\frac{\pi}{2}} \sin^4 x \, dx \approx 0.589048623$, $\int_0^{\frac{\pi}{2}} \sin^6 x \, dx \approx 0.490873852$, or any other such integral? How many would students be likely to look for a closed-form representation of 0.785398164? It need not be "something gained, something lost." For instance, asking students to express 0.785398164 in terms of $\pi/2$ would lead them to discover (on dividing 0.785398164 by $\pi/2$) that

$$\int_0^{\frac{\pi}{2}} \sin^2 x \, dx \approx \pi/4$$

This, or the instructor's queries, can motivate them likewise to discover that

$$\int_0^{\frac{\pi}{2}} \sin^4 x \, dx \approx 3\pi/16$$

and

$$\int_0^{\frac{\pi}{2}} \sin^6 x \, dx \approx 5\pi/32$$

These closed-form integrals immediately suggest the readily proved recursive relation

$$\int_0^{\frac{\pi}{2}} \sin^{2n} x \, dx = \frac{2n-1}{2n} \int_0^{\frac{\pi}{2}} \sin^{2n-2} x \, dx$$

Letting $A_{2n} = \int_0^{\frac{\pi}{2}} \sin^{2n} x\, dx$, so that $A_{2n} = \frac{2n-1}{2n} A_{2n-2}$, students would obtain

$$A_2 = \frac{\pi}{2} \cdot \frac{1}{2}, \quad A_4 = \frac{\pi}{2} \cdot \frac{1\cdot 3}{2\cdot 4}, \quad A_6 = \frac{\pi}{2} \cdot \frac{1\cdot 3\cdot 5}{2\cdot 4\cdot 6},$$

and be led to Wallis' sine formula $\int_0^{\frac{\pi}{2}} \sin^{2n} x\, dx = \frac{\pi}{2} \cdot \frac{1\cdot 3\cdot 5\cdots(2n-1)}{2\cdot 4\cdot 6\cdots 2n}$.

Here is another illustration of what might, or might not, be discovered using technology.

Example 6. "Of all pairs of positive numbers having a given product, P, which pair has the smallest sum?

Students using a numerical or graphing calculator can observe the answer for specific values P, and thereby conclude (Figure 15) that the smallest sum is $S_{\min} = 2\sqrt{P}$ when $x = y = \sqrt{P}$. Students who calculate (or use a CAS to display) the derivative of $S = x + P/x$ can readily obtain $S_{\min}$. There is not much thinking and no insight in these solutions. [At the very least, precalculus students could be asked to prove (or be shown how to prove) their answer by using the arithmetic-geometric mean inequality, and calculus students should be asked to explain before doing anything how they know that S actually has a minimum value.]

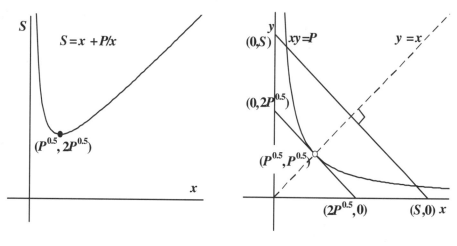

FIGURE 15   FIGURE 16

Without motivation or guidance, it is unlikely that students with "compute the answer" mentality will shift to an "explore the answer" mode of thinking. Here is an opportunity for instructors to use dynamic computer representations of the problem — to show, for example (Figure 16), that the minimum sum must occur when and only when the moving line $S = x + y$ is tangent to the fixed hyperbola $xy = P$. Reversing directions also shows that the maximum product of two positive numbers having a given sum S must occur when and only when the moving hyperbola $xy = P$ is tangent to the fixed line $S = x + y$. (See also [**13**].) Figure 16 suggests that the result carries over to three positive numbers, and this can be demonstrated by showing that the minimum sum occurs when and only when the movable plane $S = x + y + z$ is tangent to the fixed surface $xyz = P$. Now curious calculus students might want to (or be asked to) investigate how the problem can be further extended.

The lure of technology can lead to demonstrations or proofs that are devoid of insight. This is especially unfortunate if such results can be proved in ways that enrich students' mathematical understandings. The following, taken from a CAS newsletter, describes how an instructor used a computer algebra system to prove the reflective property of a parabola in a high school class whose students knowledge of trigonometry was limited.

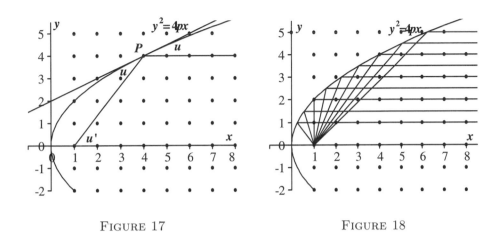

FIGURE 17   FIGURE 18

In Figure 17, the light ray is reflected by the parabola $y^2 = 4x$. Sometime or other we have heard that all reflected rays meet in the focus. Now the curve's tangent at $P(x, 2\sqrt{x})$ takes the role of a mirror, with $y' = \frac{1}{\sqrt{x}}$. Use this to show that the rays reflected at points $A(2, y)$ and $B(6, y)$ meet at the same point on the x-axis.

General solution: $u = \tan^{-1}(1/\sqrt{x})$ and $u' = 2u = 2\tan^{-1}(1/\sqrt{x})$, which gives the reflected line's slope $m = \tan\left(2\tan^{-1}(1/\sqrt{x})\right)$. Even without any sum rule for the trigonometric functions, CAS is helpful.

$$(\text{CAS output}) \; TAN\left(2 \cdot ATAN\left(\tfrac{1}{\sqrt{x}}\right)\right) = \frac{2 \cdot \sqrt{x}}{x-1}$$

Thus, the family of lines passing through the points $P\left(x_0, 2\sqrt{x_0}\right)$ is $y - 2\sqrt{x_0} = \frac{2\sqrt{x_0}}{x_0-1}(x - x_0)$. Setting $y = 0$ and solving for x, we find that $x = 1$. All reflected rays meet in the focus $F(1, 0)$. Figure 18 shows the instructor's included CAS display.

Does Figure 18 provide any more insight than the proof why this result is true? How many students could explain what exactly causes this result to be true for this parabola, and how many could say why this property is true for all parabolas? The intent of these remarks is not to disparage an instructor's well-intentioned efforts, but rather to show how much more could have been gained by introducing and building on fundamental concepts.

Example 7. Computer-generated displays as in Figure 18 can motivate students to ask if rays parallel to the y-axis reflect off the parabola $y = ax^2$ and pass through its focus (Figure 19). Since the students knew (or could be shown visually) that the parabola becomes indistinguishable from the tangent line through a point $P\left(x_0, ax_0^2\right)$ as x approaches x_0, here is an opportunity to show students how to calculate the equation of the tangent at $x = x_0$. Writing $y = ax^2$ as

$$y = a\left\{x_0 + (x - x_0)\right\}^2 = ax_0^2 + 2ax_0(x - x_0) + a(x - x_0)^2$$

and ignoring the term $a(x - x_0)^2$, which is negligible when x is very close to x_0, we find that the tangent to the graph $y = ax^2$ at $P(x_0, y_0)$ has the equation

$$y = 2ax_0(x - x_0) + y_0$$

Note, in particular, the key result that the tangent's y-intercept is $Q(0, -y_0)$.

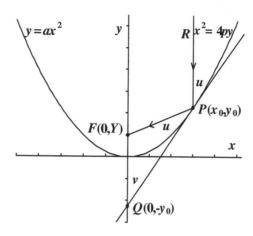

FIGURE 19

Now observe that a ray $\overline{RP}$ is parallel to the y-axis if and only if $v = u$, which is true if and only if $|FP| = |FQ|$. Squaring $\sqrt{(y_0 - Y)^2 + x_0^2} = Y + y_0$ and simplifying, we get $x_0^2 = 4Yy_0$. Therefore, $Y = p$ and $F(0, p)$ is the parabola's focus.

Students likewise can show why this property is true for the parabola $y^2 = 4px$. Using translations of the graphs $y = \frac{1}{4}x^2$ and $x = \frac{1}{4}y^2$, students can prove, or be led to prove, that the reflection property is true for every parabola $y = ax^2 + bx + c$ and $x = ay^2 + by + c$. Based on such understandings, students can use CASs to explore their conjectures, as well as confirm the reflection property for every parabola.

The informed, judicious of technology can dramatically enhance the ways mathematics is taught, learned, used, and created at all levels, from primary school, to college/university. However, to realize its fullest potential we need to address a wide variety of issues, some of which are briefly considered in the next section. See [1] for a much extended exposition of these and related issues.

4. Impact on students, faculty, and the parameters of instruction.

It is well known that a large constellation of behavioral and social factors are at work in predisposing students to success or failure in mathematics courses.

Instructional environments. The quality and quantity of interaction in instruction are important ingredients for learning. Some students prefer to work alone, some do better in small groups, and others learn best through different dynamics and forms of give and take. Instructional environments beneficial to some students may disadvantage and be counterproductive to others. What mix of which types of learning environments is better suited for whom?

Symbol sense. Increased emphasis on symbolic operation carries with it the potential for increased mystification when students have no understanding of a displayed result. How many students who differentiate $y = x^n$ can verify that their answer agrees with a CAS displayed result $y' = ne^{\ln x}/x$ or $y' = e^{n \ln x} n \ln e/x$ (based on using $y = e^{n \ln x}$)? What kinds of symbol sense should we expect of students? How can we help them discover patterns and relations that are masked by symbolic or numerical displays (decimal representations)? What danger is there that the increased emphasis on push-button symbolic computations may lead students to view mathematics as operating with symbols on computer keys?

Solution verification and reconciled representations. To what extent should students be able logically to justify or computationally to verify a symbolic or numerical solution? Should we expect students to reconcile multiple representations of a result computed by different methods? Compare, for example

$$\int \sin^3 x \, dx = \frac{\sin^3 x}{3} - \frac{2 \cos x}{3} \quad [Maple \quad 4.1], \qquad = -\frac{3 \cos x}{4} + \frac{\cos 3x}{12} \quad [Mathematica],$$

$$= -\cos x + \frac{\cos^3 x}{3} \quad [CAL \quad 2.0]$$

Mathematical exploration. Students engaged in technology-based self-directed explorations may acquire interesting mathematical results or interesting mathematical misconceptions. How much structure and guidance is appropriate for which students to engage in what kinds of explorations? What higher-order knowledge do students need to know when they have discovered something important and what makes it so?

Syllabus-student interface. Much remains unknown about the role and value that routine processes and computations play in learning mathematics. Does proficiency with straightforward, mechanical processes give students satisfaction or motivation to stay vested and continue coping with harder, more varied subject matter? How much routine, repetitive material is needed to provide students with intellectual rest stops before driving on to more demanding mathematical terrain? How will more concept-oriented, experientially based courses change our definition of what constitute remediation? Many of the classes we teach are made up of students with diverse career objectives. Thus, they may have differing predispositions towards various kinds of mathematical knowledge and ways of using it. How do we accommodate the different cognitive and affective needs of students within the same class?

Knowledge assessment. What we assess and how we do so influences students' perceptions of what is expected and how they are meeting these expectations. Although we stress understanding and critical thinking, our test questions often stress routine processes and computations exemplified by the verbs solve, sketch, evaluate, calculate, compute, differentiate, integrate, invert, etc. – precisely those mindless processes keyed to what CASs can do best. Asking students to "state and prove" also reveals no understanding of what may have been memorized. To reduce the disparity between our educational goals and assessment objectives, we need to use examination questions characterized by the verbs define and illustrate, explain, describe, compare, justify, interpret, etc. Fifteen or twenty minutes of probing discourse with a student at a computer could reveal a great deal about the student's subject specific knowledge, as well as help us gauge what students have gained from our courses by observing what they do when they do not know the answers to posed problems. In what ways will technology alter the format, administration, diagnostic or predictive utility of standardized examinations?

Impact on faculty and mathematics departments. Career development research shows that the priorities, commitments, interests, and abilities vary considerably among teaching assistants, adjuncts, beginning college instructors, professors at mid-career, and faculty nearing retirement. Thus, it may not be reasonable to expect all faculty to be willing or able to stay current in the instructional uses of evolving technologies. Which populations of teachers are or will be at risk as technology assumes greater prominence in mathematics instruction? What does this portend for the pool of people that can be hired as part-time mathematics instructors? Successful curriculum innovation requires the continuing, broadly supported efforts of a mathematics department, as opposed to ad hoc approaches where a few colleagues each use different software, and others use none at all. What are the responsibilities of a Mathematics Department to its students? To its faculty?

References

[1] Page, W. "Computer Algebra Systems: Issues and Inquiries", *Computers and Mathematics with Applications* 19:6 (1990), pp. 51-69.

[2] Smith, D. A. "Questions for the Future: What About the Horse?", *Symbolic Computation in Undergraduate Mathematics Education* (Z. Z. Karian, ed.), The Mathematical Association of America, MAA NOTES, 24 (1992), pp. 1-5.

[3] Davis, P. J. and Anderson, J. A., "Nonanalytic Aspects of Mathematics and Their Implications for Research and Education", *SIAM Review* 21 (1979), pp. 112-117.

[4] Page, W. "Count the Dots: Combinatoric Proofs Without Words", *Mathematics Magazine* 55 (1982) p. 97.

[5] Page, W. "Summing the Vertex Angles of Stars", *International Journal of Mathematics Education in Science and Technology* 22:5 (1991) 759-768.

[6] Schoenfield, A. H. "On Calculus and Computers: Thoughts About Technologically Based Calculus Curricula That Might Make Sense", Ibid [2], pp 7-15.

[7] Orton, A. "Chords, Secants, Tangents & Elementary Calculus", *Mathematics Teaching* 78 (1977), pp. 48-49.

[8] Arnheim, R. *Visual Thinking*, University of California Press (1969).

[9] Page, W. Precalculus: *A Collaborative Approach to Thinking and Doing Mathematics* (in preparation).

[10] Zorn, P. "Computer Symbolic Manipulations in Elementary Calculus", *The Future of College Mathematics*, (A. Ralston and G. Young, eds.), Springer (1983) 237-249.

[11] Page, W. "The Formula for Arc Length Does Measure Arc Length", *Two-Year College Mathematics Readings*, (W. Page, ed.), MAA (1981) 111-114.

[12] Hosack, J. "Computer Algebra Systems", *The Use of Computers in Undergraduate Instruction* (S. A. Smith et al, eds.), The Mathematical Association of America, MAA NOTES 9 (1988), pp. 35-41.

[13] Montuchi, P. and Page, W. "Behold! Two Extremum Problems (and the Arithmetic-Geometric Mean Inequality)", *The College Mathematics Journal* 19 (1988) p. 347.

30 BONNIE WAY, LARCHMONT, NY 10538, USA
E-mail address: Wxpny@aol.com

CBMS Issues in Mathematics Education
Volume **14**, 2007

Research Experiences with Undergraduates:
A discussion from the mathematical educational point of view

Chi-Kwong Li

ABSTRACT. My experience in doing research experience with undergraduates in the last 15 years will be described. We will discuss: sample problems which will connect and attract students, how to explore the strengths of students to do research, benefits gained by the students and advisors in the process. The discussion can be viewed as a follow-up and expansion of my article [**19**].

1. Prelude

It is my pleasure to share my research experiences with undergraduates in the last 15 years. One may see [**16**] and [**19**] for some background of the undergraduate research programs at William and Mary, and my involvement in a number of them. In the following, I will discuss my research experiences with undergraduates from the mathematical educational point of view.

2. The purpose of doing research with undergraduates

As mentioned in the description of the USA National Science Foundation Research experiences for undergraduates (REU) program (`www.nsf.gov/pubs/2004/nsf04584/nsf04584.txt`) the aim of the program is "to provide appropriate and valuable educational experiences for undergraduate students through research participation. REU projects involve students in meaningful ways in ongoing research programs or in research projects specially designed for the purpose. REU projects feature high-quality interaction of students with faculty and/or other research mentors and access to appropriate facilities and professional development opportunities. Active research experience is considered one of the most effective ways to attract talented undergraduates to and retain them in careers in science and engineering, including careers in teaching and educational research."

In my experience, doing research with undergraduates is indeed an effective way to enhance their interest in studying mathematics. With the research problems in minds, students are better motivated and more eager to learn advanced mathematics. Moreover, they would try to find innovative ways to apply the theory to solve problems. This active learning style always leads to deeper understanding of the results they learned and/or developed. Involving students in research is definitely a good educational tool.

In addition to the educational value, there is another motivation for me to advise undergraduate research projects. Namely, I can show more people that mathematics study is creative, beautiful, and useful. As long as the students have the proper view of mathematics research, whether they decide to become mathematicians is not so critical. Not everyone has to be a mathematician, but the mathematics community will certainly benefit if more people know that mathematicians are doing interesting and useful things.

3. Recruiting and selecting students

To have a successful undergraduate research project, it is important to make a good match between advisees and advisors. It is more likely to get a good match if students are actively involved in the decision process.

For the NSF REU eight week summer program at William and Mary, students were recruited from other institutions. When they applied for the program, they already knew that the theme of the program was matrix analysis. The eight to nine selected participating students would listen to presentations of the potential advisors in the first two days of the program, and had a meeting among themselves to determine a matching between advisors and advisees. That often led to good matches between advisees and advisors.

For other undergraduate research programs at William and Mary, students might approach me for possible research projects; I might invite outstanding students from my classes to do undergraduate research projects or honor thesis projects. In any case, before any commitment, I would try to understand students' interests and show them mine. A good mutual understanding is crucial for a successful research collaboration and positive research experiences for students (and me).

4. Selecting research topics

To select an undergraduate research topic, it is most convenient if students come with their own research problems which can utilize my research expertise in matrix analysis. In such cases, students would have strong motivation in studying the problems, and I would be able to learn more about other subjects related to my research area. Sometimes, the research team may involve advisees and advisors from different areas leading to interesting interdisciplinary research. In fact, I have conducted undergraduate research projects (sometimes with other colleagues) on topics including game theory, coding theory, cryptology, and mathematical biology; see [**2, 3, 24, 25**].

If students do not have their own research problems, I would propose a number of problems, and hope that students would be interested in some of them. Given the time constraints and limitation of the background of students, it is desirable to choose problems such that

    (1) the questions can be readily understood by students,

(2) the problems have connections to other areas,

(3) different approaches and techniques can be used in the study.

For such problems, students could quickly start the investigations with various techniques (geometric, algebraic, analytic, or computational) familiar to them. Furthermore, they could learn and apply results from other areas in the study. The exposure of students to techniques from different branches of mathematics might stimulate their interests in other research topics, which would result in more positive impacts to their future study.

Matrix analysis is a good area in which to conduct undergraduate research. Some research problems in matrix analysis do not require a lot of background to understand. Moreover, matrix analysis is related to and useful in the study of many different topics such as group theory, operator theory, operator algebras, and numerical analysis. The many different aspects of matrix analysis could attract students with different interests, and doing research on matrix analysis could lead to research opportunities in other areas. To illustrate these points let me describe a sample research problem.

Let M_n be the linear space of $n \times n$ matrices. Suppose $M, N \in M_n$ satisfy $\det(MN) = 1$, and $L : M_n \to M_n$ is defined by

$$(1) \qquad L(A) = MAN \qquad \text{for all } A \in M_n$$

or

$$(2) \qquad L(A) = MA^t N \qquad \text{for all } A \in M_n.$$

Then L is a linear map satisfying

$$(3) \qquad \det(L(A)) = \det(A) \qquad \text{for all } A \in M_n.$$

A natural question is whether every linear map $L : M_n \to M_n$ satisfying (3) has the form (1) or (2). It turns out that the answer is affirmative by a result of Frobenius [13].

The simplicity of such a question can easily draw the attention of students. Based on this result, one may ask many other natural questions such as:

(1) What kind of linear maps will leave invariant the rank function, the eigenvalues of matrices, or the row (column) spaces of matrices?

(2) What if we consider additive maps or multiplicative maps instead of linear maps?

(3) What is the structure of maps leaving invariant a certain important subsets, such as the general linear group, the set of matrices with convergent powers, the set of matrices corresponding to controllable or observable systems in control theory?

Involving students to select the research project is more likely to arouse their interest. Moreover, it could convey to students the important message that *formulating the right question is important in doing research and creating new knowledge in both pure and applied mathematics.*

5. Working on the projects

Once the students and I (and perhaps other advisors) have decided to work on a research topic, we would meet regularly to discuss the problem. We would consider different approaches to study the problem. Very often, students would follow my suggestions to work out the low dimensional cases of the problems. This was a very useful step in exposing the pattern and hidden structure of the problem leading to the solution. In some cases, students from different background would prompt me to learn some new subjects or draw my attentions to other approaches. These gave new insights and different perspectives to the problems that sometimes led to major breakthroughs.

Another important part of the project was training students to write up the research results and present the results to other people. This is indeed a very important educational component. With the modern computer software, it is relatively easy to prepare a technical paper, and do a mathematical presentation. Most students could learn the software efficiently. Some of them advanced so quickly that they ended up teaching me how to do many interesting things.

6. Results of the research

Typically, by the end of the research project, students and I would obtain a complete solution or some partial results for the research problems. Some of the results were upgraded to research papers; see the reference list. This is particularly exciting and encouraging for students. In any event, students (and I) had learned more mathematics; they acquired some experience in mathematical research; they got some training on how to write and present mathematics; they understood more about the work of professional mathematicians; they were better prepared for graduate study in mathematics (if they decide to do it). I am glad to see that most of my undergraduate research students have indeed gone on to graduate school to study mathematics and related subjects. Nevertheless, as mentioned before, as long as the students have seen a real picture of what mathematical research is about, I do not have any problem of seeing them pursue directions other than mathematics. To me, it is most rewarding to see that more young people see the beautiful, useful and creative aspects of mathematical research!

In the following reference list, names of undergraduate students are in italics.

References

[1] *M. Alwill* and *C. Maher*, Multiplicative Maps on Matrices, REU report (Advisors: C.K. Li and N.S. Sze), William and Mary, 2003.

[2] *B. Arkin*, Algebraic structures in Feistel Ciphers and an analysis of GOST, Honors Thesis (Advisors: C.K. Li and W. Bynum), William and Mary, 1998.

[3] *E. Bellenot*, Effects of Biological Invasions on Ecological Communities, REU report (Advisors: C.K. Li and S. Schreiber), William and Mary, 2003.

[4] V. Bolotnikov, C.K. Li, *P. Meade*, C. Mehl, and L. Rodman, Shells of matrices in indefinite inner product spaces, Electronic Linear Algebra 9 (2002), 67-92 (based on an REU project).

[5] R. Brualdi, *H. Chiang* and C.K. Li, A Partition Problem for Sets of Permutation Matrices, Bulletin of ICA 43 (2005), 67-79 (based on part of an honors project).

[6] *S. Chang* and C.K. Li, A special linear operator on $M_4(\mathbb{R})$, Linear and Multilinear Algebra 30 (1991), 65-75 (based on an REU project).

[7] *S. Chang* and C.K. Li, Certain isometries on $\mathbb{R}^n$, Linear Algebra and Appl. 165 (1992), 251-261 (based on an REU project).

[8] *H. Chiang* and C.K. Li, Linear maps leaving the alternating group invariant, Linear Algebra Appl. 340 (2002), 69-80 (based on an REU project).

[9] *H. Chiang* and C.K. Li, Linear maps leaving invariant subsets of nonnegative symmetric matrices, Bulletin of Australian Math. Soc. 68 (2003), 221-231 (based on part of an Honors thesis).

[10] *H. Chiang* and C.K. Li, Generalized doubly stochastic matrices and linear preservers, Linear and Multilinear Algebra 53 (2005), 1-11 (based on part of an Honors thesis).

[11] *T. Coleman*, C.K. Li, M. Lundquist, and *T. Travison*, Isometries for the induced c-norm on square matrices and some related results, Linear Algebra Appl. 271 (1997), 235-256 (based on an REU project).

[12] *C. Curtis*, J. Drew, C.K. Li, and *D. Pragel*, Central groupoids, central digraphs, and zero-one matrices A satisfying $A^2 = J$, J. of Combinatorial Theory (Series A) 105 (2004), 35-50 (based on an REU report).

[13] G. Frobenius, Uber die Darstellung der endlichen Gruppen durch Linear Substitutionen, *Sitzungsber Deutsch. Akad. Wiss. Berlin* (1897) 994-1015.

[14] *C. Hamilton-Jester* and C.K. Li, Extreme vectors of doubly nonnegative matrices, Rocky Mountain J. of Math. 26 (1996), 1371-1383 (based on an REU project).

[15] *C. Heckman*, Computer Generation of Nonconvex Generalized Numerical Ranges, REU report (Advisor: C.K. Li), William and Mary, 1990.

[16] C.R. Johnson and D. J. Lutzer, A decade of REU at William and Mary, Proceedings of the Conference on Summer Undergraduate Mathematics Research Programs, ed. by J. Gallian, 19-29, American Mathematical Society, 2000.

[17] *J. Karro* and C.K. Li, A unified elementary approach to matrix canonical form theorem, SIAM Review 39 (1997), 305-309 (based on an Honors thesis).

[18] *A.-L. S. Klaus* and C.K. Li, Isometries for the vector (p,q) norm and the induced (p,q) norm, Linear and Multilinear Algebra 38 (1995), 315-332 (based on an Honors thesis).

[19] C.K. Li, Research experiences with undergraduates, IMAGE (The Bulletin of the International Linear Algebra Society) 31 (2003).

[20] C.K. Li, *J. Lin*, and L. Rodman, Determinants of certain classes of zero-one matrices with equal line sums, Rocky Mountain J. of Math. 29 (1999), 1363-1385 (based on an REU project).

[21] C.K. Li and *P. Mehta*, Permutation invariant norms, Linear Algebra Appl. 219 (1995), 93-110 (based on an REU project).

[22] C.K. Li, *P. Mehta*, and L. Rodman, Linear operators preserving the inner and outer c-spectral, Linear and Multilinear Algebra 36 (1994), 195-204 (based on and REU project).

[23] C.K. Li, *P. Mehta*, and L. Rodman, A generalized numerical range: The range of a constrained sesquilinear form, Linear and Multilinear Algebra 37 (1994), 25-50 (based on an REU project).

[24] C.K. Li and *S. Nataraj*, Some matrix techniques in game theory, Mathematical Inequalities and Applications 3 (2000), 133-141 (based on a Wilson interdisciplinary research project).

[25] C.K. Li and *I. Nelson*, Perfect codes on the towers of Hanoi graph, Bulletin of the Australian Math. Soc. 57 (1998), no. 3, 367-376 (based on an Honors thesis).

[26] C.K. Li and *C. Pohanka*, Estimating the Extreme Singular Values of Matrices, Mathematical Inequalities and Applications 1(1998), 153-169 (based on an Honors thesis).

[27] C.K. Li, *S. Shukla*, and I. Spitkovsky, Equality of higher numerical ranges of matrices and a conjecture of Kippenhahn on hermitian pencils, Linear Algebra Appl. 270 (1997),323-349 (based on an REU project).

[28] C.K. Li and *W. Whitney*, Symmetric overgroups of S_n in O_n, Canad. Math. Bulletin 39 (1996), 83-94 (based on an REU project).

[29] S. Nataraj, Age Bias in Fiscal Policy: Why Does the Political Process Favor the Elderly?, Ph.D. thesis, Stanford University, 2002.

[30] *O. Shenker* and *K. G. Spurrier*, Notes on ray-nonsingularity, REU report (Advisors: C.K. Li and T. Milligan), William and Mary, 2003.

DEPARTMENT OF MATHEMATICS, COLLEGE OF WILLIAM AND MARY, WILLIAMSBURG, VA 23187-8795
E-mail address: ckli@math.wm.edu

CBMS Issues in Mathematics Education
Volume **14**, 2007

Problem Solving:
What I have learned from my students

James Sandefur

ABSTRACT. Most students have difficulty transitioning from mathematics courses
which are taught in a more algorithmic manner, such as algebra and calculus
often are, into more theoretical courses which require students to comprehend
and construct proofs. To understand why students have this problem and how
they can overcome it, for 4 years I have been videotaping my college math
students attempting to construct proofs of statements of varying degrees of
difficulty. These videos have given me insight into where students have problems, why they become stuck, and what support helps them make progress. In
this talk, we will discuss some video-clips and their implications for teaching
proof and problem solving. I will also share how my teaching has changed
and what impact it has had on Georgetown University math students as they
transition into our upper level courses.

1. Background

Most of our students can quickly learn the techniques we teach and can apply
them to problems that are similar to the ones we have worked in class. On the
other hand, these same students often have difficulty generalizing techniques both
to multi-step problems and to problems that are somewhat different from what
they have seen. They often exclaim "You haven't shown us how to work this." In
other words, most of our students are not adept at either problem solving or at
constructing simple proofs [1].

I will first describe what I mean by problem solving and how that differs from
constructing proofs. Consider a two-person game in which there is a pile of n
beads, and on each turn a player can pick up one, two, or three beads. The winner
is the person who picks up the last bead. If each person plays optimally, who wins
the game, the person who goes first or second, and what is the optimal strategy?
Problem solving consists of the students determining the winning strategy and
developing insight into why the strategy works. They might play the game using
different sized piles of beads. Eventually, they discover that the key is whether n
is divisible by 4 or not. If $n = 4k$, then the person who goes second should win. If
$n = 4k + 1$, $4k + 2$, or $4k + 3$, then the first person should win. The reason depends
on the fact that no matter how many beads the first player takes, the second player
can take a number of beads so that the total picked up by the two players is 4.

This is problem solving. Once the problem has "been solved", the next task is to construct a **proof** that the solution is correct. In this case, we could use induction to prove that the second player wins when $n = 4k$. Then we could prove that the first person wins as a corollary of the first result, that is, if $n = 4k + i$, $i = 1, 2$, or 3, then the first player takes i beads, and we then apply the $n = 4k$ result to the remaining pile of beads. Our students have had very little practice in constructing proofs. They think that once they have found the solution, they are finished.

In watching students try to construct proofs, it is clear that they are missing many key ideas when they don't go any further than gaining insight. For example, I might ask the students to prove the implication that if the product of two integers, nm, is odd then each of the integers must be odd. They might say that if each of the integers is odd, then the product must be odd. They might even write the equation

$$nm = (2k + 1)(2i + 1) = 2(2ki + k + i) + 1$$

and claim this proves the result. Many do not to realize that they have proven the reverse implication, that the product of two odds is odd, which is not what they were asked to show. They may not even realize the statements are different. To gain insight they should consider the false implication that if nm is even, then n and m must be even.

We have tried numerous approaches to improving our students' ability to understand and construct proofs, such as presenting more proofs in calculus and requiring a proof based course, Foundation of Mathematics. These efforts have failed to achieve their objectives for many reasons. If we didn't test our calculus students on proofs, they would not pay attention when we presented a proof. If we did test the students, they would memorize the proofs with little understanding. In Foundations, the students saw the proofs as content specific and did not generalize the approaches to their other courses. Also, many students took Foundations in their senior year, so faculty teaching other courses could not build on what was learned in Foundations. But one of the most important reasons that we failed is that none of us really knew how students learn to solve problems.

2. The Research Study

In 2001, I began teaching the Foundations course. Simultaneously, I began a research program to try to understand how students learn to problem solve, and what I could do to enhance that learning. I was reminded of a story about some scholars during the Middle Ages who were arguing about the number of teeth in the mouth of a horse. Finally, one of the scholars suggested they actually go look at a horse. So it was with me: if I was going to understand how students learned to problem solve, I would have to actually watch them solve problems.

As a pure mathematician, I was not sure where to start. Fortunately, I was aided by a small grant from the University, and the support of staff from our Center for New Designs in Scholarship and Learning (CNDLS), particularly, Susannah McGowan. Over the past 4 years, with CNDLS help, I have been conducting video Think Alouds (TA), in which I videotape students doing their homework. The particular structure is to videotape each student working on the problem alone, then bring the students together and videotape them while they continued working on the problem in a group. Someone would be there to encourage the students to verbalize what they are thinking while they work on the problem, and to give them hints or prompts if they became stuck.

Through watching and rewatching the TAs, and discussing them with others, I have gained a better understanding of our students' difficulties. Using this understanding, I have experimented with the structure of Foundations, and continued use of TAs has helped me judge which approaches are more effective in supporting students as they become independent problem solvers. In the following, I will share some of what I have learned.

3. Initial Observations

From observing my students on videotape, it appears that students 1) are more than willing to do the work we require of them, 2) get stuck near the beginning of many problems, 3) cannot change directions when they are using an unproductive approach, and 4) do not use examples to help understand either the question or what approaches might help with the answer. Let me discuss each of these points in more detail.

Observation 1: Students are willing to work. I had the misconception that poor quality or missing homework was the result of students not making sufficient effort. Early on, I discover this is not always the case. For my first TA, I asked a group of students to find all values for a and b such that the function

$$f(x) = \begin{cases} \frac{1}{ax+b} & x \neq -\frac{b}{a} \\ \frac{1}{b} - \frac{b}{a} & x = -\frac{b}{a} \end{cases}$$

has a 3-cycle, that is,

$$f(f(f(x))) = x$$

for some x. The solution is to algebraically simplify the equation $f(f(f(x))) = x$ to

$$(a + b^2)(ax^2 + bx - 1) = 0$$

For a 3-cycle to exist, we would need 3 x-values, but solving the quadratic gives only 2. Alternatively, if $a + b^2 = 0$, then we have a 3 cycle for (almost) any x. This answer makes sense, since the problem asks about a and b values, and not x values. This seemed to be a reasonably straight forward problem to me, requiring a little algebra and some thinking about the question being asked.

Each of four students was videotaped for 30 minutes working on this problem on their own. They then continued working on this problem as a group for another hour. The idea is to have each of them think about the problem separately, then let them come together to share ideas. This is the system I have used over the entire 4 years.

After working for 90 minutes, the group did not even understand the question. They would solve for x, then note that this wasn't the answer since it asked for a and b. They would then substitute some values in hoping to magically find a 3-cycle, then would go back and solve for x again. What was surprising was that the students wanted to continue working on this problem, even though they had accomplished little in the 90 minutes. Thus, I learned my first general principle that I have seen repeatedly in TA's: A lack of results does not mean there is a lack of effort. Sure, there are some students who put in a minimum amount of work or quickly stop working when they get stuck. But I have found that most of our math students are willing to put a great deal of effort into their work if they find the question interesting. The sad part is that this effort is often wasted time, with the students gaining little from the experience. From this, I developed my first goal in revising Foundations.

Goal 1: Help students spend their time more productively.

Observation 2: Students are often stuck at the very beginning of a problem. The students who were trying to determine the a and b values that resulted in 3-cycles never even understand the question being asked. In another situation, one of these students was videotaped working a graph theory problem. For 40 minutes, the student just kept repeating the question, but never made a first step.

Goal 2: Help students get started on their problems.

Observation 3: Students keep repeating the same steps, even when they clearly do not help. In watching my students work, I noticed they were like a wind-up toy car that is stuck in the corner, wheels spinning but not going anywhere. Once students decide how to approach a problem, they have difficulty trying a new approach.

One group of students was trying to show that the Power Set P_{n+1} on $n+1$ objects contains twice as many sets as the Power Set P_n on n objects. I suggested they try constructing P_1, P_2, P_3, and P_4, the Power Sets on 1, 2, 3, and 4 objects, respectively. The strategy the students used to construct each Power Set was to first list the null set, then all the sets of size 1, then all the sets of size 2, and so forth. They did not use the Power Set on 2 objects to help construct the Power Set on 3 objects.

I had thought the students would see that they could use P_2 to construct P_3 by listing P_2, all of the sets on the first 2 objects,

$$\emptyset, \{1\}, \{2\}, \{1, 2\}$$

plus all those sets with the third object added,

$$\{3\}, \{1, 3\}, \{2, 3\}, \{1, 2, 3\}$$

The students had not observed this connection between Power Sets. So I suggested that the students look for connections between the Power Set on 2 objects and the Power Set on 3 objects, again hoping they would see how one could be used to construct the next one. Instead, the students tried comparing sets according to how many elements were in the set, so P_2 and P_3 both contain the null-set, and there is one more subset of size 1 in P_3 than in P_2. This approach becomes more complicated when comparing the number of subsets with 2 or 3 elements, or when looking for the relationship between P_3 and P_4. This approach would clearly be difficult to generalize from P_n to P_{n+1}. Once these students developed a strategy for constructing Power Sets, they were having difficulty changing to another approach.

Goal 3: Help students learn how to try a variety of approaches.

Observation 4: Students avoid looking at examples and instead try to solve the general problem. One group of students was asked to show, if the integer n has an odd factor greater than 1, then $2^n + 1$ is not prime. During the individual portion of the TA, one student was juggling symbols, not getting anywhere. We then had the following conversation.

I said, "You seem to be wandering around hoping something will pop out." He replied, "Yeah, that's what I usually do." I said, "Did you think about checking a few examples to see if the statement is correct?" to which he replied, "Yeah, heh heh, ummh, that would also have been helpful for problem 3 (a problem assigned earlier)."

Once this student starting checking some values, he discovered that whenever n was odd, then 3 was a factor of $2^n + 1$. This helped him prove part of the result. Continued work with examples helped the student discover the general pattern, which his group was finally able to solve (after several more prompts to keep them going in a productive direction).

Students are not only reluctant to try examples, but when they do try examples, they tend not to reflect on how the examples can help them solve the problem, just as the group working on Power Sets did not reflect on how finding P_3 could be used to find P_4.

Goal 4: Help students learn to use examples to develop a better understanding of the problem and to reflect on examples to help them understand the general situation.

4. What helps?

Of the numerous approaches I have used to help accomplish my goals, the most successful strategies have been 1) to give prompts or hints that help the students structure their approach to a problem, 2) to have the students submit multiple drafts of their solutions, 3) to have students develop their own conjectures through the use of examples, and 4) to have students write each solution two ways, one which includes their thinking about the problem and a second that is a formal proof. Let me discuss each of these strategies in more detail.

Strategy 1: Give prompts. I have had more success with prompts than with hints. Let me explain the difference. A prompt helps the students organize their approach. They tend to be the questions that we ask ourselves when we are solving a problem, and they tend to be the same, regardless of the problem, such as

What is given?

How can I rewrite what is given in a form that is easily used, possibly using a definition?

What must I show?

How can I rewrite what I must show in a form that is usable?

What method of proof seems most likely to work, and why?

On the other hand, a hint is specific to the particular problem. It may suggest how to accomplish one of the steps of the problem. I gave the students a hint to look at the difference between the Power Set on 2 objects and the Power Set on 3 objects. As another hint, I might have suggested that the student determine common factors of $2^n + 1$ when n is odd.

What I discovered as I began teaching this course is that prompts are the questions I ask myself, almost subconsciously. To develop good prompts, I have learned to observe my own thinking as I work problems, somewhat of an internal Think Aloud, and focus on what I am asking myself as I work problems. Until I started observing myself, I didn't even realize I was asking myself questions. It had developed to the point that it was subconscious.

Let me give an example of how these questions work. Students generally do not know the difference between what is given and what must be shown, and they are also reluctant to use definitions. For example, students intuitively know what it means for an integer n to be odd, but it rarely occurs to them to use a definition of odd, such as there is an integer k such that $n = 2k + 1$. Suppose students are to show that the product of two odd integers is odd. In response to the questions, what are we given and how can we rewrite it in a usable form, the students would write, "We are given that n and m are odd. A usable form of this statement is that there are integers i and j such that $n = 2i + 1$ and $m = 2j + 1$." In response to the questions, what must we show and what is a usable form of that statement, the students would write, "We must show that nm is odd. A usable form of this statement is that there exists an integer k such that $nm = 2k + 1$." From here the students would compute

$$nm = (2i + 1)(2j + 1) = 2(2ij + i + j) + 1 = 2k + 1$$

where $k = 2ij + i + j$. What is amazing is that for many students, I need to keep repeating these questions throughout the course. It takes most students a long time to internalize these questions.

Even though the prompts seem obvious, the students tend not to think in this way. They have usually approached mathematics as a series of equations that need to be rewritten, and they do not pay close attention to the specific words in a problem, especially the words "for all" and "there exists." They start learning that if a statement begins, "for all $x \cdots$", then the method of proof will probably begin "choose $x \cdots$." If the statement includes "there exists $\cdots$", then at some point, we will probably have to find it. Some good early exercises for the students are to give them statements such as

$$p = \{\forall \, x, \, \exists \, y \text{ such that the equation is satisfied}\}$$

$$q = \{\exists \, y \text{ such that } \forall \, x, \text{ the equation is satisfied}\}$$

and ask them for which of the following equations each of these statements is true.

$$2x + y = -2$$
$$x + y^2 = 3$$
$$(x - 2)(y + 3) = 0$$

These are later followed up with the use of prompts that focus students attention on the phrasing of the problem.

When students begin to work on a proof they usually wander around with no direction. They hope for luck. It is particularly important to give prompts that help students focus on what type of approach might work. Among the types of proofs they know are direct proofs (in which we may work forwards and/or backwards), contraposition, contradiction, and induction. When I give the prompt, "what type of proof seems most likely to work and why?", the students know that: 1) if the statement is to show the existence of something (for every x, there exists a y such that), then a direct proof may work, in which we actually "find" y; 2) if the conclusion of the statement includes the word "not", then contraposition or contradiction might work (there does not exist an x such that) because it is difficult to show something doesn't exist, so let's assume it does exist and find a problem; and 3) if the conclusion is that something is true for every positive integer n, then induction might work.

Strategy 2: Multiple drafts: For difficult problems, hints will clearly help the students. The problem is that a hint may help one student and be of no use to another. In one TA, students were asked to show that a graph G on n vertices can be isomorphic to its complement G^c only if

$$n = 0 \text{ or } n = 1 \bmod 4$$

The complement of a graph on n vertices is the graph G^c which has edge uv if and only if uv is not an edge in G. The idea behind the proof is that for G and G^c to be isomorphic, they must have the same number of edges, which means the complete graph on n vertices must have an even number of edges, which can only occur if there exists an integer k such that

$$n = 4k \text{ or } n = 4k + 1$$

I gave the students the following hint. What do you know about the total number of edges in G and G^c? Answer: They are the same. At first, this hint made no sense to the students. After a short period of time, the students actually constructed some specific examples, finding isomorphic pairs, G and G^c, with 4 vertices and again with 5 vertices. They noticed that the complete graph on 6 vertices has 15 edges, which cannot be divided equally. Then one student exclaims, "Oh, so when he asks what we know about the total number of edges in G and G^c, he means the total number of edges in G and G^c." The hint finally made sense, and the students progressed quickly to the solution. This hint worked well.

As described previously, when I suggested that students look at the difference between the Power Sets on 2 and 3 objects, these students looked for the wrong connections, and the hint was of no value.

Hints work better if they are somewhat student specific. Because of this, I have instituted a multiple draft system. I know that the students will have a problem with a given deadline. The problem will be structured in several parts, with each part giving the students a prompt, such as clearly state, in a usable form, what must be shown. The students are required to type all solutions (most use Word with Equation Editor) and email the solutions to me by the deadline. For ease in grading, I have each group of 3 or 4 students send me one solution. Because it is electronic, I can give each group individual hints, depending on the problems I see with their solution. My hints and comments are embedded within the document using the Track Changes feature of Word.

Each problem is worth 100 points. For most problems, I do not expect the first draft to be correct. If the students have made a good effort and are going in a productive direction, I might not deduct any points. On the other hand, if the students are going in the wrong direction, and need a major hint, I will give a 5 or 10 point deduction, which will be deducted from the grade of the final version of the solution. If it seems that the students did not put much effort into their first draft, then I will deduct 10 points, and will not give a good hint. I want to encourage a good initial effort.

The students then have several days to write a second draft of the problem. I repeat this process, with additional possible deductions, until the students essentially have the correct solution. This way, the initial problem includes appropriate prompts, and I can individualize hints for each group of students. At the end, each student must have a solution that is correct except for minor details, but their grade may be in the 80's or even 70's if it took several major hints for them to get this solution.

This system in which each problem is graded several times is time consuming for me. Because of this, I assign fewer problems, but they are generally harder and more involved. Having solutions typed also makes the grading easier. For each problem, there are often multiple places where students make mistakes. I generally write a document with a collection of hints that might be given, and then can just copy and paste the appropriate hints into each group's paper. This also saves time.

There are other advantages to having multiple drafts. Students do not spend too much time working unproductively, since they can get feedback. To insure that each student in a group is involved, I require each draft to be typed by a different student. Having the electronic version of the solutions allows me to use some papers for illustrations in the class in later semesters. And if a student's solution is too good, I can quickly and easily compare it to solutions I have received in previous semesters.

Strategy 3: Making conjectures: Instead of asking students to prove a statement, I now try to have more problems that cause students to explore a situation and construct their own conjectures. This helps combine problem solving with construction of proofs. Students are encouraged to try to understand why the examples work by reflecting on their construction. When I began, I would have asked students to show that if n has an odd factor greater than 1, then $2^n + 1$ is composite. I now ask students to look for patterns in the factors of $2^n + 1$. They will quickly conclude that if n is odd, then 3 divides $2^n + 1$, and will prove it using induction. After some additional work, many students will observe that if $n = 2(2k + 1)$, then 5 divides $2^n + 1$. Continued work will lead students to the result that if n is not a power of 2, then $2^n + 1$ is not prime. The proof is still not easy for the students, but they get the sense of discovery, and even the weaker students can get some partial results. They also develop some ownership for the problem.

One difficulty that often arises is that students have so much fun looking for patterns, they forget to actually stop and prove some of their results. A second problem is that the problem must be worded carefully so that the students actually see some patterns. Many students are so disorganized that they may work for a long time without making any discoveries.

I believe one of the greatest shortcomings of post-secondary mathematics education is the lack of development of our students' ability to look for patterns and make conjectures. And yet, this is the basis for mathematical research.

Strategy 4: Two different types of proof: Students begin my course with only a vague notion of what a proof is. I might give them an implication, $p \Rightarrow q$. They will work from both ends until they get an equation that is known to be true. At that point, they think they have a proof. Consider the statement, "if n and m are consecutive integers, then $n^2 + m^2 - 1$ is divisible by 4." The students confuse what is given with what needs to be shown. They might turn the following in as their proof.

$$n^2 + m^2 - 1 \qquad\qquad = 4k$$
$$n^2 + (n+1)^2 - 1 \qquad\quad = 4k$$
$$n^2 + n^2 + 2n + 1 - 1 \quad\; = 4k$$
$$2n(n+1) \qquad\qquad\quad = 4k$$

so
$$k = \frac{n(n+1)}{2}$$

While a mathematician would realize this actually contains the proof since $n(n+1)$ must be even, it has become clear to me that students do not know why this is a proof. They work the problem as if n, m and k were all given constants and that they only need to check that everything balances in the equation $n^2 + m^2 - 1 = 4k$. They seem not to realize that n and m can be treated as known integers and that we must show an integer k exists that balances the equation.

I give problems that have several parts, corresponding to my prompts. The first part would be to restate what is given in an usable form (as discussed previously), and the second part would be to state what is to be shown in usable form. The third part has them show their "thinking", that is, write a solution such as the equations above. This helps them develop insight into why the statement is true. In the last part, they must construct a formal proof in which they begin with what is given and work forward until they reach what was to be shown. This last part requires the students to tie the other three parts together, and is crucial in helping students develop a better understanding into what a proof actually is.

There may be another part to the problem asking the students what proof method might work. This part usually follows the second part in which they write what needs to be shown. If they decide on contraposition or contradiction, then they would have to rework the first two parts, so that they have the contrapositive of what is assumed and what must be shown.

Strategy 5: Presentations. I have had good success with having students give group presentations. Early in the semester, groups will present simple problems, taking around 10 minutes. At the end of the semester, each group gives a larger presentation, usually consisting of the proof of a major theorem from the text and the solution to a problem. Students must learn these proofs at a deeper level than usual so they can help other students understand the problem. These presentations are similar in structure to the assigned problems discussed previously; that is, the students will describe what is given and what needs to be shown, and will present an informal proof, describing how they thought about the problem. Then they will give the formal proof. Most students now give Power Point presentations. The use of animation makes their presentation come alive. Students used to complain that they didn't get as much from student presentations as they got from my lecture. That is no longer a complaint.

Each group must meet with me twice before giving their presentation. The first meeting is so I know they are on the right track. In the second meeting, they actually give the presentation to me. This helps avoids embarrassing errors in the actual presentation. Several pointers that I give to the students are 1) make sure slides or transparencies are in large enough fonts, 2) each slide has one idea, 3) a computation is not continued from one slide to the next, 4) each slide should have very few words, and 5) they should engage the class, possibly asking questions about what the next slide should be. The fourth pointer is critical. Cluttered slides are difficult to follow. The goal is to only have the essentials on the slide and then fill in the details with the verbal presentation.

For the presentations to work, the students know that they will be responsible for the material on a final exam.

5. What Problems Remain?

Learning to teach problem solving has been one of the most difficult challenges of my academic career. After teaching this class 7 times in the past 4 years, and watching hours of videotape, I still feel I am only beginning to understand how students learn problem solving. And there are still many obstacles preventing more success.

One obstacle is finding a significant number of good problems that are at an appropriate level for my students. Many good problems can be found in texts such as [2]. More often than not, a problem that seems easy to me is too difficult for my students. Equally often, I assign problems that are too easy, and the students gain little from working them. Giving appropriate hints is also quite difficult to do. In an effort to not give away the solution, my hints still tend to be too obtuse, and consequently, not much help to the students. Giving good hints is an art that I have not mastered.

Teaching problem solving is quite time consuming. Each semester, I try some variation in an effort to reduce the time I spend either meeting with students or grading papers. The only short cut that has had some success is the use of multiple drafts. This reduces the number of students who visit my office and the grading of later drafts is usually not that time consuming since they have already been given some direction. Most short cuts I have tried have not reduced my time commitment, but have resulted in less success in my students.

Each class presentation must be carefully prepared. For the students to gain from my presentation, I must carefully construct the steps they need to take through a problem. I must make sure that my presentations clearly model what they should be doing. I must also carefully choose similar problems for them to try in groups during class. The students need this supervised practice.

When most students enter college, they are not nearly as competent problem solvers as they should be. Some of this results from the lack of time spent solving problems and reasoning in the elementary, middle, and secondary mathematics classrooms. I do get the occasional student who has had some experience in proof and problem solving, but most of our students are just beginning to learn to reason when they take Foundations. I have been somewhat disappointed in how little they can accomplish in one semester. To be successful, we must reinforce what they have learned in our other courses. This means faculty must talk among themselves and share ideas, both those that work and those that do not work. And finally, we should continue to carefully observe our students to make sure we improve in our ability to help them.

References

[1] S. Epp, *The Role of Logic in Teaching Proof*, American Mathematical Monthly, Volume 110, no. 10, December 2003, 886–899.
[2] D. Smith, M. Eggen, and R. St. Andre, *A Transition to Advanced Mathematics, 5th Edition*, Brooks/Cole Thomson Learning, 2001.

DEPARTMENT OF MATHEMATICS, GEORGETOWN UNIVERSITY, WASHINGTON, DC 20057, USA
E-mail address: sandefur@georgetown.edu

CBMS Issues in Mathematics Education
Volume **14**, 2007

Guidelines for Using Computers Creatively
in Mathematics Education

Ulrich Kortenkamp

ABSTRACT. Computers are the ultimate tool for teaching: They provide microworlds that can be explored; they can be forgiving and strict; they take account of everything that is happening; they can create maps of what the learner knows or still has to learn; they are fun to use; they provide interactive illustrations that enlighten those who use them — or at least, that's what they could be or do. There are significant drawbacks: many people do not know what they could do with them; if they know it, they probably do not know how to make them do it; and, finally, it is not validated whether it is of any didactic value to use them in the way they are used.

In this text, we present some basic guidelines that can help in designing and evaluating electronic material. Starting from an example, we identify some roles the computer can take and discuss their implications for the development of mathematics tools.

1. Introduction

CLAIM 1. *Using a computer is by no means a guarantee for better teaching.*

CLAIM 2. *Using a computer is a chance to significantly enhance teaching.*

Today, everyone — students, parents, government, university administration, just to name a few — require the use of computers in teaching, as they do not want to miss the chance for the enhancement of Claim 2. Unfortunately, taking Claim 1 into account, we are only left with a faint hope. As many teachers and professors neither want to use the computer nor know what to do with it, if we add the technical insufficiencies of many computer installations for teaching, we even might end up with

CLAIM 3. *Using a computer can be hazardous to teaching.*

This article intends to identify the advantages of new media and make some of the underlying mechanisms more visible. If you intend to (or have to) use computers in teaching, you should checkmark the framed boxes below and reflect on each of them in your context.

Supported by the DFG Research Center MATHEON.

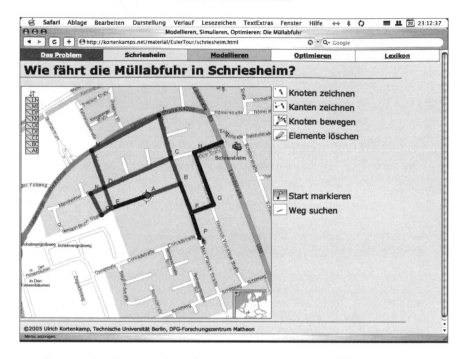

FIGURE 1. A screenshot of an applet used to teach Eulerian graphs and tours to 13-year old students. The general topic of the sequence is "What is the tour of a garbage collection vehicle?" Students can draw a graph onto a map of their hometown Schriesheim and ask for a Eulerian tour through it.

2. Exemplary Use of a Computer in Teaching Discrete Mathematics

The material that is introduced in this section has been used for students of grades 4 to 8; nevertheless, it could be adapted to university teaching as well, as it is concerned with an important basic topic from Discrete Mathematics. This activity is intended to be used for the introduction of the concept of graphs, and to explore the notion of Eulerian tours.

The general topic is the optimization of tours for garbage collection. Based on the observation that the garbage collection vehicle has to go through every street at least once — which is also sufficient, as two garbage collectors serve both sides of the street — students explore tours that do not use any street twice. First, they work on an electronic exercise sheet that shows a city map of their hometown (Fig.1). They add vertices and edges of a graph using the mouse, and they can run an algorithm that tries to find a round-trip tour that visits all edges exactly once.

The electronic exercise sheet is an HTML page with an embedded Java applet. The Java applet was created using the Visage-Extension [2] of Cinderella [4]. This exercise can run standalone from a local disc or CD-ROM or it can be put on the web. Besides a Java runtime, which is included by default on major operating systems, no software installation is necessary.

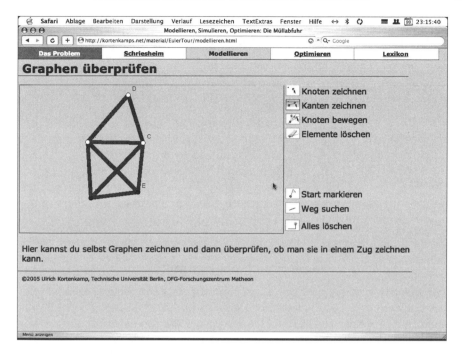

FIGURE 2. The open learning environment for drawing and testing graphs. On the left hand side we see a 5-vertex graph drawn by the student. The coloring of vertices is done automatically (see text). On the lower right there are buttons for selecting a start vertex and starting the algorithm that finds Eulerian tours.

As a next step, we let the students work with pencil and paper. They are supposed to check by hand whether a given graph admits a Eulerian tour, that is, a closed tour that visits every edge exactly once.

The solutions will not be checked by the teacher, but by the students themselves. They use the next electronic work sheet to draw the graph and ask for a Eulerian tour. If there is one, the computer will show one, otherwise the algorithm will fail and highlight a problematic part of the graph. In Fig. 2 we can see a graph drawn by a student.

During this phase students naturally will ask themselves[1] whether there is an easy way to distinguish between Eulerian graphs and non-Eulerian ones. The answer to this question is positive — any graph that contains only vertices of even degree, that is, has an even number of edges incident to it, is Eulerian, and only these. The proof of that fact is easy, and can be done by an induction argument, but discovering this conjecture is not that easy.

In this activity we have added a subliminal clue for arriving at that concept. The vertices in Fig. 2 are colored automatically in either white or black, depending on their degree. White vertices have an even degree, black vertices have an odd degree. Our experience is that students will not notice the coloring at all at first. However, when they investigate possible reasons for some graphs to be "good" and

---

[1]If they do not ask themselves, the teacher should activate this discussion

others being "bad", they can use this coloring as a first hint: Graphs that were
proved being Eulerian (using the built-in algorithm) have only white vertices.

The last part of the sequence is another electronic work sheet (Fig. 3) that opens
the problem further and can be used a starting point for other, related activities.
Students are given a graph that contains both black and white vertices, and their
task is to change the color of all vertices to white. This is always possible — a
theorem about graphs states that every graph contains an even number of odd-
degree vertices, so we can connect pairs of them with paths. As the students do
not know the theorem yet, they are invited to play a game where they should try
to give a graph that their classmates cannot complete to a Eulerian graph.

Building on this, we could either pursue different directions, or bring this sequence to an end. Possible continuations are, for example, proofs by induction
for various graph properties, shortest-path algorithms, or (weighted) matchings in
graphs.

3. Roles of the Computer

We will now discuss the various aspects of computer use in this example. We
will use the term *computer*, even though we mean all computer-like media and, in
particular, appropriate software. The first two roles are evident, but we want to
mention them nevertheless.

> **1. Computers can be used as a motivating element.**

It is widely known that using a computer at all can have a positive effect on
the motivation of students. However, that might easily change in the future when
using a computer becomes a day-to-day event, so we should not rely on it in our
teaching.

> **2. Computers can provide or enhance the visualization of concepts.**

Visualization and interactive presentation of content has become much easier
with a computer. In our example, it is really easy to demonstrate a tour on a city
map in a professional way, something which needed much more preparation (like
preparing many hand-drawn slides in advance) before. As most teachers are aware
of this publishing aspect of computers, we will not focus on it here, but instead we
will concentrate on the following, not so apparent issues.

> **3. Computers can restrict the actions of learners and thus help them to
> develop appropriate mental models of representation.**

At first thought, this might appear a drawback of the computer, and not an
advantage. However, even in an open learning environment, it is not desirable
that students be able to do everything. There might be situations in which it is
possible to work completely unrestricted, but usually this is not the case. If we
create really open situations, we have to accept that the students might not reach
the original goal (which is, in the above case, to learn about the concept of graphs
for modeling). If we accept that, the teaching might still be instructive and good,
but we risk that we — the students and teachers – end up with unsatisfactory
semi-results. I strongly disagree with the opinion that it is sufficient to think about
a problem and find some result. This assumes that anybody has both the creativity

and intellectual capacity to solve all problems. Even if students work in groups, this is not true, and one of the great advantages of humanity is the ability to store and recall others' inventions using speech and writing.

How is this implemented in the Euler Tour example? Students are allowed to draw on the city map using the computer. Of course, they could also use a pencil on a photocopy of the city map, but then they could draw anything, not only graphs composed of vertices and edges. The difference between abstract model (the graph) and drawing (the city map) could not be established that way — the graph is just another drawing.

---

4. Computers can give an immediate hands-on experience on abstract models.

The graph that is drawn on the city map is "used" directly. This creates the important immediate feedback for learning. With traditional methods, we had to rely on the students knowing how to find the right tour in advance for checking; if that were the case, we would not have to teach them. Using the computer, they can try out many more examples and get immediate, correct feedback.

---

5. Computers can act as referees.

It is difficult to supervise a group of more than 20 students who work with a computer. In particular, non-homogeneous groups pose a problem: it is not possible to check with each student his or her individual progress and give advice or hints. If we fall back to addressing the whole class, we lose the fact that each student can settle for his own learning method and speed. Or, if we restrict checking of exercises to giving the answers (either by the teacher or by a student), some students can be left with unanswered questions: Why is it wrong — or even, why is it correct what I did? The necessary temporal synchronization between the students takes away the time to answers these questions.

With the help of the computer, it is possible to overcome this. The computer can act as an authority for right or wrong, and it can even show why something is wrong. In the garbage collection example, we exhibit this by using the computer for checking the students' answers. When a graph is Eulerian, the computer can prove this by visualizing the corresponding tour. When it is not, the software will highlight problematic areas of the graph to encourage further inspection.

Also, this allows for other teaching scenarios. For example, students can play a two-person game: One person is thinking of a graph, the other person has to decide whether it has the Euler property. Without the help of the computer, we cannot be sure that the answers are correct, putting the whole educational effect of the game at risk.

---

6. Computers can give hints and guidance.

In the example, we exploit the coloring of vertices for giving an almost subliminal hint. Our experience shows that even people who know that the evenness of the valence of a vertex is important don't immediately recognize the reason for the coloring. It's just something to think about, a crystallization point for thoughts, a thought-provoking impulse. In addition, it gives a temporary nomenclature for a property of vertices — students can talk and think about black and white vertices

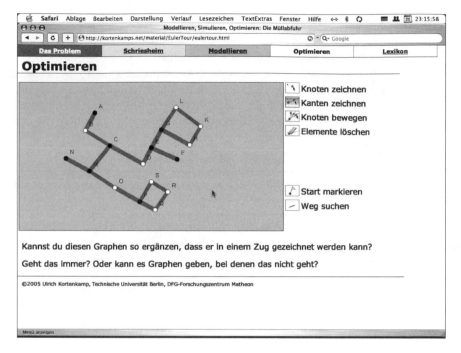

FIGURE 3. The electronic work sheet for "optimizing". The German instructions are: *Is it possible to extend this graph to make it possible to draw it without lifting the pen? Is this always possible (for any graph)? Or are there graphs that do not permit it?*

instead of vertices of even- and odd degrees. This constitutes a significant aid for developing the right concept.

7. Computers make it easy to customize material for a certain audience.

There is no doubt that computers with their word processing and desktop publishing tools made it possible for everybody to produce material that looks professional. If one has access to an electronic version of a work sheet, then it is easy to change some values, or to exchange a figure or drawing by another one. For teachers, this implies they can use their colleagues' material even if it is not exactly fit for their course. An enormous amount of preparation work can be re-used for other purposes.

The same is true for electronic material. In our example, it is easy to replace the city map with the map of another town, or a subway plan, or a milling plan for a printed circuit board.

Also, the hints described in the previous section can be omitted or changed, in order to adapt to the abilities of the students. This can be done individually for each of them.

8. Computers can show the need for analyzing the structure of a problem.

The last general role of computers we want to bring up here is another general property of introducing algorithmic thinking into schools. If we are really looking for a way to use the computer to solve a problem, we have to break it down into small parts that can be solved by basic building blocks.

In the example sequence, we used this only implicitly by using graphs as a model for street maps. If time permits, this can be explored further by examining the Eulerian Tour algorithm. What data does the algorithm need? Which decisions have to be made? It all comes down to marking edges and finding unmarked edges incident to a vertex. If we arrived at this conclusion, we can see that the graph model is perfect for answering questions like this.

4. Implementation Aspects

We cannot rely on the fact that every teacher is both willing to and able to create electronic activities him- or herself. Quite the contrary, most teachers depend on using material that has been made available to them by third parties (i.e., software manufacturers, government, or colleagues, to name the most important ones).

This section addresses both software manufacturers and software users. We highlight three important aspects of software that have to be taken into account when creating or evaluating software products.

4.1. User Interface. The user interface of a piece of software is a key component. If the software is not accessible for one reason or another, then the "inner values" cannot be revealed and are irrelevant. While this seems to be common sense, many educational software products still come with poor human-computer-interfaces.[2] This renders them useless, at worst.

It is relatively easy to check the user interface of a software product — much easier than creating it in the first place.[3] Here are some rules of thumb for judgment.

- Is the functionality of the software carefully selected, instead of just complete? Is the toolbar (if any) cluttered?
- Are there default choices in the configuration that apply to your situation?
- Does the interface comply to the user interface guidelines of the operating system you are using, i.e., is its handling and look-and-feel similar to other software on your computer?
- Has somebody taken care of making the software look visually appealing?
- Is it possible to adapt the software to your needs (see Box 7 above)?

You will probably be able to add to this list.

Unfortunately, most open-source-software[4] fails the tests above — and this is related to the answer to the meta-question: *Is anybody aware of the issue and responsible for the human-computer-interface?*

---

[2]The same applies to scientific talks. Although most people know that the scientific value of a talk cannot be recovered if its presentation is poor, they seem to rely on the inner qualities and neglect the performance.

[3]An example is the toolbar for dynamic geometry software (DGS) for which there is no good solution so far. See [**3**] for a discussion about how to move to a zero-interface for geometric constructions.

[4]This is by no means a vote against open-source-software. We just want to emphasize that this is one of the areas which definitely needs some progress in the next years.

4.2. Modularity and Programming Interfaces. Even when using new technology for teaching, the teacher is still in charge of providing the content and material. A software company cannot anticipate the special needs for all teaching/learning situations; if so, then it would be easy to provide a teacher-less package for online teaching.

This implies that a teacher has to be able to choose from the available material and rearrange it according to the pedagogical situation. Monolithic blocks of content are not suitable here. Every bit should be re-usable.

Also, there should be a way to add to the material as described in the previous section. The black-white-hints were not built into the software package used, but they are a custom add-on done by the teacher himself. As it is completely unclear what other ideas a teacher could have, there has to be a general way to extend the software, i.e. a programming interface (or API).

Again, we want to list a few rules of thumb for a first evaluation:

- Is it possible to use parts of the software independently or is it a all-or-nothing decision?
- Does the software use standard document formats like HTML or PDF, or is a separate viewer necessary that might not be available for all (current and future) platforms?
- Is there an API for custom extensions? Is it easy to learn?
- Does the software license allow for free redistribution of content created with it?

4.3. Mathematical Foundation. As we are focussing on mathematical software for mathematics education, we should not forget that we want to teach *mathematics*. This creates a dividing line between general-purpose software like media players or animation tools and special-purpose software for doing mathematics like spreadsheets, DGS or CAS.

Media players are not aware of the content they are playing, and their interaction capabilities are restricted to linking pre-produced content to certain choices. We can have a wealth of material that is interconnect by clickable links, but still this is finite and can hardly respond to every aspect that might come up during teaching. Only very closed teaching situations can afford this type of material, unless it is meant as accompanying media, e.g. material that is used as a reference.

In order to support explorative and experimenting learning, the software has to implement the mathematical concepts as exactly as possible. To give a clear-cut example, we refer to K-2 teaching: A calculator for one-digit additions can be implemented using a table that stores all problems and their solutions. Using it is similar to using a media player — we press the channel number (for $3 + 5$ we choose "channel 35´´) and get a pre-produced unit about adding three and five. A student who wants to explore addition more in-depth cannot choose a channel for $10 + 1$ as the calculator was not designed for this. An open software environment would have included the mathematical theory for addition and would be able to do all possible additions.[5]

This example may be exaggerated, but many educational software products today fail in this category! Everything which might be outside the current scope for the lesson has been omitted, as it leads to higher production costs. This is

---

[5]See [1] for a discussion of this in the context of Dynamic Geometry software.

caused by the common approach to do an implementation that works for most cases, but not in general, and to "fix" all the cases that are relevant for teaching — at least those that the software developer did think of.

Let us conclude again with the rules of thumb for software evaluation in this category:

- Is the software just playing media or does it use a structural representation of the mathematical content?
- Are special cases handled by a general theoretic approach or using a series of "if-then-statements" within the software?
- Is it possible to try experiments that were not foreseen by the software developer?
- Is unexpected user input handled as an error, not at all, or in a reasonable way?

5. Conclusion

As we have seen, there are many ways of using a computer to enhance teaching, some of which are well-known, while others are much subtler. Our contribution here was to identify a few concepts, generalize them, and make them accessible for other situations.

In Sec. 3 we discussed three main components of software development that are areas worth of inspecting when evaluating (or implementing) software. In order to support the roles of the computer identified before, these areas constitute key components.

6. Acknowledgments

I would like to thank for the opportunity to present this work at the 1st KAIST International Symposium on Enhancing University Mathematics Teaching in May, 2005. Parts of this work have been supported by the DFG Research Center MATH-EON in Berlin. Many thanks to Dirk Materlik for his work within the Visage project, and to Brigitte Lutz-Westphal for fruitful discussions.

References

[1] Kortenkamp, U. *Foundations of Dynamics Geometry* Dissertation, ETH Zurich, 1999, http://kortenkamps.net/papers/1999/diss.pdf
[2] Kortenkamp, U. and Materlik, D. Visage. A software package for visualizing graph algorithms using interactive geometry software. See http://cinderella.de/visage.
[3] Kortenkamp, U. and Materlik, D. *Pen-based input of Geometric Constructions.* Proceedings of MathUI 2004, http://kortenkamps.net/papers/2004/Scribbling-article.pdf.
[4] Richter-Gebert, J. and Kortenkamp, U. *The Interactive Geometry Software Cinderella.* Springer-Verlag, Heidelberg, 1999, http://cinderella.de.

DEPARTMENT OF COMPUTER SCIENCE, UNIVERSITY OF EDUCATION SCHWÄBISCH GMÜND, 73525 SCHWÄBISCH GMÜND, GERMANY
E-mail address: Ulrich.Kortenkamp@ph-gmuend.de

CBMS Issues in Mathematics Education
Volume **14**, 2007

Suggestions from the Real World
on Improving Math Education

Leon H. Seitelman

ABSTRACT. Because the goals and culture in business and industry in the United States are dramatically different from those in academia, the training that enables the mathematics professional to succeed in a nonacademic setting requires attention to skills that are not usually developed in the course of formal mathematical education. Using first-hand experience as a guide, this paper discusses some of the contrasts between the two environments, spotlights the ways in which the industrial applied mathematician contributes, and presents ideas for adapting mathematical training to serve the needs of graduates with industrial career aspirations. Recognizing the problems that currently exist in retaining students at all levels in mathematics courses, a number of suggestions are presented for improvement of mathematics curricula at all academic levels.

Overview

Considerable effort (and substantial funding) has gone into the study and improvement of mathematics pedagogy – i.e., teaching styles and learning models – and the replacement of traditional K-12 curricula by applications-focused alternatives. Some of this work has supported the substitution of problem-based case studies that develop the necessary mathematical concepts, as needed, for the previous formal proofs and disciplinary (analysis, geometry, algebra) alignments. In addition, a school of thought that focuses on student-led discovery of mathematics has also emerged. Until very recently, much less attention has been devoted to the issue of mathematical content in the education of teachers. But the issue of teacher preparation is critical, because students need to understand the importance of mathematics in preparing for academic and career choices, and, if they have never learned them, teachers cannot tell their students about the meaningful connections of mathematics with the real world applications that will keep those students involved in mathematics courses. This content issue needs to be addressed in greater depth, and the retraining of mathematics teachers already in the schools, particularly with respect to the applications of mathematics, has to become a priority item. Students will be well served by restoring much of the previous emphasis in K-12 mathematics education, which emphasizes rigorous thinking – a skill much needed for both vocational and personal success – and by improving the mathematical understanding of teachers of mathematics.

At the college level, mathematics has to serve a dual purpose: to prepare the next generation of mathematicians and mathematics teachers, and to provide other disciplines with the mathematical training and understanding needed for their students to be able to use, and understand, the technology associated with their respective subjects. In particular, this means that mathematics departments need to work cooperatively with the scientific and engineering disciplines that are the main "consumers" of mathematics courses, to define and deliver courses that are appropriate for their needs. From a client/provider standpoint, this kind of complementary synergy is natural; from the vantage point of a discipline that relies on the enrollment (and tuition) stream of other departments to make possible the low enrollment advanced courses in mathematics, it is essential. In light of the experience at the University of Rochester a few years ago, where the bread-and-butter pre-engineering courses were in jeopardy of being taught within the engineering departments themselves, with concomitant loss of tuition credit hours, it is obvious that indifference or inattention to the stated needs of client departments represents not only a marketing disaster, but potentially a financial calamity as well. If it is to survive and thrive in the future, mathematics must rethink its relationship with, and responsibility to, the rest of the academic community.

The "math wars" of a few years ago were the result of a "perfect storm" of competing and conflicting interests: the concern of the professional mathematics community about whether current pre-collegiate preparation of students threatened the pipeline of future mathematicians, and the reluctance of the mathematics education community to acknowledge for a long time that content knowledge in teacher training was in fact a legitimate concern. The highly fractious, often acrimonious exchanges that followed the release of the first draft of the NCTM Standards set back the common cause of the mathematics community, because the general public does not distinguish between the factions in the relatively tiny mathematics community, and therefore concluded that this group, not known for its public outreach, cannot even get along professionally. Given the importance of mathematics to the future of science and technology, and the economy in general, it is imperative for the various interests to resolve to work together respectfully to solve the problems that have been identified, and restore public respect and support for the profession.

Introduction

This paper discusses how things are actually done in industry, and the personal and professional skills that enable a mathematics professional to succeed in that environment. It presents suggestions for improving mathematics education, at all levels, to make the preparation of mathematicians, scientists and engineers, and nontechnical individuals, more appropriate to what they need to fulfill both their vocational responsibilities and their obligations as citizens. The perspective presented is that of a trained mathematician with long experience in private industry and extensive interest and involvement in mathematics education.

Industrial Work

Understanding the skills needed in the business world requires an appreciation of how industrial work is performed. The clear distinctions between academic concerns and commercial constraints frame the cultural issues. With this insight, it is possible to draw conclusions about the kind of preparation that is required in industry.

Much of the contrast between the two environments stems from the way in which things are done, and how people interact, which is, in turn, critical to getting things done. While many industries share common concerns, however, it is important to realize that, "One size does *not* fit all." Different industries do things differently. Maturity of both the company and the technical area under development plays an important role in explaining these differences. In general, however, many skills are useful for success in all industries, and this paper will strive to identify them. Finally, we will identify some of the newer curriculum development that has been undertaken in recent years, to support the training needs of particular industries.

Ideas to Improve Math Education

The second goal of this paper is to suggest a few ideas to improve mathematics education, at all levels. Some of these are distinctly different from what is currently fashionable opinion.

In the United States, too many students begin to make poor mathematics course choices, i.e., "drop out" of serious mathematics study, beginning in middle school. Part of this decision-making may be the result of being unable to make meaningful connections with real applications in much of the K-12 mathematics curricula. Because of the building block nature of mathematical preparation, in which advanced courses assume the foundation of previous study, underprepared students who decide in high school that they would like to pursue careers in technical fields are confronted with the realization that they are unable to do so, because their mathematical preparation is lacking. The belief, "I'll never use this stuff in real life," that leads to mathematical underpreparation, becomes a delimiter for a student's future.

It seems obvious – at least, to this author – that the state of affairs can be improved if more real applications of mathematics are introduced into pre-college education. Unfortunately, teachers don't know how mathematics is used, because their preparation places little (if any) emphasis on it. Teachers in the U.S. can't teach applications, because, too often, they never learned any. So the best way to improve the situation is to encourage change in the way teachers are exposed to real applications of mathematics, which can then be taught to their students, and help to sustain greater student interest.

At the college level, many mathematics departments have historically been enclaves of researchers, who interact primarily – or even exclusively – within their own department, participating only in a very limited way with departments outside the discipline. This needs to change, if mathematics is to preserve its vitality and viability.

Finally, at the graduate level, graduate education needs to evolve, to provide the kind of training that graduates will find most helpful to their future professional careers.

Theorem: In the Real World, there are *no* closed form solutions

First, a little information about the real industrial world.

The only clients who brought well posed problems, with closed form solutions, into my office were there to solve the homework problems in their evening master's degree courses. Problems in industry are posed in the language of the product that gives rise to them. If the industry is engineering, the practitioner's goal is to determine the important elements of the problem, develop or improve or correct or otherwise update whatever model has been developed, use or collect data to validate the model, and then translate the results back into the language of the discipline that gave rise to the problem.

Solutions are not complete when the existence of a solution is proved, or when the algorithm for the solution has been formulated. Only when the actual numerical answer is presented to the client in the nomenclature of the application is the problem completed.

In a new problem area, the mathematical models themselves may be incomplete, or flawed. Data can be of high or low quality, adequate or not, and may quite possibly not be in a form appropriate for the analysis. Finally, projects almost always have challenging time constraints, driven by competitive pressures, or technical commitments, or other factors beyond the control of the practitioner.

Oh, yes, and there is one more constraint. An answer *is* required.

In a word, the environment is demanding. Because industry must also show a profit to survive and thrive, it is also unforgiving.

Attributes of Industrial Problems

Real world concerns are demanding. Problems are complicated. Some can be of a few weeks' duration, but the biggest ones can last months, or even years. (One project, to predict aircraft engine performance under all conditions, lasted for the better part of a decade!) Most efforts require the worker to delve into fields that are outside of mathematics. Not surprisingly, there's a good deal of modeling of various phenomena, and even more remodeling, as the understanding of the problem proceeds, and becomes more complete. Of course, extensive computing can (and usually does) result, with a parallel focus on data collection and numerical analysis of whatever procedures are chosen or developed.

For large scale computation projects, efficiency can be an important concern. Of necessity, the work can result in publishable research, although proprietary issues may make this kind of recognition problematical. But the job always involves learning new things, and applying them in new contexts. Finally, the need to be able to communicate – the important conclusions of the work to non-mathematicians and non-scientists – especially management (often, the biggest challenge) is often the most important skill for the practitioner.

A Contrast in Environments

So there's a real difference between academia and industry. Academia is concerned with *process* issues – developing proofs, ensuring uniqueness, demonstrating optimality of procedures and proving rates of convergence, and so forth, while in industry the focus is always upon understanding and solving problems in a *cost effective* way, producing a good enough answer to develop a product that meets the design requirements, i.e., that is "good enough" for the task intended. Naturally, approximate methods play an important role on the practical scene.

A cynic might say that academia is focused on the micro: becoming more and more familiar with increasingly specialized subject matter. Certainly this is the public perception of mathematics in the United States. The public thinks of mathematicians, when it thinks of them at all, as really smart people, who think up beautiful thoughts in isolation – think of Andrew Wiles, in his attic, for a decade – and who publish articles about obscure subjects in arcane journals, with circulation limited to very few people outside of the authors' immediate families.

In industry, by contrast, the goal is to somehow integrate whatever is known from whatever fields are needed to solve whatever problem is presented so that a product can be produced. This requires people to work in a team environment to blend their respective knowledge bases in a way that will get an answer. In further contrast to the academics, because of the commercial interests involved, much of this creative work will never see the light of the publication day. (So while rewarding, in a lot of ways industrial work can be quite limiting.)

More Contrasts

There is a quite a bit of diversity in the kind of mathematical expertise that is required by the various industry groups. ("One size does *not* fit all.") Mature industries, for example, have an extensive experience base, and current work must be "grafted" on to that existing knowledge, and be compatible with it. Most often, this history is very helpful, teaching how product development can be usefully and effectively pursued. Legacy systems, or technology developed over the years, were used to design the previous generation of products; experienced "practititioners of the art" developed rules of thumb, and other ideas, that become entrenched as gospel in product design.

But with this technological record comes institutional inertia. The tendency to rely on the body of knowledge and procedures developed over the years is compelling, even when the methods employed are inefficient, or do not really apply to the new problem. At the same time, whatever is developed has to be "back-compatible," i.e., must be consistent with the technology that is displaced. In particular, this means validating new procedures for existing test data, and sometimes reconciliation with service experience.

The situation is quite different for emerging industries, which are often just developing the knowledge and techniques for new fields and new products. Here, there is more "making it up as you go along." The situation can be considerably more chaotic, as design work may not fully precede manufacturing, and the incorporation of service experience presets major feedback loops to both. To compound matters, technical understanding may be limited at the outset. Finally, task scheduling may be extremely aggressive, because market realities may make the underlying product development subject to budget constraints driven by tenuous external funding, and outside pressures from competing products.

Four Problems (I've Worked On)

To provide a sense of how all these considerations play out, I'd like to describe work on four problem areas that my work involved, and the challenges they presented.

Fan blade loss and containment. Aircraft engine manufacturers have to design against the very remote possibility that a fan blade may crack off during flight. This is not simply far-fetched; although the requirement for operation states that aircraft runways must be macadam, in many third world countries the reality is that there is a lot of debris (e.g., pebbles) in many airports, and all of this material is sucked into the plane's jet engines on takeoff. In extreme cases, a blade might snap off. Control of the displacement of the rotor center line is imperative, if further destruction to the remaining blades is to be avoided.

Similarly, the companion "containment" problem must be solved. This problem considers the fate of the blade that has snapped off. The imperative here is to demonstrate that the engine casing is strong enough to keep the broken blade inside the engine (hence, contained).

The mathematical problems here are primarily of numerical integration. Calculation of the maximum deflection of the rotor shaft of the affected stage is needed for the blade loss problem, while the containment problem is a study of case response to impulse loading.

Compressor and turbine blade design systems. The study of blade shapes focuses on the smooth fairing of blade date provided by the fluid dynamics programs. This leads to work in several areas: spline fitting (particularly for blades with significant camber, or twist, where the Bernoulli small slope assumption for cubic splines is no longer valid); surface design, using parametric fitting; and visualization, to ensure design validation, machinability and minimum weight.

"Reverse engineering" of chamfering machine. This was an attempt to model the undocumented methods underlying the Sheffield gear chamfering machine to produce uniformly chamfered gears. The Sheffield Company, which previous supplied both the chamfering bit and the patented machine that was used to make the chamfers, had gone out of business, leaving no record as to how the chamfering bit was designed from knowledge of the gear geometry. Solution of this problem necessitated working in the shop to develop a simulation of the actual chamfering machine, in order to determine the appropriate cutting tool that would produce the required chamfers.

"On wing" balancing of fan rotor assemblies following in-flight damage. This problem arose as the Boeing 777 neared launch. The radically new fan blades varied dramatically in weight, and balancing of the fan stages was needed. Even more, the problem of replacing blades damaged in flight by whatever spare blades were available at regional airport facilities was daunting, since the blades varied widely in weight. The goal was to rebalance the stages with as little rearrangement of the blades as possible, since the removal and remounting of each blade was a 15 minute operation, and the desire was to avoid failing to meet schedule.

The work on these last two projects led to U.S. patents.

Lee's "Cliff's Notes" on Electronic History

Development of numerical procedures has become more extensive, and more widely applied, over the past forty or so years. At the risk of over-simplification, it's my contention that considerable algorithmic development took place in the 1960's; collections of these were assembled into software libraries in the 1970's;

systems were developed in the 1980's to permit a user to set up mathematical problems, which would then be solved by the appropriate library routines; physical problems could be formulated, and 1990's software would then model and solve them; and now technology is under development to provide the specifications for part design, which involves setting multiple requirements, and then deriving the associated physical problems and solving them.

These developments could take place because the technology was becoming progressively more sophisticated. The advent of open architectures made the sharing of computer codes possible, and widespread. The need for increased efficiency was driven home in the U.S. by the automotive industry success in Japan, which showed that increased design and manufacturing efficiency was a necessity for healthy industry.

As a result of this sea change, much more sophisticated computing has been brought to bear on many industrial problems, and systems have been developed each of these steps that have removed the user further and further from the core computational and theoretical problems underlying the solution. When problems arise in the solution, the user is basically unable to make a knowledgeable judgment about what went wrong, or where the technology (i.e., programs) was inappropriate for the purposes intended. In other words, the user becomes a *consumer* of technology, rather than an informed practitioner. This makes students, who understand the limitations and strengths of the programs that they use, a progressively endangered species. To mitigate against this misuse of technology, the mathematics instructor has to be the "gatekeeper of last resort" for intelligent and appropriate use. So we have a responsibility to teach the limitations and shortcomings of the packages we use, rather than encouraging students to overdose on the use of them.

The Future Success of Mathematics Departments Depends on Their Evolution

Many mathematics department in the U.S. are dependent upon engineering and other disciplines to provide the enrollments for their "Math for Engineers" and other service courses. These courses guarantee the departmental revenue for the low enrollment graduate-level courses that serve the mathematics department's own graduate students. Preserving that enrollment base is an imperative.

It is crucial that these service courses support the needs of their customers. The risk is, as recent history at the University of Rochester attests, that if their needs are not served by the math department, those customers may choose to teach these courses themselves, with potentially serious consequences to the mathematics department. (At Rochester, after the smoke cleared, there were fewer permanent faculty embers in the math department.) Therefore, it is crucial to work with client disciplines to find a satisfactory middle ground between their practical needs, and the cultivation of the logical and mathematical rigor that a user community (dependent upon software, if not simply addicted to it) ought to respect.

It is unacceptable to try to dictate the content of courses to clients, and communication – especially, active listening – must become the normal mode of operation. Unfortunately, my best guess is that this will require substantial change on the part of the mathematics department, since mathematicians are not exactly legendary for their listening abilities, or their tact in approaching others. *Nevertheless, change is an imperative, not an option.*

Tenure, Employment and Education Reform

Tenure comes without an expiration date. That means that people don't have to retire – at least after the mid-1990's, when the rules changed for faculty over 70. And they didn't.

This meant that the much-heralded "shortage" of mathematics Ph.D.'s, which had been predicted (or promised, depending upon your age), did not materialize. Faculty lines were not looking for replacements, since their holders did not retire. Worse yet, when faculty members did retire, they were increasingly replaced by adjunct faculty, primarily to save money.

Respect for nonacademic employment has progressed from non-existent to minimal. Part of this "tolerance" might well be the result of the realization that full-time academic employment in the current environment is not a realistic expectation. But make no mistake – it's still regarded as second-class work, in too many mathematics departments.

The strength of tenure is that it provides the faculty with the opportunity to make dramatic and effective changes; the weakness of tenure is that, regardless of the need for change, there's no imperative for the faculty to make it. The isolation of the faculty from the competitive marketplace means that they are ill-prepared to understand the changes that need to be made, or to understand the importance of these changes for their students.

Curricula need to be expanded to prepare students for the world of work outside the walls of academia. There are many exciting opportunities for excellent mathematics in a variety of new industries. Faculty commitment is needed for developing courses of study that will help their students succeed in that environment, but for too many faculty members, the academic paradigm is all they know. It is a pity that this limited world-view is increasingly inappropriate for their students.

New Graduate Programs in Business and Industry

In the last decade, a number of *interdisciplinary* graduate programs have been launched to improve industrial competitiveness. The Alfred P. Sloan Foundation provided the seed money for many of them. These new programs, at least 11 of which are in mathematics-related fields, show great promise for providing mathematics students interested in industrial work with the training needed for success.

But What About K-12 Mathematics?

All of the above speaks to the issue of how post-secondary mathematics education can be improved. But the situation in K-12 is decidedly different.

In the United States, mathematics has long been presented in a less than favorable light. Although no one would think of boasting that he or she were unable to read, the inability to do simple mathematics, like balancing a checkbook, is publicly presented as nothing unusual. Mathematicians are often depicted as social misfits, and the brunt of jokes – a development that may in fact be made more plausible by our interpersonal skills – and the problems that we solve are almost always presented in the public press as being both inaccessible and irrelevant to the ordinary person (Wiles proves Fermat's last theorem; "Largest composite number is factored" [an actual New York Times headline]; Four color conjecture is true!;

Progress made on one of Hilbert's 100). Most people believe that, while computing may be valuable, mathematics is a dead subject that was only interested to dead Europeans. Since many in the mathematics community are reluctant to emphasize the importance of mathematics knowledge to the growth of technology and the economy, these stereotypes persist. Mathematicians really have a social and cultural problem, and it is hardly surprising that U.S. student performance in mathematics continues to lag behind that of many other industrialized countries.

But this situation need not persist. We have the opportunity to show how an appreciation of mathematics helps us understand our world. When students learn that knowledge of mathematics can be useful and have interesting applications, their achievement will reflect the greater interest.

Examples abound in real life. To cite just a few from the past few years in the public policy arena, we have: relating cell phone usage to automobile accidents, and appropriate remedies; establishing a link between cell phones and brain cancer; understanding the risk of shark attacks off the Florida coast, or roller coaster amusement park accident rates; deciding whether mammograms are effective, or carry risk; deciding solutions to Social Security insolvency; evaluating the meaning of SAT scores after their renorming in the mid-90's; reconciling global warming and *rising* temperatures in Antarctica; and determining the forensic reliability of fingerprint or DNA evidence, or Florida recount statistics. Besides checkbook balancing, budgetary planning, lease vs. buy decisions, evaluating mortgage alternatives, and other bread-and-butter issues use the mathematical training

The point, of course, is that some knowledge of mathematics, and some familiarity with mathematical thinking, can help *everyone* understand a great many issues and phenomena in the modern world. But we can only ingrain these ideas in the public consciousness by upgrading the K-12 mathematics education to emphasize the importance of mathematical thinking in modern occupations, in personal life, and for responsible citizenship

K-12 Politics Is An Obstacle

Unfortunately, current K-12 teacher training and continuing education programs emphasize the study of pedagogy rather than the mastery of content. Schools of education typically control the education of future teachers, and long have resisted the efforts of many in the formal mathematics community to ensure that teachers of mathematics, especially those in secondary education, are sufficiently trained in mathematics courses. Although the needs of those students who will become the next generation of mathematicians and engineers are decidedly more rigorous than those who will not, it is certainly true that all students need the rigor of mathematical thinking to understand the modern world, and to fulfill their obligations as productive citizens. To demand less of them, is to deny them a full place in society.

It is imperative to incorporate more real applications in student materials, to reinforce the idea – not currently apparent – that mathematics is important in everyday life. And especially, that the mental discipline that mathematics fosters in its students can in fact be carried over in other fields to better understand the policy tradeoffs that influence many choices, and, in some cases, the validity of important ideas. In other words, that mathematics is not simply a diversion for the mathematicians.

We need to update the way we train teachers to reflect this goal. Currently, this is neither a priority, nor a reflection of practice. Leiping Ma's thesis comparing the training of Chinese and American mathematics teachers should not have been controversial, since it was hardly surprising, but its political implications made it, for a long while, unacceptable to the mainstream in the mathematics education. Until they adopted its conclusions.

There Is Light at the End of the Tunnel

Attitudes are adversarial, and change slowly – perhaps, glacially – in mathematics. Respect for applied mathematicians by those in the pure mathematics community has taken a generation (and still is not pervasive, in my judgment). The formal mathematics establishment has been unable – and in some cases unwilling – to establish a respectful relationship with the mathematics education community. That community, in turn, shows little sustained interest in establishing a meaningful dialog with the mathematicians, ignoring many of their well intentioned suggestions, adopting them without bothering to acknowledge the input when all else fails. A better solution – one that better serves students – is possible.

Applications-focused input can revitalize mathematics curricula, spark student interest and imptove achievement. If the strengths of the mathematics community can be harnessed to work cooperatively for long-needed improvements, the effects on American education will be both positive and sustainable.

It only requires the will – and the committment – to change. The question is: Do we really have either?

110 CAMBRIDGE DRIVE, GLASTONBURY, CT 06033-1379, USA
E-mail address: LSeitelman@aol.com

CBMS Issues in Mathematics Education
Volume 14, 2007

Spreadsheets in the Mathematics Classroom

Robert S. Smith

ABSTRACT. *Excel* and other such electronic spreadsheet programs have found their way in to a variety of undergraduate mathematics courses. In this paper we will demonstrate some spreadsheet uses in a variety of undergraduate courses from precalculus to abstract algebra.

1. Introduction

Initially the electronic spreadsheet was used in mathematics teaching to implement algorithms that relied upon iterative procedures, [1] and [2]. However, since the early 1990s the spreadsheet has reached far beyond its initial application and has embraced many different areas of the mathematical sciences. This greater utility has come with increased functionality and ease of use. The spreadsheet is now at home in finite mathematics [5], precalculus [9], calculus [11], [12], and [13], differential equations [4], statistics [8], linear algebra [6], abstract algebra [10], and numerical analysis [6], just to name a few. In this note we will illustrate how the spreadsheet can be used in some of these areas.

2. Graph Transformations with Spreadsheets

A solid foundation in functions is essential to beginning mathematics students. Students need to be able to visualize a graph based upon its formula representation, and conversely. This is especially true in studying graph transformations. A spreadsheet is a wonderful tool to help students grasp and understand function transformations – horizontal shifts $(F(x - a))$, vertical shifts $(F(x) + b)$, vertical stretches and compressions $(cF(x), c > 0)$, horizontal stretches and compressions $(F(dx),\ d > 0)$, reflections about the x-axis $(-F(x))$, reflections about the y-axis $(F(-x))$, and compound transformations $(cF(d(x - a)) + b)$. Instructors are using spreadsheets such as "Transformation" to illustrate these concepts and to provide examples, while students are using spreadsheets for drill, practice, concept reinforcement, and discovery.

3. Derivatives and Rate of Change

In a casual discussion with a colleague, the question arose as to what knowledge a student should take away from a beginning calculus course. The colleague said that he wanted his students to know how to compute the standard derivatives of

	A	B	C	D	E	F	G
1			**Transformations of F(x) = x³ - x² - 4x**				
2							
3	**x**	**F(x)**	**cF(d(x-a))+b**	**a =**	-1	**c =**	2
4	-10	-1060	105.75	**b =**	0	**d =**	- 1/2
5	-9.9	-1028.71	101.03725				
6	-9.8	-998.032	96.448				
7	-9.7	-967.963	91.98075				
8	-9.6	-938.496	87.634				
9	-9.5	-909.625	83.40625				
10	-9.4	-881.344	79.296				
11	-9.3	-853.647	75.30175				
12	-9.2	-826.528	71.422				
13	-9.1	-799.981	67.65525				
14	-9	-774	64				
15	-8.9	-748.579	60.45475				
16	-8.8	-723.712	57.018				
17	-8.7	-699.393	53.68825				
18	-8.6	-675.616	50.464				
19	-8.5	-652.375	47.34375				
20	-8.4	-629.664	44.326				
21	-8.3	-607.477	41.40925				
22	-8.2	-585.808	38.592				
23	-8.1	-564.651	35.87275				
24	-8	-544	33.25				

the course. From the author's point of view, this is not enough. Students should know what a derivative is! We would suggest that computation of the standard derivatives should be augmented by computing derivatives from the definition, and by studying the difference quotient function,

$$F_h(x) = \frac{F(x+h) - F(x)}{h},$$

that approximates $F'(x)$. To get a better feeling for the derivative, perhaps calculus students should analyze $F_h(x)$ as h varies. Our sense is that by taking the multi-pronged approach suggested heretofore, students will get a deeper and more balanced view of the derivative of a function. The spreadsheet "Derivative" can be made dynamic by installing a slider to vary h [**7**]. Using this slider, students can watch the function $F_h(x)$ converge to $F'(x)$.

Spreadsheets can also be useful in approximating the rate of change in a discrete data set. For example, consider the following problem:

> A set of temperatures in degrees Celsius taken hourly from midnight to midnight is given below. Plot the data and approximate the tangent line at 1:00 p.m. as accurately as you can.

Hour	0	1	2	3	4	5	6	7	8
°C	6.5	6.1	5.6	4.9	4.2	4.1	4.0	4.8	6.1
Hour	9	10	11	12	13	14	15	16	17
°C	8.3	10.0	12.1	14.3	16.0	17.3	18.2	18.8	17.6
Hour	18	19	20	21	22	23	24		
°C	16.0	14.1	11.5	10.2	9.0	7.9	7.0		

It is interesting to see what students will do with such an open-ended problem. Most students would probably make a graph like the one in the first "Temperature"

	A	B	C	D	E	F
1	Derivative of $F(x) = -(2x^3 + x^2 - 4x - 3)/10$					
2						
3			h =	2	1.3	0.6
4	x	F(x)	F'(x)	$F_2(x)$	$F_{1.3}(x)$	$F_{0.6}(x)$
5	-4.0	9.9	-8.4	-4.6	-5.748	-7.092
6	-3.9					-6.674
7	-3.8					-6.268
8	-3.7					-5.874
9	-3.6					-5.492
10	-3.5					-5.122
11	-3.4					-4.764
12	-3.3					-4.418
13	-3.2					-4.084
14	-3.1					-3.762
15	-3.0					-3.452
16	-2.9					-3.154
17	-2.8					-2.868
18	-2.7					-2.594
19	-2.6					-2.332
20	-2.5					-2.082
21	-2.4					-1.844
22	-2.3					-1.618
23	-2.2					-1.404
24	-2.1	0.8712	-1.826	-0.306	-0.656	-1.202
25	-2.0	0.7	-1.6	-0.2	-0.508	-1.012

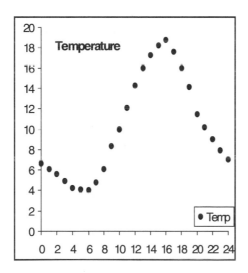

spreadsheet, calculate the slope of the secant line between the data points $(12, 14.3)$ and $(14, 17.3)$, and conclude that the desired slope is approximately 1.5. Hence the tangent line would be $y = 1.5x - 3.5$.

Solutions to this problem are constrained only by the creativity and resourcefulness of the students. A more thoughtful student might construct the parabola that passes through the points $(12, 14.3)$, $(13, 16.0)$, and $(14, 17.3)$, $y = -.2x^2 + 6.7x - 37.3$, and compute the tangent line to the parabola at $(13, 16.0)$. While each

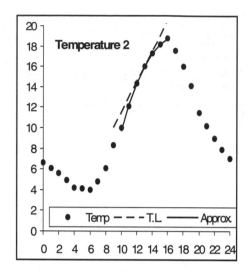

solution yields the same tangent line, we would certainly want to commend the student who did the parabolic approximation for such an insightful approach.

4. Approximating Zeros of Functions

A natural application of spreadsheets in mathematics is implementing algorithms that rely on iterative procedures. An example of this application is numerically approximating zeros of a function. Finding zeros of functions (or solving equations) is a fundamental application of mathematics that is spread across many disciplines. However, determining a function's zeros can be a nontrivial activity for students-even if the function is a simple polynomial of degree $n \geq 3$. A fortiori, solving an equation such as $2 \cos x = 2 - x$, can be positively daunting. Yet, the well known Newton-Raphson method will effortlessly find the solutions to this equation and the zeros of a variety of functions. While this method is widely applicable, it is not foolproof and can fail in a spectacular way, as we will demonstrate.

A spreadsheet implementation of the Newton-Raphson method to solve an equation could be as follows:

(1) Write the equation in the form $f(x) = 0$.
(2) Make a table of values of the function or a graph of the function so that one can identify an interval over which $f(x)$ has a zero.
(3) Select a value, x_1, which is close to the zero. This will be the first approximation of a zero of $f(x)$.
(4) Compute the second approximation of a zero of $f(x)$, as follows:

$$x_2 = x_1 - \frac{f(x_1)}{f'(x_1)}.$$

(5) Repeat (4) to compute $x_3, x_4, \ldots$. Use the general iterative scheme to compute

$$x_{n+1} = x_n - \frac{f(x_n)}{f'(x_n)}, n \geq 1.$$

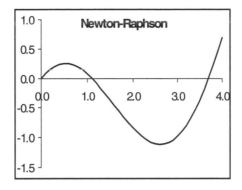

	A	B	C	D	E	F	G	H	I	J	K
1			Newton-Raphson Method applied to F(x) = 2cos(x)+x-2								
2											
3	n	x_n	$F(x_n)$	$F'(x_n)$	Iterate		n	x_n	$F(x_n)$	$F'(x_n)$	Iterate
4	1	0.4846	0.25432	0.06829	-3.2395		1	0.4847	0.25433	0.06811	-3.2492
5	2	-3.2394979	-7.2299	0.8045	5.74733		2	-3.2491736	-7.2376	0.78525	5.96774
6	3	5.74732607	5.46699	2.02116	3.04245		3	5.96774347	5.86906	1.62047	2.34592
7	4	3.04245046	-0.9477	0.80204	4.2241		4	2.34592316	-1.0537	-0.4287	-0.1122
8	5	4.22409736	1.28586	2.76627	3.75926		5	-0.1121532	-0.1247	1.22384	-0.0102
9	6	3.75926163	0.1288	2.15827	3.69958		6	-0.0102455	-0.0104	1.02049	-0.0001
10	7	3.69958413	0.00294	2.05897	3.69815		7	-0.0001029	-0.0001	1.00021	-1E-08
11	8	3.69815452	1.7E-06	2.05654	3.69815		8	-1.058E-08	-1E-08	1	-3E-16
12	9	3.69815367	6E-13	2.05654	3.69815		9	-3.179E-16	0	1	-3E-16
13	10	3.69815367	0	2.05654	3.69815		10	-3.179E-16	0	1	3E-16
14											
15	n	x_n	$F(x_n)$	$F'(x_n)$	Iterate		n	x_n	$F(x_n)$	$F'(x_n)$	Iterate
16	1	0.4848	0.25434	0.06794	-3.2589		1	0.4850	0.25435	0.06758	-3.2785
17	2	-3.2588995	-7.2452	0.76592	6.20046		2	-3.2785033	-7.2598	0.72703	6.70699
18	3	6.20046408	6.19363	1.16525	0.88521		3	6.70699064	6.53005	0.17754	-30.075
19	4	0.88520572	0.15147	-0.5401	1.10150		4	-30.074618	-31.62	-0.9476	-63.444
20	5	1.16155809	-0.0420	-0.0040	1.11051		5	-63.443958	-63.807	2.14918	-33.755
21	6	1.11050603	-0.0011	-0.7918	1.10915		6	-33.75497	-37.145	2.43826	-18.521
22	7	1.10914622	-8E-07	0.7906	1.10914		7	-18.520056	-18.028	0.35438	34.0447
23	8	1.10914418	-5E-13	-0.7906	1.10914		8	34.0447232	30.302	0.01877	-1580.4
24	9	1.10914418	0	-0.7906	1.10914		9	-1580.4264	-1584.4	0.59221	1094.94
25	10	1.10914418	0	-0.7906	1.10914		10	1094.94462	1092.75	-0.9901	2198.63

If the process produces wildly fluctuating iterates, then the process fails. Otherwise successive iterates will tend to stabilize rapidly, in which case a reasonable approximation of the zero will be found.

EXAMPLE 1. Let us try to approximate the solutions to $2\cos x = 2 - x$. First, let us set $f(x) = 2\cos x - 2 + x$. It is clear that there are no zeros of $f(x)$ for $x < 0$ or $x > 4$. A graph of $f(x)$ suggests that zeros can be found in neighborhoods of $0, 1$, and 3.5. Indeed, if we take $x_1 = 0, x_1 = 1$, or $x_1 = 3.5$ then the algorithm rapidly produces the approximations $0, 1.1091$, and 3.6982, respectively. In this example, it is perhaps more interesting to investigate the instability of the method. Since $f'(.5)$ is close to zero, it is reasonable to look for instability in a neighborhood of $x = .5$. The spreadsheet "Newton-Raphson" illustrates that small changes in x_1 can produce radically different results. Indeed, in the interval $(0.4845, 0.5001)$, one can choose x_1 so as to find each of the three zeros and also choose a value x_1 of so that the Newton-Raphson method diverges.

	A	B	C	D	E	F	G	H
1	**Distributive Laws for Boolean Algebra**							
2								
3	$x \vee (y \wedge z) = (x \vee y) \wedge (x \vee y)$							
4								
5	x	y	z	y∧z	x∨(y∧z)	x∨y	x∨z	(x∨y)∧(x∨z)
6	0	0	0	0	0	0	0	0
7	0	0	1	0	0	0	1	0
8	0	1	0	0	0	1	0	0
9	0	1	1	1	1	1	1	1
10	1	0	0	0	1	1	1	1
11	1	0	1	0	1	1	1	1
12	1	1	0	0	1	1	1	1
13	1	1	1	1	1	1	1	1
14					*			*

5. Boolean Algebra

One day while presenting a seminar on Boolean algebra and switching circuits to some first-year students, the author proved one of the distributive laws for a binary Boolean algebra using a spreadsheet. The students surely doubted the wisdom of this approach. Why would anyone try to invoke the use of a spreadsheet in a Boolean algebra proof? Without stretching the imagination too much, one can see that a spreadsheet approach in "Boolean Algebra" can be applied to any switching function and consequently has immediate application to the design and analysis of switching circuits.

Let us recall that if $(B, \vee, \wedge, ')$ is a Boolean algebra then for all $x, y, z \in B$, the following distributive laws hold:

$$x \vee (y \wedge x) = (x \vee y) \wedge (x \vee z)$$
$$x \wedge (y \vee x) = (x \wedge y) \vee (x \wedge z)$$

To prove that the first distributive law holds, all we need to show is that if

$$f(x, y, z) = x \vee (y \wedge x) \text{ and } g(x, y, z) = (x \vee y) \wedge (x \vee z)$$

then $f(x, y, z) = g(x, y, z)$ for all $x, y, z \in \{0, 1\}$. A proof of the first distributive law is constructed in the spreadsheet "Boolean Algebra."

Note that the entries in cells D6 and E6 are "=min(B6, C6)" and "=max(A6, D6)," respectively. The values for $f(x, y, z)$ are found in column E. The entries in cells F6 and G6 are "=max(A6,B6)" and "=max(A6,B6)," respectively. The values for $g(x, y, z)$ are found in column H.

6. Abstract Algebra

American students often think of abstract algebra as one of the most difficult undergraduate courses in the mathematics curriculum. Among the challenges encountered by these students are the notions of binary operations, semigroups, groups, and subalgebraic structures. One way to make these notions less formidable is to study them using a spreadsheet. Here is an exercise that helps students come to terms with these concepts.

Consider the semigroup $(S, \cdot)$ where S is the set of integers modulo 28 and the binary operation is multiplication modulo 28. Construct the Cayley (multiplication) table for this semi-group. Determine $\langle 3 \rangle$, the subsemigroup of $(S, \cdot)$ generated by

	A	B	C	D	E	F	G	H	I	J	K	L	M
1						**Abstract Algebra**							
2		3	9	27	25	19	1	5	13	17	11	15	23
3	3	9	27	25	19	1	3	15	11	23	5	17	13
4	9	27	25	19	1	3	9	17	5	13	15	23	11
5	27	25	19	1	3	9	27	23	15	11	17	13	5
6	25	19	1	3	9	27	25	13	17	5	23	11	15
7	19	1	3	9	27	25	19	11	23	15	13	5	17
8	1	3	9	27	25	19	1	5	13	17	11	15	23
9	5	15	17	23	13	11	5	25	9	1	27	19	3
10	13	11	5	15	17	23	13	9	1	25	3	27	19
11	17	23	13	11	5	15	17	1	25	9	19	3	27
12	11	5	15	17	23	13	11	27	3	19	9	25	1
13	15	17	23	13	11	5	15	19	27	3	25	1	9
14	23	13	11	5	15	17	23	3	19	27	1	9	25

3, and determine $\langle 3, 5 \rangle$, the subsemigroup of $(S, \cdot)$ generated by the subset $\{3, 5\}$. Is either of these subsemigroups a group?

Building the Cayley table for $(S, \cdot)$ facilitates the construction of $\langle 3 \rangle$ or any other subsemigroup. To build the Cayley table for $(S, \cdot)$, enumerate from 0 to 27 down column A beginning in cell A3. Install "=$A3" in cell B3 and copy down to cell B30. Copy B3 through B30, select B2 to AC2, and then implement Edit → Paste Special → Transpose → OK. Now, clear cells B3 to B30. Install "=mod($A3*B$2, 28)" in cell B3 and copy to cell AC30 to complete the table.

To produce a Cayley table for $\langle 3 \rangle$, simply clear column A and place the powers of 3 in column A. Once a Cayley table for $\langle 3 \rangle$ is constructed, it is a simple matter to augment this table to produce the subsemigroup $\langle 3, 5 \rangle$. The student can easily discern that both $\langle 3 \rangle$ and $\langle 3, 5 \rangle$ are groups, and that $\langle 3 \rangle$ is a subgroup of $\langle 3, 5 \rangle$. This Cayley table can be used to generate all subsemigroups and all groups within $(S, \cdot)$. Such exercises will help to reinforce basic algebraic notions such as closure, identity, generators, subsemigroups, subgroups, and groups.

7. Conclusion

The electronic spreadsheet is an easy to use and versatile pedagogical tool. Many students learn to use spreadsheets in courses outside of mathematics, and this is good career training. However, when students do mathematics with a spreadsheet, they benefit in two ways: they enhance their mathematical experiences and gain a dynamic new perspective on the uses and analytical power of this software tool. With a variety of built-in mathematical and statistical functions and excellent graphics [3], the spreadsheet is a powerful instrument for teaching and learning in many areas of the mathematical sciences.

References

[1] Arganbright, Deane. The electronic spreadsheet and mathematical algorithms. The College Mathematics Journal 15 (1984), 148-157.

[2] Arganbright, Deane. *Mathematical applications of electronic spreadsheets*, McGraw-Hill, 1985.

[3] Arganbright, Deane. *Spreadsheet Curves and Geometric Constructions*, CRC Press, 1993.

[4] Beare, Richard. *Mathematics in Action*, Chartwell-Bratt, 1997.

[5] Comer, Stephen. The use of spreadsheets in finite mathematics. *Proceedings of Conference on Technology in Collegiate Mathematics*, Addison-Wesley, 1989, 129-132.

[6] McLaren, David. *Spreadsheets and Numerical Analysis*, Chartwell-Bratt, 1997.
[7] Neuwirth, Erich and Arganbright, Deane. *Mathemematical Modeling wtih Microsoft Excel*, Brooks/Cole, 2004.
[8] Piele, Donald. *Introductory statistics with spreadsheets*, Addison-Wesley, 1991.
[9] Sandefur, James. Technology, linear equations, and buying a car. The Mathematics Teacher 85 (1992) 562-567.
[10] Sjöstrand, David. *Mathematics with Excel*, Chartwell-Bratt, 1994.
[11] Spero, Samuel. *The Electronic Spreadsheet and Elementary Calculus: Graphing and Numerical Methods*, Harper Collins, 1991.
[12] Smith, Robert. Spreadsheets as a mathematical tool. Journal on Excellence in College Teaching 3 (1992) 131-148.
[13] Smith, Robert. Spreadsheets at Joint Meetings in Baltimore, UME Trends 4 (1992) 1-3.

DEPARTMENT OF MATHEMATICS AND STATISTICS, MIAMI UNIVERSITY, OXFORD, OH, 45056-3414, USA

E-mail address: smithrs@muohio.edu

CBMS Issues in Mathematics Education
Volume 14, 2007

Incorporating MATLAB® into University Mathematics Programs

Alexander Stanoyevitch

ABSTRACT. MATLAB®, an acronym for "MATrix LABoratory", is the most extensively used mathematical software in the general sciences. Other software packages, such as Maple and Mathematica are also popular, but more so in mathematics departments than in other fields. The latter two software packages work symbolically, whereas as MATLAB, in its default mode, works in floating point arithmetic, which is much faster for performing computations with sufficient accuracy for most applications. For instances where symbolic functionality is required, MATLAB offers access to the Maple kernel (which is built in), and thus can offer the best of both worlds. With its superb graphics and user-friendly interface, MATLAB is an ideal software to enhance university mathematics courses. Indeed, because of its wide use in industry and the research sciences, a university education in mathematics without MATLAB could pose a serious disadvantage to a student's potential for landing suitable employment.

We will discuss the implementation of MATLAB into a variety of courses in the university curriculum, spanning from individual use by a single faculty member to full-scale adaptation by a mathematics department in its programs. After our general implementation summary, we will present a detailed example of incorporating MATLAB in the solution of a family of problems concerning air travel logistics that could be presented in courses ranging from the precalculus-level all the way up through upper-level mathematics courses (depending on the degrees of detail and analysis that are presented). Our focus is primarily geared to undergraduate curricula.

1. How I Began to Work MATLAB® into My Courses

The story of how I started using MATLAB in my courses is somewhat atypical, and can perhaps serve as motivation for those having hesitations on making such a transition. My doctoral research was in pure mathematical analysis and at my first post at the University of Hawaii, I continued with my pure mathematical research and was teaching math courses governed by departmental syllabi that were quite traditional. There were no specific technology requirements, but instructors could use it at there own discretion, as long as there was time to cover the required topics. For many courses, the syllabi were too ambitious to allow much digression into technology. I was learning that showing the students interesting applications of the theory was a most effective motivator for them to appreciate (and thus more thoroughly study) the mathematical theories and concepts being presented. I thus began planning my lessons to include an increased emphasis on applications, while still covering all of the theory. I began using the Maple® and Mathematica® software for some research inquiries as well as in teaching demos.

I subsequently found an interesting challenge at the University of Guam when they were looking for a new faculty member who would be primarily responsible for teaching their numerical and applied mathematics courses. Ordinarily such positions are filled by candidates who completed their doctoral work in such a field, so I was eager to take on this exciting opportunity. The only problem was that the software they were using at the time was MATLAB, with which I had no experience. My initial impression was a bit negative on using this software over one of its symbolic counterparts (like Maple or Mathematica). This impression was partially fostered from the attitudes that were widely prevailing among many pure mathematical circles that symbolic software (like Maple or Mathematica) were the ONLY real tools that should be used for mathematical work. Well, my new career thus got off to a rough and busy start, having to quickly become adept with this new computing platform. As I began to learn and use MATLAB, however, I became increasingly impressed with its speed, power, ease of use, and state-of-the-art graphical capabilities. I also came to understand why MATLAB is the software of choice in nearly all of the scientific fields. Rather than using **symbolic arithmetic** (in its default setting), which works in expandable precision to keep answers exact, MATLAB works in a **floating point arithmetic** that limits the size and number of digits in its calculations. These limits conform to meet the rigors of the IEEE[1] double precision standards, which are sufficient for most practical purposes. After all, if we are computing, say a minimum eigenvector of a certain (symmetric) matrix, is it really necessary to know the number, say, to 150 digits? Pure mathematicians often scoff at anything less than exactness, but in practical situations, such objections are often purely academic. In any case, MATLAB does have symbolic functionality available for instances where one (feels) it is necessary. The basic symbolic functionality is included in the Student Version of MATLAB, and it is available with the so-called Symbolic Toolbox add-on to the professional version. The Symbolic Toolbox gives MATLAB users access to the Maple kernel. Although it is tempting to work symbolically, the trade-off is that calculations are much more expensive (time-consuming). Indeed, in my first MATLAB-based textbook [Sta-05a] on the subject of numerical ordinary and partial differential equations, although symbolic functionality is discussed, its use was extremely minimal, and the text could be made essentially independent of it.

The many benefits and versatility of MATLAB began to motivate me to use it in more than just the originally intended classes in numerical and applied mathematics. I began incorporating it, to various degrees, in most all of my math classes. This semester, for example, I am making extensive use of MATLAB for the first time in a course in abstract algebra. Students these days are seeking to use their computers in any way possible to help them learn. I am finding that the incorporation of MATLAB brings my courses to higher levels in that it enables students

---

[1]IEEE is the acronym for the Institute for Electrical and Electronics Engineers, Inc., a nonprofit professional association of more than 350,000 individual members in 150 countries. Their standards were carefully developed to help avoid some problems and incompatibilities with earlier floating point systems.

to perform more independent research that would otherwise not have been feasible at the undergraduate level.

2. How Can You Implement MATLAB into Your Courses?

Many math departments are gravitating towards including a MATLAB component in their curriculum. Once this is done, courses can be organized in an efficient manner with some core MATLAB-based courses giving students preparation to jump into more advanced courses with a solid MATLAB foundation behind them. If you are in such a department, this section may be skipped. The next best thing would be a department with other faculty already using MATLAB in their courses. This would be a middle-ground that could eventually lead up to the first sort of curriculum structure. If you are in such a department, your colleagues can be valuable resources not only to consult with on their experiences, but to begin to organize sequences of math courses that build up and nicely complement MATLAB implementation. Such courses could, for example, be made part of an "Applied Mathematics Track" that would constitute one of several tracks in which students could earn a bachelors degree in mathematics. Graduate programs are often more specialized, making it easier to build around a particular computing platform; this is why our focus is geared towards undergraduate curricula.

Now we are left with the remaining situations where no one else in your department is currently using MATLAB, and your department may or may not even have a license for it. Through discussions with other mathematics department chairs and administrators, I am finding that most will support such innovative goals in teaching relating to bringing a high-power computing platform (like MATLAB) into the curriculum. What would be required, initially, would be a classroom license for a sufficient number of computers in a computer lab. These licenses are quite affordable (go to www.mathworks.com, the website for MathWorks, the company that sells MATLAB, for more detailed information) and include permission for all instructors to install the software on their personal computers to use (only) for class preparations. Additionally, a few additional licenses (a minimum of, say, four or five) would need to be purchased for the student computer lab. These licenses are more expensive, but can be set up on a central server that would allow any machine to run it as long at the maximum number of licenses is not exceeded at any given time. Finally, you should instruct your student book store to order some copies of the Student Version of MATLAB, as many students will prefer to use it on their own computers (these licenses are kept affordable, and the last time that I checked they ran under US\$100).[2] You might first begin using MATLAB in an easy-to-use course such as linear algebra (it is great with matrices), or numerical analysis.

In the isolated use of any technology in any (mathematics) course, one must also address the trade-off with time needed to introduce the technology being taken from the limited time of the semester (or quarter). I have faced this issue myself in an assortment of courses where I had wanted to use MATLAB, but some (or all) of the students had no MATLAB (and some no programming) experience. Personally, I feel that when I teach my students MATLAB, it is worthwhile to teach them at least some of the associated rudimentary programming as well. I can usually give such students an adequate preparation in two weeks of class instruction. The

---

[2]MathWorks will even send instructors interested in using MATLAB a complimentary copy of the Student Version; see their website for details.

exact material (and homework exercises) that I cover will vary with the course, but I always cover at least the following core material from [Sta-05b][3] : Chapter 1 (MATLAB Basics), Chapter 3 (Introduction to M-files[4]), Chapter 4 (Programming in MATLAB), Sections 5.1-2 (Floating Point Arithmetic), Sections 7.1, 3, and 4 (Matrices and Linear Systems), and Appendix B (Symbolic Computations).[5] After this, by carefully including computational problems in the assignments, the students will continue to become more adept with MATLAB while they use it to help learn the material of the course proper. Many of MATLAB's built-in M-files are open source, so students can look at these to continue to learn efficient programming ideas, and modify existing programs to better meet their needs.

I should add that since MATLAB has such a wide variety of built-in functions, it is also possible to use it without having the students do any programming (some scientists use it in this way as well). Some (MATLAB experienced) instructors will write MATLAB programs themselves specifically for the course and provide them to the students as learning tools, and many will share them with other interested instructors and/or students. Web searches on free MATLAB material will reveal the vast amounts of programs and documents that are available. A good example of this is Rice University Professor John Polking's M-files pplane and dfield. Over the past decade, he has continually developed these user-friendly, high-level, graphically enhanced M-files for analyzing phase-planes and direction fields in ordinary differential equations. He makes them freely available for educational purposes, along with instructions for their use (on his web site). He has also co-written a supplementary book [Pol-03] for standard courses in ordinary differential equations that elaborates on their use, as well as many of MATLAB's built-in functions for solving ordinary differential equations. MathWorks maintains a website [Mat-05] with descriptions of an ever-expanding list of over 800 textbooks that use the MATLAB software to various degrees in an assortment of subjects.

Currently I am using MATLAB, to various extents, in most all of the courses that I am teaching. The usage of MATLAB in my courses ranges from minimal (e.g., an occasional in-class demo for a lower-level class in finite mathematics, on, say, the shipping logistics material in Section 3, or on cryptology), to higher-level involvement requiring students to write programs to solve difficult problems in the class. MATLAB proficiency also makes it easier to get students involved in capstone or interdisciplinary research/dissertation projects. Presently, for example, I have a student in my discrete structures class writing a paper on ant colony methods in combinatorial optimization (these can serve as effective heuristics in difficult problems such as the traveling salesman and vehicle routing problems). I have also made extensive use of MATLAB in an abstract algebra course. Surprisingly, even in such a symbolic and abstract subject, MATLAB's floating point system (restricted to integer arithmetic) is impressively adequate for all but the most technical applications (e.g., in professional-level security cryptography). The abstract concepts can be made more concrete with the resources of MATLAB. Long computations, that would have otherwise been unfeasible, can be carried out to glean greater insights

---

[3][Sta-05b] contains the general core introduction to MATLAB culled from my larger numerical analysis textbook [Sta-05a].

[4]M-files are simply programs written for MATLAB; the programming language of MATLAB is similar to the C-family.

[5]Much of this material is of a tutorial nature, and so can be assigned as homework.

into the subject. For example, the paper [Mak-02] shows many interesting ways to experiment with a wide variety of matrix groups and rings using MATLAB.

Perhaps one of the most important reasons to learn a software like MATLAB is that so many (in fact, most) interesting mathematical problems do not have an exact analytical solution, or it is not feasible to find one. In such cases, simulations can be used to obtain approximate answers to any degree of accuracy. I have used simulations extensively in an upper-level probability course, and have also recently taught a MATLAB-based special topics course in simulation using the (non-MATLAB) textbook [Ros-02]. Even when there is an exact answer that the student needs to find (in a homework problem, say), a student (or teacher) may get stuck or go in the wrong direction with a tricky problem, but a simple simulation can point them in the direction of the correct answer. Simulations provide an excellent example of the superiority of floating point arithmetic for certain computational tasks. Results improve with running large numbers of trials, and floating point arithmetic gives us this speed whereas symbolic computations would proceed at much slower pace, keeping very exact track of all of the incidental quantities. Sometimes a program can model such a complicated natural phenomena that it is helpful to have a graphically enhanced program to check that things are working as planned. MATLAB's superb graphics capabilities allow for this. It is important to realize, however, that graphical output also eats up a lot of resources, so that a good scheme might be to first write a graphically enhanced program (for a difficult model), use it to check and demonstrate the accuracy of the model, and then disable the graphics so as to be able to do longer and more repeated runs of the program. Such a project was carried out in [Sta-04], where a graphically enhanced MATLAB program was developed to analyze the most effective way to control a traffic intersection.

3. A Particular Example of a Family of Problems

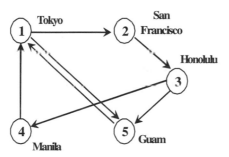

FIGURE 1. A small shipping network

In this section we present details of an example of some problems relating to the logistics of air shipping. Many of the concepts we will introduce have applications in the tourism and travel industry. Most of the ideas will be motivated by a series of practical questions. The basic prerequisites are minimal, so the material can be presented in wide variety of courses. Suppose that a Pacific Rim air shipping company has connecting flights between five cities as shown in Figure 1. The ideas will work for networks of any size, but such a small one will allow us to verify the concepts geometrically.

The information contained in such a network can be represented using a 5×5 **incidence matrix** A, where each of the entries of A is either 0 or 1 as determined by the following rule:

$$a_{ij} = \begin{cases} 1, \text{ if there is a direct flight from city } \# \, i \text{ to city } \# \, j \\ 0, \text{ if there is no direct flight from city } \# \, i \text{ to city } \# \, j \end{cases}$$

Thus we obtain the incidence matrix A:

$$A = \begin{array}{c} \\ \\ \#1 \Rightarrow \\ \#2 \Rightarrow \\ \#3 \Rightarrow \\ \#4 \Rightarrow \\ \#5 \Rightarrow \end{array} \begin{array}{ccccc} \#1 & \#2 & \#3 & \#4 & \#5 \\ \Downarrow & \Downarrow & \Downarrow & \Downarrow & \Downarrow \\ \left[\begin{array}{ccccc} 0 & 1 & 0 & 0 & 1 \\ 0 & 0 & 1 & 0 & 0 \\ 0 & 0 & 0 & 1 & 1 \\ 1 & 0 & 0 & 0 & 0 \\ 1 & 0 & 0 & 0 & 0 \end{array}\right] \end{array}$$

Such a spreadsheet can easily be queried as to the existence or nonexistence of a direct flight between any distinct pair of cites. Of course, the graph could tell us the same information, perhaps even more easily. But for a large network, as for example the network of all of FedEx's airport hubs, such a diagram would be a dizzying mess, and the incidence matrix would be the best way to store and access the information. If this were the only novelty of incidence matrices, they would not be worth discussing in this section. It turns out that the square of the incidence matrix tells us something quite interesting about the network (and thus furnishes a great answer to the common question students ask when first learning how to multiply matrices: "Why would anyone invent such a complicated way to do it?")

QUESTION 1: What do the entries of the matrix A^2 tell us about the shipping network?

Answer: The (i,j) entry of A^2 equals the number of ways that one can fly from (row) city $\#i$ to (column) city $\#j$ using **exactly two** flights. More generally, the entries of A^M (M a positive integer) count the number of ways to go from row city to column city using **exactly M** flights.

The proof of these facts is not hard (using the definition of matrix multiplication and induction), and would make a suitable exercise in a linear algebra course, but for a lower-level class, the result can just be stated and demonstrated, as we do next.

For the network of Figure 1, and its incidence matrix A, we compute: $B = A^2$, and $C = A^3$, and interpret the entries b_{31}, b_{12}, and c_{12}.

Using MATLAB, we enter the incidence matrix A, and compute B, C, and D.

```
>> A=[0 1 0 0 1; 0 0 1 0 0;0 0 0 1 1;1 0 0 0 0;1 0 0 0 0];
>> B=A^2, C=A^3
```

$$\rightarrow B = \begin{array}{ccccc} 1 & 0 & 1 & 0 & 0 \\ 0 & 0 & 0 & 1 & 1 \\ 2 & 0 & 0 & 0 & 0 \\ 0 & 1 & 0 & 0 & 1 \\ 0 & 1 & 0 & 0 & 1 \end{array} \qquad \rightarrow C = \begin{array}{ccccc} 0 & 1 & 0 & 1 & 2 \\ 2 & 0 & 0 & 0 & 0 \\ 0 & 2 & 0 & 0 & 2 \\ 1 & 0 & 1 & 0 & 0 \\ 1 & 0 & 1 & 0 & 0 \end{array}$$

Since $b_{31} = 2$, we see that there are 2 ways to go from City #3 (Honolulu) to City #1 (Tokyo) using exactly two flights. From Figure 1, we see that these two routes are: #3→#5→#1 (with a stop in Guam) and #3→#4→#1 (with a stop in Manila). Similarly, $b_{12} = 0$ means that there is no way to go from City #1 (Tokyo) to City #2 (San Francisco) using exactly two flights (check Figure 1 to convince yourself), although there is a direct flight. The entry $c_{12} = 1$ indicates that there is precisely one route that goes from City #1 (Tokyo) to City #2 (San Francisco) and that uses exactly three flights. The reader can verify using Figure 1 that this unique route is:

$$\#1(\text{Tokyo}) \to \#5(\text{Guam}) \to \#1(\text{Tokyo}) \to \#2(\text{San Francisco}),$$

demonstrating that these matrices count literally all possibilities. Of course, programs can be easily designed to weed out such inefficient routes.

QUESTION 2: The owner of the (or any) shipping network would like to know the worst (maximum) number of flights we would actually need to be able to ship from any city to any other city. We define this number (a positive integer) to be the **worst-case-scenario number** of the directed network. How can this be computed?

In case no student raises their hands to offer an answer, ask the following follow-up question that should lead them in the right direction.

QUESTION 3: What do the entries of the matrix $D = A + A^2$ tell us in terms of the shipping network?

Answer: Since the entries of D simply sum the corresponding entries of A (the number of direct flights) and A^2 (the number of 2-segment flights), the entries of D thus tell us the number of ways to go from row city to column city using either one or two flights, or **at most two** flights.

For example, we compute $D = A + A^2$, and then interpret d_{31}.

```
>> D=A+B
            1   1   1   0   1
            0   0   1   1   1
→ D =       2   0   0   1   1
            1   1   0   0   1
            1   1   0   0   1
```

Here, $d_{31} = a_{31} + b_{31} = 0$ (no direct flights) + 2 (2 two-flight routes indicated above) = 2.

By the same token, it follows that the entries of the matrix $S = A + A^2 + \cdots + A^M$ indicate the number of ways to go from the row city to the column city using **at most M** flights. This leads to the following algorithm for answering Question 2, which is easily programmed into an M-file.

Algorithm: Computation of Worst-Case-Scenario Number of a Directed Network:[6]

Step 1: Form the incidence matrix A. If all nondiagonal entries are 1, this means there is a direct flight between any two pairs of cities and the worst-case-scenario number of the network is 1. Otherwise, move on to Step 2.

---

[6]We assume that the network is **connected**, meaning that any city is reachable from any other city. This assumption gives an upper bound of $n - 1$ for the worst-case-scenario number of an n-city network (Why?).

Step 2: (*Iterative Step*) Continue adding increasing powers of A: $A + A^2$, $A + A^2 + A^3$, ... until we obtain a matrix that has no nonzero entries except possibly on the main diagonal. The resulting exponent M of the last power added will be the worst-case-scenario number.

We point out that since the zeroth power of (any square) matrix A, A^0, is defined to be the identity matrix I, we can extend the network interpretation of powers of the incidence matrix A to include the zeroth power. (With zero flights, we can only go from a city to itself.) With this extended interpretation, the above algorithm can be slightly simplified if we include the zeroth power of A in the sums; this allows us to stop as soon as ALL of the matrix entries are nonzero.

As an example, let's now compute the worst-case-scenario number of the directed network of Figure 1. We have already computed A and $A + A^2$; neither satisfies the nonzero requirements, so we continue with the above algorithm:

```
>> A+A^2+A^3, ans+A^4
                1  2  1  1  3                    4  2  2  1  3
                2  0  1  1  1                    2  2  1  1  3
→ ans =         2  2  0  1  3     → ans =        4  2  2  1  3
                2  1  1  0  1                    2  2  1  1  3
                2  1  1  0  1                    2  2  1  1  3
```

Thus we find the worst-case-scenario number of the network is 4. From the second-to-last matrix, we see that there is only one ordered pair of cities (#5 → #4) that would need a full four flights since the row 5 column 4 entry is the only nondiagonal zero entry. The reader can verify with Figure 1 that there is no way to fly from City #5 (Guam) to City #4 (Manila) using less than four flights in this network.

QUESTION 4:   (a) The owner of the shipping company of Figure 1 would like to investigate the possibility of adding a new flight to the existing schedule (one new arrow) in such a way that the worst-case-scenario number could be brought down as much as possible. Can the worst-case-scenario number be brought down in this way, and if so, what would be the possible flights to add that would bring it down as much as possible? (b) Answer the same question for two new flights.

Answer: Part (a): There is a simple strategy here. Adding a single new flight to the network simply corresponds to a new incidence matrix with one of the previous zero nondiagonal entries being changed to one. We can simply compute the new worst-case-scenario numbers of all such modified incidence matrices and keep track of those that are less than 4 (the worst-case-scenario number of the original network that was computed in the preceding example). The ones that are as low as possible are the ones that we are interested in. So that we can solve not only this question, but the same one on any network, it is useful to write a MATLAB program to accomplish this task. We apply such an (easily written) program to the incidence matrix under consideration.

(MATLAB input:) >> AddOneFlt(A)

(MATLAB output:)

By adding one new flight, the worst-case-scenario $\rightarrow$ ans =   1 3
number of the network can be reduced from 4 to 3.   1 4
The segments that will achieve this   2 4
reduction are stored as the output matrix.   5 2
                                                                            5 3
                                                                            5 4

Thus, the worst-case-scenario number can be reduced to (as low as) 3 by adding one new link and there are six ways to achieve this reduction. These six links are listed above. For example, the first one: [1 3] corresponds to a new direct flight being added from City #1 (Tokyo) to City #3 (Honolulu).

Part (b): The strategy here is similar. Adding two new flights corresponds to changing two zero nondiagonal entries of the incidence matrix to ones. The worst-case-scenario numbers now need to be checked. We need only record the ones whose worst-case-scenario numbers are less than 3 (the lowest it could get from using one new flight). An M-file can be written in a similar fashion to that used above, but now we will need four nested "for loops" to run through all of the possible ways of adding two new flights (each new flight requires two indices). Once this is done, and the reader runs it on the data of this problem, he/she will find that the worst-case-scenario number cannot be reduced below 3 for any two new flights that are added.

QUESTION 5: Are the above programs practical for general (larger) network routing problems?

Answer: The simplest way to start to understand this question is to run the programs with larger networks. What happens if we try to answer the above questions for the 23-city network shown in Figure 2?

Running the (MATLAB) programs on a PC, we would promptly find the worst-case scenario number to be eight and that by adding one new flight it could be lowered to as low as seven (in 63 different ways). To find that with two new flights it could be further lowered to six (in 22 different ways), the program starts to take a while to execute, and you would probably want to leave it running while you went out to lunch. If you tried to find out how much lower the worst-case scenario number could be brought down to using three new flights, you would need to let the computer work over a long weekend. The programs for adding new flights mentioned above, although theoretically sound, are rather brute-force in nature since they simply recompute the worst-case-scenario number for all of the new possibilities. It thus becomes important to analyze our algorithms and make them as efficient and elegant as possible.

These issues lead us to the very important concept of **complexity** of an algorithm. Complexity measures the approximate size of the amount of computation needed to run an algorithm with input size n, and is usually expressed in the form of a **big-O estimate**, $O(f(n))$, where $f(n)$ is a "simple" function of n.

To say an algorithm works in $O(f(n))$-time means that with an input of size n, it will take less than $C \cdot f(n)$ logical (or arithmetic) operations, where C is some positive constant. Ideally, we seek big-O estimates that are sharp in the sense that examples of the problem (with input size n) can be found that will take more than $c \cdot f(n)$ logical operations, for another positive constant c (and thus no

AIR FREIGHT DAILY SCHEDULE

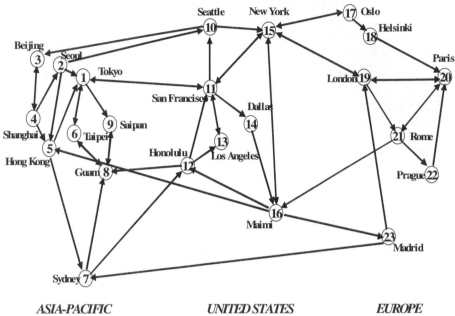

FIGURE 2. A moderately-sized shipping network

smaller function can be used in the big-O estimate). An algorithm is said to run in **polynomial time** if it admits a big-O estimate of the form $O(n^p)$ for some positive integer p. Polynomial time algorithms are considered to be good algorithms, but, of course their runtimes can increase significantly for larger exponents p, as well as a large value of the (invisible) constant C. Each of the algorithms mentioned for the above shipping route problems run in polynomial time, but some of them are still too slow for even moderately sized networks. (The exponents p increase quickly with the number of new flights we look into adding to the network.) Many important problems (e.g., the traveling salesman problem) do not yet have algorithms that can even run in polynomial time. The biggest single issue in algorithms is to design them to function as efficiently as possible. For an advanced class that has learned to program in MATLAB, one could end this lesson on network routing with a (difficult) question of the following sort (ideally given as an extra-credit problem):

QUESTION 6: Assume that the following costs (for shipping a 100 lb parcel) are associated with flights in the the 23-city network of Figure 2: Flights within any of the three regions (Asia-Pacific, United States, and Europe) cost $100. Flights from one region to an adjacent region (i.e., Asia-Pacific to/from US, or US to/from Europe) cost $200 and the Madrid to Sidney flight costs $300. The only exceptions are that flights between Guam and Honolulu or Guam and Taipei cost $300. Also, for each such shipment, the company must pay a $2 airport tax to each airport used. Using this information, create a MATLAB M-file: [price routes] = LowestPrice(i,j) The two input variables, i and j, denote the numbers of the origin and destination cities, respectively, for shipping a parcel. The first output variable, price, will be the lowest possible price for shipping the parcel, and the second output variable, routes, will be a matrix of the corresponding routes to achieve this lowest price (each such route will have the same number of flights–Why?). For example, if you run LowestPrice(19,22), the output should be price = 206, and routes = [19 21 22], indicating that the cheapest way to ship from London to Prague would be to do through Rome and the cost for such a shipment (for one standard parcel) would be \$206 (=2 × \$100(airfares) + 3 × \$2(taxes)). Your program should be able to run in less than 5 seconds (on any decent computer) for any pair of inputs.

The simple price structure in this problem allows for a variety of creative thinking and solutions. Initially, this problem might seem much more complex than that of adding one or two good flights. It turns out, however, that a very efficient algorithm exists for finding lowest prices in any such network. This algorithm was discovered by Edsger W. Dijkstra[7], a Dutch computer scientist in the 1950s. Dijkstra's algorithm runs in $O(n^2)$-time, where n is the number of cities. It can be geometrically described as follows: Staring at the origin city $\#i$, we release a green fluid (representing cost) that flows along unused edges at a rate of \$1/hour. This continues until all edges have been saturated (assuming the network is connected). The minimum cost of getting from city $\#i$ to ANY other city $\#j$ is simply the time it takes for the green fluid to reach vertex $\#j$. Shortest paths can be kept track of in a straightforward fashion (by tracking predecessor cities). Dijkstra's algorithm remains one of the best for determining minimum costs in general network problems.

References

[1] [Mak-02] Mackiw, George, Experiments with finite linear groups using MATLAB, in *Innovations in Teaching Abstract Algebra* (MAA Notes, #60), Edited by Ellen Maycock and Allen C. Hibbard, Mathematical Association of America, Washington, DC (2002)

[2] [Mat-05] MathWorks' continuously updated website containing descriptions of MATLAB based textbooks (currently contains over 800 titles): www.mathworks.com/support/books/

[3] [Pol-03] Polking, John, *Ordinary Differential Equations Using MATLAB, Third Edition*, Prentice-Hall, Upper Saddle River, NJ (2003)

[4] [Ros-02] Ross, Sheldon, *Simulation, Third Edition*, Academic Press, San Diego, CA (2002)

[5] [Sta-04] Stanoyevitch, Alexander, Minimizing lost time at automobile intersections, *Proceedings of the Summer Simulation Conference (2004)*, 48-53, Edited by Agustino G. Bruzzone and Edward Williams, The Society for Modeling and Simulation International, San Diego, CA (2004)

[6] [Sta-05a] Stanoyevitch, Alexander, *Introduction to Numerical Ordinary and Partial Differential Equations Using MATLAB*, John Wiley & Sons, Hoboken, NJ (2005)

[7] [Sta-05b] Stanoyevitch, Alexander, *Introduction to MATLAB with Numerical Preliminaries*, John Wiley & Sons, Hoboken, NJ (2005)

---

[7]Edsger W. Dijkstra (1930-2002) was a Dutch computer scientist who studied physics at the University of Amsterdam where he obtained all of his university education and his PhD in 1959. He became very interested in computer programming during his studies well before this was a recognizable line of work. In fact, in 1957, when he put computer programming as his profession in his marriage license, the authorities would not accept it. (He was still able to get married, but changed his profession to physicist.) He became a professor of mathematics at the Eindhoven University of Technology (in the Netherlands) in 1962 until 1973 when he moved to become a research fellow for the Burrows Corp. In 1984, he moved to the US to become a professor of computer science at the University of Texas at Austin.

DEPARTMENT OF MATHEMATICS, CALIFORNIA STATE UNIVERSITY - DOMINGUEZ HILLS, CARSON, CA 90747, USA

E-mail address: astanoyevitch@csudh.edu

CBMS Issues in Mathematics Education
Volume **14**, 2007

A CAS Supported Environment for Learning And Teaching Calculus

Elena A.Varbanova

ABSTRACT. Some aspects of our experience in integrating CAS Derive into undergraduate mathematics education are represented. The emphases is on how tools like computer algebra systems can be converted into mathematical instruments to strengthen a traditional methodology of teaching mathematics. To illustrate our experience selected topics and examples in Calculus that make use of CAS Derive are considered.

"Challenge is energy of life"

1. Introduction

The abundance of technology in the twenty-first century makes the introduction of new tools into the university mathematics education natural and inevitable. Nowadays no self-respecting university lacks a computer supported teaching and learning environment.

Choosing appropriate tools is an important issue because human activity depends upon the environment. Converting tools into effectively integreable instruments is another real issue [3]. Adressing these two issues allows universities and teachers to make various admissable decisions that are influenced by such different factors as educational goals, priorities and limitations.

As for computer algebra systems (CAS), their great power and potential are "addressed" to mathematics teachers' creativity and sense of novelty. We have to appreciate man's over-seeking spirit for designing and developing one of the most challenging tools that we have ever had for doing mathematics. However, the implemented symbols, notations, functions and terminology of mathematics cannot automatically transfer mathematical knowledge to learners and enhance their feeling for mathematics. As with other technological tools, the use of CAS requires teachers to take a professional attitude. Methodological principles and teachers' capabilities to put these principles into practice in a CAS supported environment can give CAS vitality.

2. Tradition and Technology - Challenges and Concerns

Traditional mathematics education in Bulgaria, as a whole, has proved to be successful. Understandably, we Bulgarian mathematics teachers have respect for our tradition and our predecessors. But we are keen to exploit technology and to be good successors as well.

On the one hand, good tradition makes us feel free to develop mathematics education in ways enabling it to incorporate technology. On the other hand, we are concerned that the impact of technology not turn into "Deep Impact" (American movie, 1998; "deep" has been translated as "lethal" or "fatal"). That is, the impact should by no means result in damaging a good system and replacing an effective methodology by a pseudo-methodology.

The engineering students at the Technical University of Sofia are prepared in mathematics by four service courses called Mathematics 1, 2, 3 and 4. Calculus is a major part of mathematics needed by engineers.

In 1996 I did my own investigations about possible applications of CAS Derive (DOS version) in my teaching. I found that it closely corresponded to my understanding of the need for software-related curricula in undergraduate mathematics for non-mathematics students. As the work of practicing engineers is dominated by computers and software tools, we decided to start with the integration of Derive into the teaching and learning of calculus. Our decision was aimed at equipping from an early stage undergraduate students to meet the challenges of the digital world.

Derive was initially introduced at the Faculty of Mechanical Engineering during the academic year 1997/98. Until then we had only traditional classroom-delivered undergraduate mathematics courses; software packages like Maple, Mathematica, Matlab had not been used for undergraduate teaching.

3. Why Is Mathematics Service Teaching Hard and Challenging?

Mathematics service courses are designed for, and taught to, non-mathematics students, that is, students who, in general, are not going to become mathematicians. What is specific in the teaching of such courses is that mathematics is to be considered and taught as a tool, not as a goal. Although the subject matter (mathematics) is the same, the goals of learning are different and different kinds of activity are appropriate.

Therefore, the mathematics teachers involved are not supposed to teach mathematics in the way they have been taught. Moreover, they have to help students learn how to implement mathematics in achieving their own goals. Experienced teachers know that each of these tasks is neither trivial, nor easy. Above all, the teachers are expected to use technology supported learning environments effectively for their courses.

4. The Key Role Of The Activity "Problem Solving" - In A Successful Mathematics Service Teaching

To "know something" means to be able to apply it where and when necessary. Otherwise, we could call such knowledge "futile knowledge", and the learning of it would appear to be "learning in vain" instead of "learning for knowing". "Apply" is to be understood in a broad sense.

For the student to learn mathematics knowledge and develop an ability to apply this knowledge, it is necessary that s/he becomes good in the basic activity in mathematics education known as "Problem Solving". Faced with the reduction of class time for lecturing, teachers have to put more emphasis on this activity.

This activity gives the student some quiet time for reflection on the material in question and shows up the student weaknesses in her/his thinking which s/he may remedy. In the process of solving problems, students' understanding itself undergoes further development.

By watching students' work in classes and laboratories the teacher can see the kind of material that they can go into, the sort of components that they do or do not pick up, their mathematical ideas, and their interpretation skills. Thus, the teacher can observe the "trajectory of the student's knowledge/learning" and provide the appropriate support at the right moment to help students make progress [2].

The role of the teacher in this activity is most important for the student's confidence in, and satisfaction of, doing mathematics. Any failure of the teacher in this activity can put students off mathematics for life. On the contrary, a successful activity will create an atmosphere where students could develop 'a life-long love' for mathematics.

5. How can CAS contribute to enhance mathematics service teaching? A Bulgarian Experience With CAS Derive - A Dynamic Unity Of Tradition And Technology

In the beginning we were really not too sure how Derive could support and enhance our teaching. What was sure was that teachers and students felt inspired by the broad range of opportunities to create a new learning environment. It was our aim to find a way of fully exploiting CAS potential to serve mathematics education with maximum benefit and minimum complications arising from its application.

The Derive approaches that we have developed for the teaching and learning of some basic topics in mathematics have been published in a few papers [6 - 10]. As the tool imprints its mark on the subject, we have been developing the activities within the potential and limitations of the Derive version in use. With the course of time we have accumulated experience in making better use of the advantages of Derive. What actually happens when using CAS is described in a paraphrase of the saying about the scalpel and the surgeon: "Far from investing the world with his vision, the computer user is mastered by his tool"[4].

Our strategy of integrating CAS is based on the general methodological principles of systematization and consistency of subject content, accessibility, visualization, personalization, and students' conscious involvement in learning.

There are three problems to address: 1) to select topics, questions and problems suitable for a CAS-supported environment; 2) to find a good balance between the work done using classical paper-and-pencil methods and those which use CAS; 3) to find an effective combination of traditional teaching-learning processes and the process of doing and learning mathematics in a CAS environment.

To overcome some limitations of traditional modes of teaching and learning, we use Derive to help students go into deeper understanding of:

- topics where graphics displays facilitate the learning process;
- newly introduced concepts having multiple use in later sections of mathematics courses;
- difficult to master topics where conceptual prototypes enhance the teaching and learning.

As the concept of function is the key concept in calculus, computer class sessions involve activities related to it. Below are some basic activities that we carry out with application of Derive:

(1) The relationship between the behaviour of the graph of a function and the signs of its first and second derivatives [7](Fig.1).

(2) The concept of approximation in various contexts: Taylor/Maclaurin series; polynomial approximation of a function (Fig.2,3,4,5); approximate analytical and numerical solution of ordinary differential equations (ODE); approximate root of an equation; numerical integration.

(3) Definite integral: properties; application.

(4) Double integral: outer and inner limits of integration; application [9].

(5) Functions of two variables: critical points and their nature [8]; types of limits [6] – the distinctions between necessary condition, sufficient condition, necessary and sufficient condition.

(6) First order ODE: general (exact) solution; approximate analytical solutions; numerical solution [10].

In the activity presented in Figure 1, a student's work is reduced to straightforward commands of *DERIVE*. Through experimentation s/he could re-invent a new portion of knowledge. The following activities have been posed by the teacher:

(a) Formulate a general statement about the relation between the behaviour of a function and the signs of its first and second derivative.

(b) Determine geometrically the intervals where the function under consideration is increasing/decreasing, convex/concave; the points of maximum or minimum, the points of inflection. To confirm your results use Derive and refer to your answer of (a).

#1: $y = x^2 \cdot e^{-x}$

#2: $\dfrac{d}{dx}(x^2 \cdot e^{-x}) = x \cdot e^{-x} \cdot (2 - x)$

#3: $\left(\dfrac{d}{dx}\right)^2 (x^2 \cdot e^{-x}) = e^{-x} \cdot (x^2 - 4 \cdot x + 2)$

#4: $\left(\dfrac{d}{dx}\right)^2 (x^2 \cdot e^{-x}) = e^{-x} \cdot ((x - 0.5858) \cdot (x - 3.4142))$

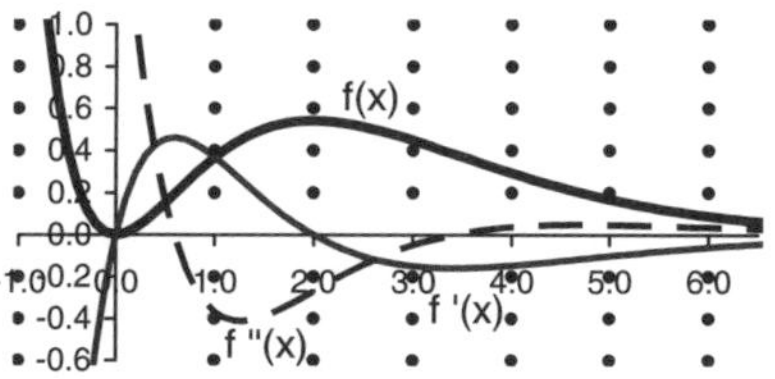

#5:   SOLVE$(x \cdot (2-x) > 0$, x, Real$) = 0 < x < 2$

#6:   SOLVE$(x^2 - 4 \cdot x + 2 > 0$, x, Real$) = (x < 0.58578 \lor x > 3.4142)$

FIGURE 1

The activity involving the application of Derive in learning the newly introduced concepts of Taylor/Maclaurin polynomial approximation, the remainder of a series, and the error of approximation have been carried out as shown in Figures 2, 3,

4, 5 and 6. The work in Figure 2 aims at a student's conceptual understanding of the new mathematical object, namely Taylor polynomials. Other questions and activities posed by the teacher are inserted into the worksheets.

#15:   TAYLOR(SIN(x), x, 0, 3) = x - 0.16666·x^3

#16:   TAYLOR(SIN(x), x, 0, 10)= 2.7557·10^{-6}·x^9 - 0.00019841·x^7

  + 0.0083333·x^5 - 0.16666·x^3 + x

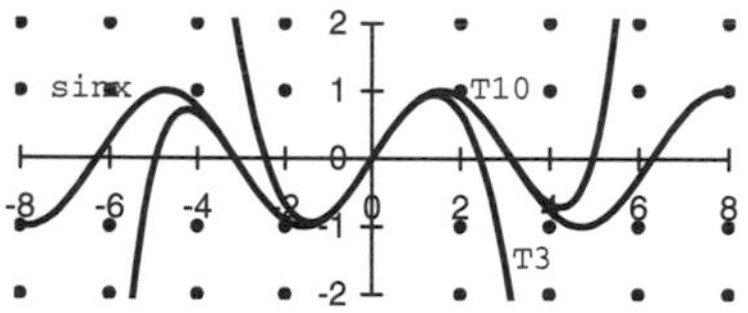

FIGURE 2

#1:   y = x^2·e^{-x}

#2: $\frac{d}{dx}(x^2 \cdot e^{-x}) = x \cdot e^{-x} \cdot (2 - x)$

#3: $\left(\frac{d}{dx}\right)^2(x^2 \cdot e^{-x}) = e^{-x} \cdot (x^2 - 4 \cdot x + 2)$

#4: $\left(\frac{d}{dx}\right)^2(x^2 \cdot e^{-x}) = e^{-x} \cdot ((x - 0.5858) \cdot (x - 3.4142))$

#5:   SOLVE(x·(2-x) > 0, x, Real) = 0 < x < 2

#6:   SOLVE(x^2 - 4·x + 2 > 0, x, Real) = (x < 0.58578 ∨ x > 3.4142)

FIGURE 3

Question 2:   Given the order of approximation and desired accuracy. Find the maximum width of the interval for x. Let n = 3 and max error = 0.0005

#22: $\frac{x^5}{5!}$ ≤ 0.0005

#23: $\frac{x^4 \cdot |x|}{120}$ ≤ 0.0005

#24:   SOLVE$\left(\frac{x^4 \cdot |x|}{120} \leq 0.0005, x, \text{Real}\right)$

#25:   -0.56967 ≤ x≤ 0.56967

FIGURE 4

```
Try with the error = 2.6666.10∧(-6) obtained in
Question 1(a) and get the initial interval [0.2,0.2]
```

#29: $\dfrac{x^4\cdot|x|}{120} \leq 2.6666\cdot 10^{-6}$

#30: $\text{SOLVE}\left(\dfrac{x^4\cdot|x|}{120} \leq 2.6666\cdot 10^{-6},\ x,\ \text{Real}\right)$

#31: $-0.19999 \leq x \leq 0.19999$

```
Question 3: Find graphically the intervals for which it is
reasonable to use the polynomial approximations obtained.
```

FIGURE 5

In Figure 5 the "reverse" question to those in Figure 3 has been especially designed to point out the necessity of reflecting on the results obtained (or of controlling the work done) by CAS. The Russian proverb "Trust but Check Up/Verify" proved to be useful in doing mathematics with CAS.

Question 4 in Figure 5 cannot be solved analytically. The graphical capabilities of CAS make this additional activity possible.

```
Question 4: Given the interval for x: [-π/2,π/2]
            and the max error = 0.001.
            Find the order of approximation, n.
```

#32: $\text{SOLVE}\left(\dfrac{\left|\frac{\pi}{2}\right|^n}{n!} \leq 0.001,\ n,\ \text{Real}\right)$

#33: $1000\cdot\left(\dfrac{\pi}{2}\right)^n - n! \leq 0 \leq n! \ \lor\ n! \leq 0 \leq 10$

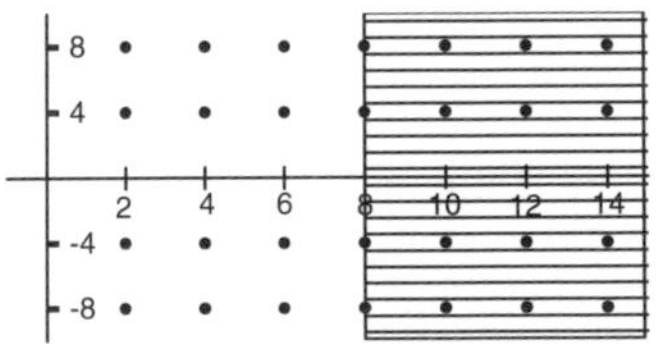

#34: $\text{TAYLOR}(\text{SIN}(x),\ x,\ 0,\ 8) = -0.00019841\cdot x^7 + \dfrac{x^5}{120} - \dfrac{x^3}{6} + x$

FIGURE 6

Our experience in combining traditional and CAS supported approaches to teaching other topics in calculus are represented in [6 – 10].

6. More of Problem Solving

Problem solving could aim at achieving some mathematics learning objectives or at obtaining only the solution needed for solving other problems. In the latter case the computer can be used as a problem solver. In the first case a series of related problems progressing in difficulty has to be constructed.

The increased use of technology and the increased demand for the online delivery of courses [5] make important the ever-present question "HOW to solve problems?". The general answer should be "NOT just ANYHOW". With or without technology general principles have to be observed [2]:

- the process of solving must be clear, exact and concise;
- the process of solving should go "From simple to complex, from known to unknown, from easy to difficult".

Here I will share examples together with related questions about how to approach the problem. These questions reflect my understanding of how to teach "solving problems in a proper way".

Example 1. Differentiate the following function: $f(x) = \tan^{-1}\left(\sqrt{\frac{1-\sin x}{1+\sin x}}\right)$.

Question: Use Chain Rule, CAS, or simply follow the general rule "First simplify", linking old and new knowledge and skills? CAS is helpful for both the geometrical interpretation of the result and discussing the points of discontinuity.

Example 2. (a) Solve the integral: $\int_0^3 \sqrt{9 - x^2}\, dx$.

Question: Use the substitution method or integration by parts (as it is solved in almost all textbooks), or simply recall the geometrical meaning of definite integral, use the Derive library function PlotInt, and let students calculate the area even without writing?

(b) To apply the above mentioned principle "From simple to complex,..." give the students a series of integrals and introduce the substitution method using appropriate integrals:

$$\int_0^c \sqrt{c^2 - x^2}\, dx \quad \Rightarrow \quad \int_0^c \sqrt{2cx - x^2}\, dx \quad \Rightarrow \quad \int_c^{c+r} \sqrt{r^2 - (x-c)^2}\, dx \quad \Rightarrow$$

$$\int_0^c x\sqrt{c^2 - x^2}\, dx \quad \Rightarrow \quad \int_0^c R(x, \sqrt{c^2 - x^2})\, dx \quad \Rightarrow \quad \int_a^b R(x, \sqrt{c^2 - x^2})\, dx$$

Example 3. Solve the integral: $\int \frac{\cos x}{1+\cos x}\, dx$.

Question: Use the substitution method or "...from known to unknown,..."? Let students compare this integral to integrals solved earlier and having the same structure of the integrand: $\int \frac{x}{1+x}\, dx = x - \ln|x+1|$, $\int \frac{x^2}{1+x^2}\, dx = x - \tan^{-1} x$.

In all activities CAS is useful as a self-assessment tool.

7. Conclusion

Mathematics teaching and learning is a skill-and-habit-forming process. Hence, it makes its mark on the learners for life [1, 2]. Technology-meets-tradition activities can contribute to enhancement of the results of this process.

A powerful tradition and technology can go hand in hand to achieve a threefold educational goal:

- make students think better than they did before

- help students acquire a life long habit of doing things in a proper way
- enhance students' understanding of the role of mathematics in the everyday life.

With students actively and interactively involved in the learning process, teachers can find out what mix of which types of learning environments are better suited for a particular topic or kind of problems.

References

[1] De Bono, E. (1984) *Teaching thinking*, Penguin Books, London.

[2] Ganchev, I., Kolyagin, Y., Kuchinov, Y., Portev, L. and Sidorov, Y. (1996) *Methodology of mathematics education*, MODUL, Sofia.

[3] Guin, D. and Trouche, L. (1999) *The complex process of converting tools into mathematical instruments. The case of calculators*, International Journal of Computers for Mathematical Learning, Vol.3 (3)

[4] Noss, R. and Hoyles, C. (1996) *Windows on mathematical meaning – learning cultures and computers*, Kluwer Academic Publishers.

[5] Selden, A. (2005) *New developments and trends in tertiary mathematics education: Or, more of the same?*, International Journal of Mathematical Education in Science and Technology, Vol. 36, Nos. 2-3.

[6] Paneva-Konovska, J.D., Varbanova, E.A.(2005) *Approaching the limits of functions of two variables using DERIVE*. Proc. International Symposium "Education For Everyone", Vol. I C, Varna.

[7] Pankov, I., Varbanova, E.A. and Watkins, A.J. (1998) *Teaching and learning mathematics with technology – a Balkan experience*. 11th Int.Conf. on Technology in Collegiate Mathematics, New Orleans, USA.

[8] Todorov, M. and Varbanova, E. (1999) *Application of DERIVE in the investgation of explicit functions of two variables*, Proc. Summer School "Appl. of Maths in Engineering'24", Herron Press, Sofia.

[9] Varbanova, E.A., Patel, M.K. And Marinova, D. (2001) *Tradition and innovation in teaching and learning double integral*, Proc. ICTMT5, Klagenfurt.

[10] Varbanova E. and Stoynov Y. (2003) *DERIVE-Approach to first order ordinary differential equations*, Proceedings of the XXIX International Summer School "Applications of Mathematics in Engineering and Economics", Sozopol.

DEPARTMENT OF MATHEMATICAL ANALYSIS AND NUMERICAL METHODS, TECHNICAL UNIVERSITY - SOFIA, SOFIA 1000, BULGARIA
    E-mail address: elvar@tu-sofia.bg

CBMS Issues in Mathematics Education
Volume **14**, 2007

Experience with Blended Learning:
IT Support Inside the Classroom and Beyond

Gabriele E. Uchida

ABSTRACT. Today, continually improving IT infrastructure including network access being more readily available, instructors are more and more encouraged to take advantage of these new possibilities and to integrate them into their courses. Experimenting with tools which enhance collaborative working and enable ubiquitous access to course material shows interesting new approaches, makes courses more interactive and can motivate students and instructors. The paper will report on some of the issues encountered in using a particular collaborative working tool - Basic Support for Collaborative Working (*BSCW*) – as a supporting platform integrated into the design of specific courses and report about faculty and student viewpoints.

1. Introduction

Recent advances in information technology, especially the general availability of Internet access for almost everybody, enable and indeed even require new approaches in knowledge acquisition and teaching. Learning is getting more interactive and group-oriented using communication over the Internet. We first give some insights on our motivation for introducing computers and internet technology into our courses in an attempt to provide a holistic scenario, and to discuss what our expectations were. Thereafter, we describe the early adaptor phase of those newly deployed tools. For us, since it was readily available and easy to use, the *BSCW* file sharing system was an obvious choice. Similar experiences can be found in [**3**]. Finally, after a first set of courses have been completed, valuable experience has been gained and therefore necessary adjustments or even new approaches can be planed and implemented for the next set of courses.

2. Motivation

The starting points for our new teaching experience were changing circumstances and unsatisfactory situations. Before increasing the use of IT support in our courses, we had common face-to-face lectures and in addition workshop-like courses to enable or enhance the understanding of theoretical concepts by way of practical exercises. This was mainly achieved with exercises to be done at home and subsequent class gatherings, where students presented and discussed their results in front of their class colleagues. Due to constantly rising numbers of students, and the larger workshop groups that resulted, this procedure became increasingly difficult, especially since involving, and even more motivating, all participating students proved to be a challenge not easily met.

The diverse knowledge background of the students was an additional difficulty on the way to designing a successful teaching environment. Students came from varying branches of study (e.g. Economics, Management Science, Business Informatics, Computer Science, Statistics, etc.) and had to be instructed in one class. So given the constantly improving IT infrastructure, it seemed like an obvious idea to make use of these new technologies to cope with our problems.

Up to this point we usually offered printed materials and supporting documents, which required a considerable organisational effort on behalf of our department staff. So the first idea was to bring these documents into an electronic form and put them *online*, so that students could download them using these new, but simple *Websites*.

FIGURE 1.   Electronic Chalkboard

In addition, the department was able to use an *Electronic Chalkboard* (see Figure 1) in the classroom. This enabled instructors to use the *Online-Handouts* as a basis for their lectures (making classical chalkboard or overhead projectors almost obsolete). For the workshop groups the *shared workspace* software *BSCW* has enabled students to upload their homework and present their results during class with much more case, as electronically prepared documents could now be used. This itself triggered completely new types of homework, such as exercises using Excel sheets, which are impossible to present with chalk or even with overhead-slides. This new approach also improved various organisational aspects. Scheduling became somewhat easier, since quite a lot of the load was now completed by the students themselves. Instead of handing over their homework on paper or e-mail, students now upload their work into dedicated folders and have access wherever internet access exists, such as from class, from diverse labs, from home or their working environment, thus, making work for many of them much easier. Instead of personal e-mail communication between student and instructor, a discussion group can be used, which proves especially useful concerning questions and answers many students might have.

Slowly integrating new technologies into our teaching efforts brought us to a procedure nowadays called *Blended Learning*. This describes a teaching and learning situation that combines different delivery methods, since *People are not single-method learners*, as Elliot Masie puts it in [4]. Commonly, *Blended Learning* is known as a mix of face-to-face classroom activity, live e-learning, software and file sharing, and sometimes self-paced learning. The challenge is now to find an appropriate mix for a particular course, considering the intention of the course and the different knowledge background of the students. There is definitely no single formula that guarantees successful learning and sound motivation. We tried to bring more flexibility into the course in order to motivate all students and at the same time easing some of the organisational load experienced so far.

The *shared workspace* software was chosen, because it was readily available, and it was already installed and maintained on one of the departments servers by a very dedicated colleague. In addition it seemed to be very easy to use and to adapt to our needs. *BSCW* [2] – Basic Support for Cooperative Work – is a software that enables collaboration over the Web using a browser as thin client! It is a *shared workspace* system which supports document upload, event notification and group management, just to mention the most basic features. In general, schools and universities receive royalty free licences for educational purposes. In addition there is a public *BSCW* Server at *http://bscw.fit.fraunhofer.de/* that can be used for explorative purposes, which proves to be very useful for the first steps to be taken. One gets accustomed with the system in a risk free environment and afterwards has gained enough insight to decide over its usefulness for one's own purposes.

3. Implementation

In accordance with local custom, we deploy or increase use of IT infrastructure in our courses gradually. It therefore took some time to get students and instructors as well accustomed to this new form of communication.

As a very first step, while keeping up traditional teaching methods in the classroom, additional teaching material for an introductory Operations Research course was made available by the instructors downloadable from their personal webpages.

Students could access these materials freely by way of the Internet and therefore could make use of them outside the classroom.

In a second step, we requested students to get more involved and become more active. They were encouraged to upload the results of their homework and use a discussion group to resolve minor organisatorial problems and obtain answers to questions which arose while solving their homework. Most of these activities were add-ons to the regular face-to-face courses, and were used outside the regular classroom activity, although it was possible to present uploaded homework in the classroom through the Electronic Chalkboard, as mentioned above. This was especially useful as soon as we initiated new types of homework, such as developing Excel models and showing how to solve these with the Excel's Solver Add-In.

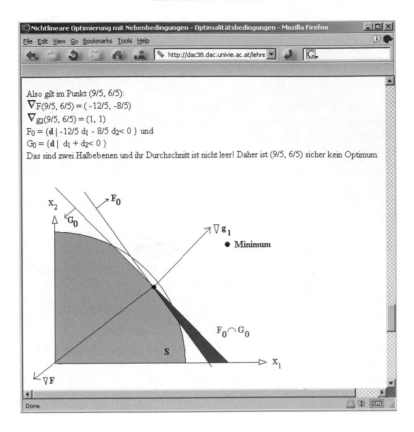

FIGURE 2.   Screenshot "Teaching Material Operations Research"

In a third step, the new tools were totally integrated into the regular course work supporting a special course for modeling and solving optimization problems. Again the starting knowledge and skills of our students were rather diverse.

During face-to-face classes, material, examples and exercises were being uploaded to the common workspace by the instructor one by one in well prepared units. Exercises were then subsequently worked out by students and after an adequate time, exemplary solutions were presented (on the workspace) to give immediate feedback. Since the course took place in a PC Lab with Internet access, every student had their own computer and access to the common workspace, which was updated during the lesson, as already mentioned. In addition, it was possible for the students to transfer their work done during the classes to their own directories, in order to document their work and access their solutions for follow-ups whenever and wherever they found it to be necessary. Since all instruction material remained online, all students could work at their own pace, and the instructor had time to answer specific questions or to support weaker students. Outside the classroom homework was to be done and uploaded to the workspace. In addition to all these collaborative features, with the consent of the respective authors, we could make copyrighted software tools available and restricted to the course and its participants, something which otherwise would not have been possible.

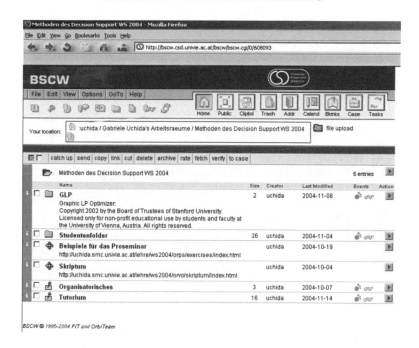

FIGURE 3.   Screenshot "BSCW Server Course Page"

Students with lesser knowledge and fewer skills were supported and motivated to continue their studies at home to catch up with their more knowledgable colleagues. On the other hand, students with a higher degree of previous knowledge were given additional units and profited by this system as well.

To use *BSCW* successfully, initially only very few simple steps have to be accommodated. Details can be set aside for later. To be able to use a *BSCW* server as a user you have to be *invited*, followed by an e-mail containing an invitation with a specific internet-link. In clicking on this link, one is prompted to enter a username and a password. From then on, a login to the server is possible. Instructors need to have authorisation to invite users to their courses, a right the *BSCW* administrator usually grants the instructors. Once given, one creates a new folder (see Figure 4) for one's course, and all invitations and resulting users are connected to this folder and all its subfolders. In a very similar manner, discussion groups or tasks can be created. Uploading files of any other type of information is now possible in a like manner directly using a browser (see Figure 5) without the need for any special programs. After these preliminary steps, inviting students to this newly created workspace (course) is immediately possible by addressing them on behalf of their e-mail address (see Figure 6).

By the time they activate their invitation and subsequently activate their account, students can use the workspace, that is, the folder they were invited to and all subfolders.

4. Lessons learned

Our main concern was a constantly increasing workload [5]. It certainly is true that implementing new technologies takes up a considerable amount of time

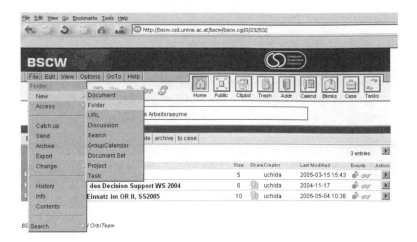

FIGURE 4.   Screenshot "BSCW Server: Create a new folder"

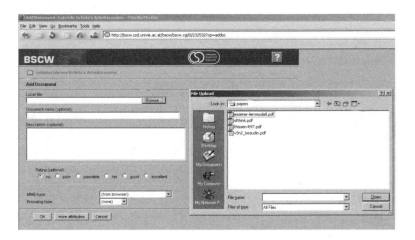

FIGURE 5.   Screenshot "BSCW Server: Upload a new file"

and requires an especially high commitment. Nevertheless, *BSCW* is an easy to use tool, which does not need too much time to get acquainted with. At first it seems feasible to reuse existent documents and make them available in an electronic form, i.e. downloadable from the Internet. No specialized design for (interactive) e-learning courses seems necessary, but a smooth and slow transition from classical teaching to e-learning should be allowed for. The workflow itself can be held very similar to traditional courses, but then again, there is potential to enhance the degree of interaction of IT support and classroom courses gradually.

¿From the students' viewpoint, the work was done with a lot of enthusiasm, perhaps due to its newness. Sometimes groups of students got so involved that it was difficult to urge students to leave the PC lab and give way for the next course – this had never happened before. Students were very curious about the new possibilities and most of them indulged in trying out new features, mainly the new possibility of asynchronous work [**1**], [**6**], where files are available from

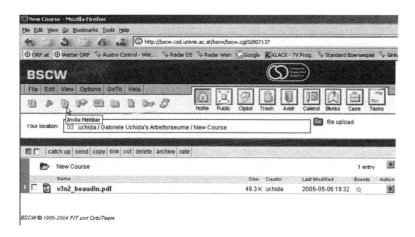

FIGURE 6.   Screenshot "BSCW Server: Invitation of new members"

everywhere (especially also from at home). At first the discussion group was not accepted by the course members, since it is not anonymous, and there seemed to be reservations about instructors being able to read their postings. Last term, however, an intensive tutorial service was installed and now communication between students themselves and between students and the teaching assistant are quite well established. Another fact to be pointed out is that students can view the work of their colleagues. At first it obviously seemed a severe drawback to the instructors who feared an increased possibility of fraudulent activity. But after a while we noticed that students invested quite some time in studying the solutions of their colleagues and therefore increased their expertise. Naturally some cheating attempts took place at first, but after adequate reprimand it worked satisfactorily, especially after the students noticed that uploaded solutions of their colleagues very often contained errors or inaccurateness, hence simple copying was not a reliable tactic. Then again, the availability of fellow students with more experience could be put to use and sometimes helped to obtain a jump-start in solving the problem.

Some experiences and good advice: It is really very important to give out strict rules concerning structure and naming conventions right from the beginning, even if they seem ridiculous at first. This procedure can reduce instructors' workload dramatically. If at all possible, the use of teaching assistants is really very helpful, and with larger groups, even essential, especially when a course is taught in a new form for the first time. Since many detail questions will arise again and again, a discussion group dealing with these is very helpful. To gain acceptance you will have to assure a risk-free environment, otherwise students will shy away, thinking the instructor will incorporate the postings into the grading. A very useful feature of *BSCW* for the instructor is the so-called Daily Report, where all the activities are logged and concise overview shows what and how much students are working. All in all, we were able to assist the students more flexibly, especially in courses with participants from heterogeneous academic backgrounds and knowledge. Supplying students with exercises to be solved in their own speed, leaves time to support weaker students during class. Faster students complete more exercises and study them in greater detail, whereas weaker students do fewer exercises with instructors supporting them from time to time. A whole wealth of creativity is available in combining all these potential options given by the system.

A problem specifically with our mathematical courses was the missing or incomplete IT competence of our students. To solve and present mathematical problems it obviously is necessary to write formulas or draw some graphics. It turned out, that many students were not able to use programs like *Word Formula Editor*, *TeX* or similar tools to write these formulas. Even more, students had great difficulties using simple graphical programs to at least make sketches or simple graphical illustrations. One possible way out was scanning handwritten exercises and uploading these scans to the workspace, but regrettably most of the time the quality was poor and due to a lack of skills, scans were made in a much too high resolution, resulting in huge files and increased upload/download time. For the same reason (missing possibility to write formulas in an easy and straight forward way) discussion groups and chat forums are definitely difficult to use especially for this area, therefore communication on these subjects is rather cumbersome and time consuming.

5. Conclusions

Positive points in our experiences: *BSCW* is an extremely easy to learn and use environment. In contrast to some other systems that we have dealt with, it is not necessary to invest an increased amount of time to instruct students in using the system. Due to the thin client principle, no special software is required - a simple web browser is sufficient to access all documents and tools worldwide, as long as Internet access is available. This enables cooperation (even internationally) in a very straight forward and easy way. Another feature that *BSCW* provides is a Closed Environment. The group has a common workspace visible only to invited members. Since some materials or even software tools have restrictions concerning their distribution (i.e. for a specific course only, but not for worldwide access), this enables distribution and especially utilization which on the other hand would not be possible, if it were not a Closed Environment.

Some problematic points: Setting up a course can take some time mainly due to organisational problems. To organise a group, all members have to be invited to the common workspace using their email address. During the beginning of a fresh term many students seem to be unable to activate their university mail account, leading to unnecessary delays. As already mentioned above, uploaded files are visible to the whole group. Since it was not possible to assign different exercises to every student some cheating attempts took place at the very beginning. This problem could be settled, or rather settled itself, as soon as some students copied incorrect solutions and in addition got reprimanded. A feature missing in the educational version and only available in the commercial version is some kind of workflow support. This could greatly enhance the *Blended Learning* approach.

What are our next steps? After having experimented with this simple and easy tool, we will try out other, more complex platforms, such as *WebCT Vista* or perhaps *Blackboard*. First experiences with *WebCT Vista* have already been made. There are a wealth of new possibilities, but the time required to learn all features in detail will be considerable. The interface is much more complicated and uses *Java Applets* which imparts a dependency upon what version of the *Java Virtual Machine* is currently installed on the client, if any, and therefore cannot be regarded as a thin client solution in its classical form. On the other hand, one gains interesting new features allowing us to create quizzes, self-assessment tests and many ways to provide feedback not available in *BSCW*. Nevertheless, in a first comparison students preferred *BSCW* due to its uncomplicated interface and thin client architecture.

We are interested in, and would like to encourage, international cooperations in the field of *Blended Learning*. It certainly would be an interesting experience to design, produce, maintain and perhaps even hold a course internationally scoped based on a collaborative architecture, such as *BSCW*, without limitations on time-zones and locations.

References

[1] Beaudin, B.P.: *Keeping Online Asynchronous Discussions on Topic*, Journal of Asynchronous Learning Networks, 3 (2), 1999

[2] *BSCW Manual*, available online: http://bscw.fit.fraunhofer.de/bscw_help-4.2/english/

[3] Jefferies, P. and Constable, I.: *Using BSCW in Learning and Teaching*, Educational Technology and Society 3 (3) 2000

[4] Rossett, A. (ed.): *The ASTD E-Learning Handbook*, McGraw-Hill, New York, 2002

[5] Thompson, M.M. : *Faculty Self-Study Research Project: Examining the Online Workload*, Journal of Asynchronous Learning Networks, 8 (3) 2004

[6] Wegerif, R. : *The social dimension of asynchronous learning networks*, Journal of Asynchronous Learning Networks, 2 (1) 1998

INSTITUTE OF SCIENTIFIC COMPUTING, FACULTY OF COMPUTER SCIENCE, UNIVERSITY OF VIENNA, AUSTRIA

E-mail address: gabriele.uchida@univie.ac.at

CBMS Issues in Mathematics Education
Volume **14**, 2007

On the mathematics courses
for social science majors

Sung-Ock Kim

ABSTRACT. Teaching mathematics to non-math majors at the undergraduate level needs special care. We will discuss goals, contents and teaching of mathematics courses for social science majors with a focus on economics, business, and management on the basis of analyzed data.

1. Introduction

Mathematics for undergraduate students whose majors are not mathematics could be a totally different subject from mathematics for mathematics majors.

The students' motivation for studying mathematics is different. The fact that they prefer social sciences to other subjects already means that they have a somewhat different character. So, to teach the basic subjects of mathematics for university students whose majors are not mathematics, mathematicians who are well trained in mathematical thinking should give special care.

We will discuss what kind of special care is needed from the viewpoint of goals, content and the method of teaching.

2. Goals of teaching mathematics to non-math majors

In general, it is said that the goal of teaching mathematics to undergraduate students whose majors are not mathematics is twofold.

One is to ensure that they can get some of the tools and techniques from mathematics that are needed for their own majors. The Wharton School of the University of Pennsylvania requires three courses as a general education requirement. These are two introductory economics courses and one mathematics course. The description of the mathematics course says that "Mathematics, like economics, is an important tool in approaching business courses."

The other is to enable them to develop skills in mathematical thinking so that they can apply them to solve problems in their own disciplines.

To find out what students think about the goal of learning mathematics, a survey was conducted at Handong Global University in May, 2005. The first question "What is your goal of studying math?" was given with the following 4 choices: 1) to develop logical thinking, 2) to use for major (I realized the need of math), 3) to use for major (recommended by faculty members or others) 4) other than the above (write:)

A total of 77 students replied as shown in the following table: 5) is the percentage of the numbers of students who chose both 1) and 2) or both 1) and 3).

	goals of learning math	reason for taking the course
1)	21 % (16)	8 % (7)
2)	44 % (34)	41 % (35)
3)	20 % (15)	33 % (28)
4)	10 % (8)	14 % (12)
5)	5 % (4)	4 % (3)
T	100 % (77)	100 % (85)

The numbers in ( ) mean the number of students who responded.

The second question asked the reason for taking the course "Mathematics for Economics, Business and Management" with the same 4 choices. This course is intended to be taken by sophomores with majors in economics, business and management in the first semester of an academic year. The prerequisite of the course is calculus of one variable functions (polynomials). This course is recommended (but not required) as a prerequisite for major courses. The students who responded to this survey were taking the course. Less than 20 percent of them are sophomores and most of them are juniors and seniors.

According to the survey, 21 percent replied that they would study mathematics to develop their logical thinking. But only 8 percent of them expect to get their logical thinking developed through the course they are taking. One reason for such low expectation could be the title of the course: Mathematics for Business, Management and Economics.

If the two goals of teaching mathematics are implemented in separate courses like "mathematics as a tool" and "mathematical thinking", each course might attract students with appropriate expectations, and hence they might tolerate some difficulties without reluctance.

Another result that we can observe is that more than 40 percent of the students realized that they needed to learn more math. This high percentage could happen because about four fifths of them are juniors or seniors. This suggests that if mathematics courses are taught after they learn some topics in their own majors, then they can be easily motivated to study mathematics. Instead of teaching mathematics separately from their major courses, teaching those courses using tools and techniques from mathematics as a team with faculty members of those departments would be another option to try.

3. Teaching Mathematics

3.1. Contents of teaching. When one discusses teaching, it is natural to think about what to teach and how to teach. In this section, we discuss the contents of teaching. For this purpose, we examined the curricula of various institutions.

The programs for economics, business and management provided by the department of mathematics usually include two courses of calculus.

The main topics of these two courses are as follows:

1) The first calculus course: calculus of one variable and applications (maximum and minimum, exponential and logarithmic functions, area, Taylor's theorem and approximations).

Some institutes include infinite series and some do not. This might be because the undergraduate level of these majors deals with only geometric series and uses at most the ratio test to check the convergence of an infinite series, and even that rarely appears.

2) The second calculus course: functions of several variables, partial derivatives, constrained and unconstrained optimization, differential equations.

Some institutions include multiple integrals, introductory linear algebra and matrix theory with application. The Wharton School of the University of Pennsylvania includes elements of probability and statistics and applications in the second course of calculus.

It seems that for an undergraduate course, the Sloan School of MIT in the United States requires more mathematics than any other. It requires calculus of one variable, multivariable calculus (including vector calculus), and linear algebra for its management major.

Most business schools require only the first calculus course, while the other is optional. For graduate school in both economics and business, courses of microeconomic theory and macroeconomic theory are required, and the second calculus course and linear algebra provide basic tools for those theories.

In the home page of the undergraduate program of MIT Department of Economics, one can find the following statement: "The level of mathematics mastery among undergraduates allows economics courses to be taught at a high level" (http://econ-www.mit.edu/). So the amount of learning in mathematics required for economics, business and management depends on the academic level which a student pursues.

Currently, human society is experiencing extremely fast changes due to the development of technologies. This influences not only calculus reform but also continuous mathematics reform as R. Douglas predicted ([4]). The calculus courses listed above might change sooner or later in the direction of reducing topics in order to enable students to engage more deeply in mathematics as pointed out in [8] .

3.2. Methods of Teaching. A way of presenting the contents mentioned in the previous section can be observed through the examination of textbooks. By reviewing some textbooks ([1], [2], [3], [5], [6], [7], [10], [11], [12]) we can see that there are two different styles:

1) Introduce mathematics and then show some examples of applications.

2) Introduce practical problems and derive mathematical theories.

The first style is logically well ordered and could be preferred by a mathematician.

The books of the second style (cf. [3], [7]) came out after the so-called calculus reform in the United States of America. In the preface of [7], the authors say that a basic principle of writing the book is "the way of Archimedes: Formal definitions and procedures evolve from the investigation of practical problems." This principle seems to be adequate for the characteristic of empirical sciences like business.

The learning style of students could be an important factor to be considered when we decide a way of presenting the contents. Their preference for business or management rather than to other subjects might have some relation with their learning style.

To check this claim, a survey was conducted at Handong Global University using selected questions from [9] in May, 2005. The answers to the following four questions out of ten questions given in the survey show a significant difference between the students whose majors are social sciences (most of them are double majors in economics and business) and the students whose majors are engineering (two thirds of them are freshmen who are going to choose majors in engineering):

1. If I were a teacher, I would rather teach a course (a) that deals with facts and real life situations. (b) that deals with ideas and theories.

2. I prefer courses that emphasize (a) concrete material (facts, data). (b) abstract material (concepts, theories).

3. I prefer to get new information in (a) pictures, diagrams, graphs, or maps. (b) written directions or verbal information.

4. I like teachers (a) who put a lot of diagrams on the board. (b) who spend a lot of time explaining.

Question	Social science	Engineering
1-(a)	67 % (45)	45 % (15)
1-(b)	33 % (22)	55 % (18)
2-(a)	55 % (36)	30 % (10)
2-(b)	45 % (29)	70 % (23)
3-(a)	83 % (55)	66 % (21)
3-(b)	17 % (11)	34 % (11)
4-(a)	52 % (33)	47 % (14)
4-(b)	48 % (30)	53 % (16)

The above results show that students in social sciences prefer concrete materials like facts and data from real life situations to theories and concepts, while students in engineering (including the students who are going to major in engineering) prefer theories and concepts. Although such an outcome has been expected, it carries some meaning that we could provide actual data.

We were able to obtain other data that might show the effect of using a computer projector for teaching. It was heard that most students in engineering were not in favor of using an overhead projector instead of writing on the board in mathematics or physics classes. The course "Mathematics for Economics and Business" was taught by the author in the first semester of both academic years 2004 and 2005. There were two classes of the course each year. One class was instructed in English and another in Korean. In the year 2004, a computer projector was used in both classes except for the section of integration by substitution because the lecture notes were not ready in time. On-line lecture notes were provided ahead of class in both years. In the second midterm, three problems similar to the problems in 2004 about Gauss-Jordan elimination and determinants were given. Also, the problem of computing $\int_1^2 \frac{x}{x^2+1} dx$ was given in both years. The results were as follows:

The percentage of the number of students who got right answers for all 3 problems and 1 integral problem, respectively.

	2004 (28)	2004 (56)	2005 (35)	2005 (80)
	English	Korean	English	Korean
3 problems	50 %	74 %	26 %	52 %
1 integral	43 %	47 %	35 %	55 %

The number in ( ) means the number of students in class.

In the class taught in English, most students are Korean except for two or three foreigners. Most of these Korean students are not fluent in English.

It seems that projecting the lecture notes in class helps students to understand the contents better, at least when the lecture notes are available ahead of time.

4. Conclusion

The characteristics of each discipline could be reflected in the style of teaching. Mathematicians are very logical. More than 50 % of new Ph.Ds get teaching positions each year according to AMS survey. In [8], Schoenfeld claims that mathematicians have to use what they know; just knowing isn't enough.

A little bit of training as a teacher might have a large effect on teaching. We suggest implementing a program concerning teaching within a mathematics Ph.D. program. Currently, it is known that more than 80 institutions from among 171 universities and colleges in Korea have some sort of teaching and learning center. This could be an indication that not only mathematics, but also other Ph.D. programs, should include a program about teaching. It may save much time and effort to improve undergraduate education.

References

[1] T. Bradley and P. Patton, *Essential mathematics for economics and business(2nd)*, Wiley, Ltd, 2002
[2] F.S. Budnick, *Applied Mathematics for Business, Economics and the Social Sciences(3rd)*, McGraw-Hill, 1988.
[3] J. Callahan and K. Hoffman, *Calculus in Context*, Freeman and Company, 1995
[4] R.G. Douglas, The first decade of calculus reform, *UME trends*, 6(1995), no.6, 1-2
[5] J.H. Fife, *Calculus for business and economics*, Macmillan, 1994
[6] M. Hoy, J. Livernois, C. McKenna, R. Rees and T. Stengos, *Mathematics for economics(2nd)*, The MIT Press, 2001
[7] D. Hughes-Hallet, A.M. Gleason, P.F. Lock, D. Flath, et al., *Applied calculus for business, social sciences, and life sciences*, Wiley, Inc., 1996
[8] A.H.Schoenfeld, What do we know about mathematics curricula?, *J. of mathematical Behavior*, 13(1)(1994), 55-80
[9] B. Solomon and R. Felder, Index of Learning Styles Questionnaire, www.engr.ncsu.edu/learningstyles/ilsweb.html
[10] K. Sydsaeter and P.J. Hammond, *Mathematics for economic analysis*, Prentice-Hall,Inc., 1995
[11] D. Varberg and W. Fleming, *Applied Calculus for Management, Social, and Life Sciences*, Prentice-Hall, 1991
[12] S.Warner and S.R. Costenoble,*Finite Mathematics and Applied Calculus(2nd)*, Brooks/Cole, 2001

GLOBAL LEADERSHIP SCHOOL, HANDONG GLOBAL UNIVERSITY, POHANG 791-708 THE REPUBLIC OF KOREA
E-mail address: sokim@handong.edu

CBMS Issues in Mathematics Education
Volume **14**, 2007

On Mathematical Contents of
Computer Science Contests

S.O. Shilova and N.V. Shilov

1. Introduction

Science Olympiads and similar contests bring a spirit of competitiveness to science education. They benefit the best students, and engage them with research. Simultaneously, Science Olympiads and contests challenge faculty to enhance their teaching so that regular students can enjoy the Olympiad and contest problems.

Computer science contests have become very popular with undergraduate students in recent years. Perhaps the Association for Computing Machinery International Collegiate Programming Contest (ACM ICPC) is the most popular contest world-wide. The initiative was born at early 1970's in the United States, evolved to the North America Computer Science Competition, and then was formally inaugurated in 1977 at the first World Final ACM ICPC. The overall number of participants of annual multi-level contests (at local, sub-regional, regional and final levels) is about several tens of thousands from more than 1,300 universities in 68 countries. Seventy-eight teams took part in the 29th Annual World Finals of the ACM ICPC, April 3-7, 2005, in Shanghai, China. In our home country, Russia, the reputation of this Contest is so high that early this year President Vladimir Putin awarded the organizers of North-East European Regional ACM ICPC the National Educational Award [8].

The basics of the ACM ICPC format follow. Every contest team consists of three undergraduates together with a computer. A team has to solve 8-10 'real-world' problems in a five-hour competition. Team members jointly rank the difficulty of the problems, design formal models of them together with algorithms that solve the formalized problems, implement the algorithms, test the resulting programs, and submit the programs to a jury. The jury designates a program as being correct if the program successfully exercises a number of preliminary designed test data suites. All problem statements are provided with samples of test data and a range of admissible data values. However, the teams have no access to the jury test suites. Each incorrect submission is fined by a penalty. At the end of the contest, teams are ranked by the number of correct submissions, and (if several teams have

---

This work is supported by Brain Korea 21 Project, The school of information technology, KAIST in 2005.

the same numbers) by the value of penalties for incorrect submissions. (Please refer to [7] to learn more about the ICPC).

Unfortunately, ACM ICPC and many other computer science contests have become much more about programming than about science. They have become more similar to a technical sport than to the Science Olympiad due to the limited role of the research and innovation component in these contests. It seems that

- the art of formal problem modeling,
- contestants having a cookbook of algorithms in their heads
- contestants having rapid typing skills in their hands

are the three cornerstones of success in these contests. Of course, all these listed skills are related to computer science proficiency. The art of modeling is especially important, since it is about research skills, not about technical skills. This research component puts the computer science contests in line with such Science Olympiads as the Mathematics and Physics Olympiads.

However, the research component in computer science is not limited to the art of modeling. In particular, it includes formal mathematical proofs of model properties and program correctness. Moreover, sometimes without these proofs, the utility of a program that 'solves' a problem is very conventional in spite of successful and extensive program testing.

At this talk we present a number of particular problems that fit the Mathematics Olympiad and computer science contests format simultaneously. In the case of the Mathematics Olympiad, the problems are about existential proofs. In the case of computer science contests these problems are about algorithm design and implementation, but they cannot be considered correct without a formal proof. The proofs in these cases can be carried out in pure traditional mathematical style, or in a computer science way, that is, in a manner that is mathematically strict but is computer science in nature. We believe that these problems can help to overcome some alienation that occurs when gifted computer science students consider mathematics as being too pure, and talented mathematics students consider computer science as being too poor. We hope that mathematics faculty and students can extend this list by providing a number of computer science contest problems that require formal proofs for validation.

2. Sample Problems

Computer science is a branch of science like mathematics, physics, or biology. This branch of science has its own objects of study and methods of research. Of course, this particular branch can adopt ideas, approaches, and methods from other branches. The progress of quantum computing in the last decade is the most popular example of how another branch of science can benefit computer science. But in return, computer science can fertilize other branches of science, too. Perhaps the advance of bioinformatics is the most recent evidence of a contribution of this kind.

At the same time, the common example of the contribution of mathematics to computer science is theoretical computer science. It is possible to say that theoretical computer science is the study of mathematical models of algorithms, data structures, programs, etc. with the use of mathematical logic, abstract algebra, topology, etc. This leads to advances in program and temporal logic, cryptography, domain theory, etc. In contrast, there are few examples when ideas, approaches and methods of theoretical computer science contribute to advances in mathematics. Nevertheless, there are a number of Olympiad-level mathematical problems in which theoretical computer science can give new insights, by interpreting these problems in a computer science manner. In the new incarnation, mathematical problems become computer science contest problems, where a working program is the primary target, but where the formal proof of algorithm correctness is absolutely necessary (in contrast to modern computer science contests where judging relies upon testing).

We have discussed already two sample problems of this kind in [**3, 2**]. Please refer to the cited papers for the full story, but let us sketch the formulations of these problems in the following format:

Math:: Mathematical Olympiad problem first,

Comp:: Computer Science contest problem next.

The first Mathematical Olympiad problem that can be solved with aid of theoretical computer science and that can be transformed into a computer science contest problem is the following Fake Coin Puzzle [**3**]:

Math:: All valid coins have an equal standard weight, but a fake coin has another weight. Is it possible to identify a unique fake in a set of 14 coins, where one fixed coin is known to be standard, by balancing them at most 3 times?

Comp:: Write a program that inputs a number of coins M and a balance limit N and outputs

- 'impossible', if it is impossible to identify a unique fake in a set of M coins, where one fixed coin is known to be standard, balancing them N times;

- an executable program that implements an interactive scenario for fake coin identification otherwise.

(Assume that all test data range [1..150].)

We would like to remark now (in addition to discussion in the cited paper) that without a formal proof of the correctness of the program's algorithm, the program can not be determined to be correct due to the following reasons:

- test data ranges in [1..150] for testing a program in a feasible time;

- identification strategy for test data in this range can be developed by manual tuning a trichotomy;

- the trichotomy is not the right strategy in the general case.

The next problem is the Harbor Dispatcher Problem.

Math:: There are N black and N white points on the plane. Every three of them are non-collinear. Prove that it is possible to connect black and white points in a 1-1 manner by intervals without intersections.

Comp:: There are N piers in a harbor and N vessels in its area. The positions of all piers are fixed. The initial positions of all vessels are known. Every vessel can move to every pier directly (i.e. in a straight line). A dispatcher has to assign an individual pier to every vessel. Every vessel must move to the assigned pier by the most direct route. To exclude collisions, intersections of these routes are prohibited. Write a program that inputs initial positions of vessels and piers and assigns an individual pier for every vessel. (Assume that in test data N ranges in [1..100] and that all coordinates of positions range in [0..1000].)

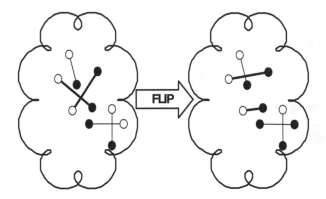

```
VAR X : coupling;
X:=initial;
WHILE not good(X) DO X:=flip(X)
```

FIGURE 1. Heuristic search algorithm and illustration how 'flip' works

Of course, a formal model for the computer science Harbor Dispatcher Problem is a set of N black and N white points in the plane without any collinear triples, and we have to find a pair-wise intersection-free interval coupling (a 'good' coupling). Hence, a straightforward mathematical approach to the Harbor Dispatcher Problem consists in the following steps:

- proving the existence of a good coupling;
- extracting an algorithm from the existential proof;
- implementing the algorithm.

In principle there are several ways to prove the existence of a good coupling in a pure mathematical way. They lead to different algorithm designs for a good coupling construction. However, there is also a pure computer science heuristic search approach to the Harbor Dispatcher Problem (Fig. 1). The idea of the heuristic search is trivial: start with some initial coupling and try to resolve local conflicts (i.e. eliminate local intersections) by flipping. Please refer [2] for a proof of the total correctness of this algorithm. Observe that without a proof the heuristic search algorithm is of very small value. (Unfortunately, computer science contests do not take proofs in to account.) Let us remark also, that the total correctness of the heuristic search algorithm is also a proof of existence of a good interval coupling.

3. Sylvester Problem

A problem that we would like to address in this section is a well-known problem of J.J. Sylvester (1814-1897) [5, 4]. The following story is a citation from [4]:

> Here is the question that Sylvester originally raised in 1893 in a journal known as the Educational Times:
>
>> Prove that it is not possible to arrange any finite number of real points so that a right line through every two of them shall pass through a third, unless they all lie in the same right line.

Sylvester used the term "right line" for straight line. Furthermore, two points which are the only two points on a line of a point/line configuration C have come to be known as ordinary lines. Today, we would state the result, in a way similar to the way that Paul Erdös (1913-1996) did when he made the conjecture, about 40 years later:

> If a finite set of points in the plane are not all on one line then there is a line through exactly two of the points.

(Let us emphasize that the problem was published in an educational journal [6]. More than one hundred years later we discuss the problem at the 1st KAIST International Symposium on Enhancing University Mathematics Teaching.)

Below we reformulate P. Erdös variant of J. Sylvester problem as a Mathematical Olympiad problem and as a corresponding computer science contest problem:

Math:: There is a finite set of points on the plane that are not collinear simultaneously. Prove that there exists a pair of points in the set that is not collinear with any other point in the set.

Comp:: A Flatland is a perfectly flat country where every two cities are connected by a road that is an interval of a straight line. It is apparent that some roads can intersect under some angle, some can not meet at all, some can be a part of other roads, etc. For example, at a map of Flatland in Fig. 2 there are 5 cities (1, 2, 3, 4, and 5) and 10 roads ([1,2], [1,3], [2,3], [1,4], [1,5], [4,5], [2,4], [2,5], [3,4], and [3,5]). In this example roads [2,5] and [3,4] intersect, roads [2,3] and [4,5] do not meet, roads [1,4] and [4,5] continue each other, road [1,2] is a part of road [1,3]. A magistral is a road that is not a part of any other road. A magistral connects all cities along it. For example, road [1,3] in Fig. 2 is a magistral that connects cities 1, 2, and 3; road [3,5] is also a magistral that connects cities 3 and 5. It is known that there are at least 2 magistrals in Flatland. Write a program that inputs the positions of cities in Flatland and outputs a magistral that connects perfectly two cities in Flatland. (Assume that in the test data the number of cities ranges in [1..100] and that all coordinates of city positions range in [0..1000].)

Of course, a formal model for the computer science Flatland Problem is a set of points in the plane that are not collinear simultaneously. Hence, a straightforward mathematical approach to the computer science problem consists in the following steps:

- solving the Sylvester problem;
- extracting algorithm from an existential proof;
- implementing the algorithm.

Please refer [**5, 4**] for a mathematical solution of the Sylvester problem. This mathematical solution leads immediately to the algorithm that searches for a pair of disjoint points $a, b \in F$ such that

$$\min_{c \in F \backslash L(a,b)} d(c, L(a,b)) = \min_{\substack{x \neq y, \, x, y \in F \\ z \in F \backslash L(x,y)}} d(z, L(x,y))$$

where

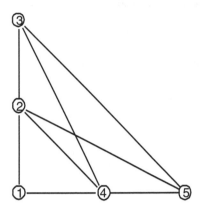

FIGURE 2. Sample map of Flatland

- F stays for the set of points (i.e. cities in Flatland),
- $L(x, y)$ stays for the straight line between disjoint points x and y (i.e. 'extended' roads between cities x and y),
- $d(z, L(x, y))$ stays for the distance between the line $L(x, y)$ and a point z outside this line.

We will not discuss the above mathematical solution for the Flatland Problem further. In contrast, in the next section we develop a computer science solution for the Flatland Problem and exploit it for solving the Sylvester problem.

4. Solving Flatland Problem

We are asked to write a program that finds a magistral in Flatland that connects perfectly two cities. In other words, the program must output a pair of cities 'a' and 'b' such that interval [a,b] is a magistral that does not contain any other city except 'a' and 'b'. Thus, it makes sense to introduce two data types CIT and MAG in which values are all cities and all magistrals in Flatland respectively.

What are the operations that can use arguments of these data types or return values of these data types? Two operations have been discussed already:

- 'freeway' operation fw: MAG → BOOL returns TRUE if the magistral contains two cities at most, and FALSE otherwise;
- 'magistral' operation mg: CIT×CIT → MAG returns a magistral that contains both argument (cities).

It is also natural to assume that we know at least two cities in Flatland

- 'initial cities' constants ia, ib: _→ CIT are simply two fixed cities

so that we can start from these cities and a magistral that contains them.

What else can we use in the solution of the Flatland Problem? Have we used everything that is provided by problem statement? - Of course, not: we have not yet utilized the fact that there are at least two different magistrals in Flatland! How we can use this information? - For example, in the following manner:

```
VAR m: MAG;
VAR a,b: CIT;
m:=mg(ia,ib);
WHILE not fw(m)
DO
    a:=sc(m);
    b:=(lf(m) OR rt(m));
    m:=mg(a,b)
OD
```

FIGURE 3. A preliminary design for the Flatland Problem

- 'side city' operation sc: MAG → CIT returns a city that does not belong to the argument (magistral).

It also makes sense to introduce some other operations:

- 'left' and 'right' operations lf, rt: MAG → CIT; they return the utmost (opposite) cities of the argument (magistral).

For example, for the map depicted in Fig. 2 we (can) have:

- fw([2,3])=FALSE but fw([2,5])=TRUE;
- mg([1,2])=mg([1,3])=mg([2,3])= [1,3];
- ia can be city 1 and ib can be city 2;
- sc(mg([1,2]))=sc([1,3]) and it can be city 4 or city 5;
- lf(mg([1,2]))=lf([1,3]) and it can be city 1 or city 3;
- rt(mg([1,2]))=rt([1,3]) and it can be city 1, if lf([1,3])=3;
- rt(mg([1,2]))=rt([1,3]) and it can be city 3, if lf([1,3])=1.

A preliminary version of a heuristic algorithm for the Flatland Problem is represented in Fig. 3. In this design (_OR_) stays for a non-deterministic choice of an 'appropriate' end of a current magistral. A heuristic behind this design is very simple: let [x, y] be a magistral with utmost end cities x and y; for sure we have only cities x, y, and another city z outside this magistral; hence we can search for a new candidate for a 'freeway' magistral among mg(x,z) and mg(y,z); hopefully, one of these two options leads to success.

5. Solution for Flatland problem

Observe that if some computation of the algorithm in Fig. 3 terminates, then the final value of variable 'm' is a magistral that contains perfectly two cities (due to loop condition 'not fw(m)'). Hence, we should take care regarding algorithm termination. With this idea in mind, let us sketch in brief how computer science proves algorithm/program termination.

There exist a number of techniques for proving termination. One of them was developed by the laureate of the 1978 ACM Turing Award, Robert W. Floyd. His method is based on mappings to well-founded sets. It can be briefly described as follows.

A well-founded set (WFS) is a partially ordered set $(D, \leq)$ without infinite decreasing sequences $d_1 > d_2 > \ldots$. Assume that F is a total mapping from the configurations of a program/algorithm into a well-founded set. If each iteration

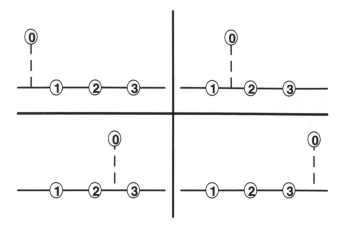

FIGURE 4. Relative positions between cities and magistral

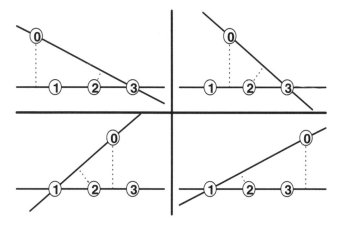

FIGURE 5. How to select next magistral and next side city

of every loop decreases the value of the function F, then it guarantees program termination. (Please refer to a comprehensive textbook [1] for details.)

The above description of method of R. Floyd gives us a clue for how to determinize a non-deterministic assignment b:=(lf(m) OR rt(m)) in the preliminary design: the right choice must decree some value...

Observe that the WHILE-loop is executed if and only if the current magistral is not a freeway, i.e. the magistral contains at least 3 cities. Let these cities be 1, 2, and 3. Hence, there are 4 opportunities for the relative positions of a side city 0 and cities that belong to the magistral (Fig. 4). Observe again, that if to select city b in $\{1,3\}$ so that city 2 lies in between the base of the perpendicular from side city 0 to the line $L(1,3)$, then $d(2, L(0,b)) < d(0, L(1,3))$ (Fig. 5). Hence, it makes sense to determine the choice '(lf(m) OR rt(m))' by another operation:

```
VAR m: MAG;
VAR a,b,c: CIT;
m:=mg(ia,ib);
a:=sc(m);
WHILE not fw(m)
DO
    b:=bs(a,m);
    c:=nx(b,m);
    m:=mg(a,b);
    a:=c
OD
```

FIGURE 6. Final design for Flatland problem

- 'best' operation bs: CIT×MAG → CIT returns the utmost city of the second argument (magistral) such that there exists another city in between this utmost city and the base of the perpendicular from the first argument (side city) to the line of the magistral.

For example, in the Fig. 5, bs(0,[1,3])=3 in the first row and bs(0,[1,3])=1 in the second row. Observe also, that it would be better to use 2 as a side city for new magistral instead of any other. So it also makes sense to define a corresponding operation:

- 'next' city operation nx: CIT×MAG → CIT returns a city of the second argument (magistral) that is closest to the first argument (utmost city).

For example, in the Fig. 5, nx(1,L(1,3))=nx(3,L(1,3))=2 always.

The final design of a heuristic algorithm for the Flatland Problem is represented in Fig. 6. Of course, the final design is not a 'formal' refinement of the preliminary one (Fig. 3). But we hope that readers are convinced by our informal development that leads us from Fig. 3 to Fig. 6. The last thing that we have to do in this section is to prove that the algorithm in Fig. 6 solves the Flatland Problem.

PROPOSITION 1. *If there are at least 2 magistrals in Flatland then the algorithm in Fig. 6 always terminates with a magistral that connects perfectly 2 cities as a final value of the variable 'm'.*

PROOF. Assume that Flatland has at least 2 magistrals.
Let D be

$$\{d(z, L(x,y)) \; : \; [x,y] \text{ is a magistral, and } z \text{ is a city outside } [x,y]\}$$

where (as in the above)

- $L(x,y)$ is the straight line between points x and y,
- $d(z, L(x,y))$ is the distance between $L(x,y)$ and a point z.

Observe that D is a finite (since set of cities is finite) subset of $\mathbf{R}^+ = \{r \in R : r \geq 0\}$. Let $\leq$ be the standard linear order on real numbers $\mathbf{R}$. Then $(D, \leq)$ is a well-founded set.

Let F: CIT×MAG → D be a mapping

$$\lambda[x,y] \in \text{MAG}. \; \lambda z \in \text{CIT}. \; d(z, L(x,y)).$$

Then every iteration of the WHILE-loop in Fig. 6 decreases value of F as follows from definition of operations 'bs' and 'nx' and Fig. 5.

Hence, in accordance with the method of R. Floyd, the algorithm in Fig. 6 always terminates. A final value of the variable 'm' must be a magistral that connects perfectly 2 cities, since the condition of the WHILE-loop is 'not fw(m)', that is, the loop must iterate while the magistral connects 3 or more cities.   □

6. Conclusion

We have designed an algorithm for the Flatland Problem based on some heuristics about useful data types and the method of R. Floyd for algorithm/program termination. Then we proved algorithm correctness and termination formally in terms of method of R. Floyd. Thus, we can claim that our solution of Flatland problem is absolutely computer science in nature and mathematically rigorous at the same time.

Let us remark that without a proof the algorithm cannot be judged as correct, basically because it is just a local heuristic search. Observe also that a formal proof of algorithm correctness implies the solution for mathematical problem of J. Sylvester (in formulation of P. Erdös). Thus, our study provides additional evidence of opportunities to apply the theory of computer science to mathematical problem solving (at the Olympiad level in particular).

Unfortunately, popular computer science contests do not take proofs in to account, and hence the joy, art, and science of mathematical algorithm development and validation remains out of their scope. But we would like to hope that Mathematics and Computer Science faculty can work together toward developing a better attitude to the mathematics contents of computer science contests. We believe that it will enhance both mathematics and computer science university teaching.

The first question is: What things are worthwhile to do? – We think that it worthwhile to work together towards developing a special competition in popular computer science contests for the best algorithm design, analysis and verification, and towards the best constructive solution in Mathematics Olympiads. We are encouraged by Science Olympiads that have competitions both in theory and practice. In particular, International Physics Olympiads for secondary schools [9] promote theoretical and experimental competitions:

> The competition shall be conducted over two days, one for the theoretical examination and one for the experimental examination. There will be at least one full day of rest between the examinations.
>
> The theoretical examination shall consist of three theoretical problems and shall be of five hours total duration.
>
> The experimental examination shall consist of one or two problems and shall be of five hours total duration.

We also remark that it make sense to think about special prizes for theory and practice. The experience of the Academy of Motion Picture Arts and Sciences with plenty of award[1] categories is a good example of diversity of this kind in the arts.

The next question follows: What can be done right now? – We are sure that it is possible to include into the problem sets of computer science contests some advanced

---

[1]For Best Picture, for Best Director, for Best Actor, for Best Actress etc.

problems that really require mathematically rigorous proofs. Simultaneously, the programs of computer science contests should provide post-competition tutorials for team members. These tutorials should address how to solve the advanced problems, and why mathematic proficiency is essential for these problems.

References

[1] Apt K.R., Olderog E.R. Verification of Sequential and Concurrent Programs, Second Edition. Graduate Texts in Computer Science, Springer-Verlag, 1997.

[2] Shilova S.O., Shilov N.V. Etude on theme of Dijkstra. ACM SIGACT News, v.35, n.3, 2004, p.102-108

[3] Shilov N.V., Yi K. How to find a coin: propositional program logics made easy. In Current Trends in Theoretical Computer Science, World Scientific, v. 2, 2004, p. 181-214

[4] Malkevitch J. A Discrete Geometrical Gem. AMS Feature Column Monthly Essays on Mathematical Topic. July-August, 2003, at URL: http://www.ams.org/featurecolumn/archive/index.html.

[5] Pach J., Agarwal P. Combinatorial Geometry. Wiley-Interscience 1995

[6] Sylvester, J. J. Educational Times, 46, No. 383, 156, March 1, 1893.

[7] Assosiation for Computing Machinery – URL http://acmicpc.org ACM International Collegiate Programming Contest – URL http://icpc.baylor.edu/.

[8] Decree On 2003 Annual National Educational Awards of President of Russian Federation (In Russian). January 26, 2005, at URL http://www.kremlin.ru/text/docs/2005/01/83056.shtml.

[9] Statutes of the International Physics Olympiads (version accepted in 1999 in Padova). At URL http://www.jyu.fi/tdk/kastdk/olympiads/

INSTITUTE OF MATHEMATICS, RUSSIAN ACADEMY OF SCIENCE, NOVOSIBIRSK, RUSSIA
E-mail address: shilov61@inbox.ru

DEPARTMENT OF COMPUTER SCIENCE, KOREAN ADVANCED INSTITUTE OF SCIENCE AND TECHNOLOGY, DAEJEON, 305-701, KOREA WHILE ON LEAVE FROM A.P. ERSHOV INSTITUTE OF INFORMATICS SYSTEMS, RUSSIAN ACADEMY OF SCIENCE, NOVOSIBIRSK, RUSSIA
E-mail address: shilov@ropas.kaist.ac.kr & shilov@iis.nsk.su

CBMS Issues in Mathematics Education
Volume **14**, 2007

Curriculum for Teaching How Mathematics is Applied to Real World in Teacher Education Course at a Japanese College

Masahiro Narita

ABSTRACT. Materials for teaching mathematics in primary and secondary education in Japan generally place little emphasis on applying mathematics to various phenomena in the real world. As the result, many prospective teachers in Japan do not know how mathematics is applied in the real world, are not interested in mathematics, and have a negative image of mathematics. Thus, they tend to teach mathematics in inappropriate ways at primary and secondary schools. It is important to change prospective teachers' attitudes toward mathematics. In order to do so, many interesting teaching materials are needed for students in teacher education courses. I have developed teaching materials on examples about applications of elementary linear algebra, such as simple calculations of matrices and vectors related to various phenomena. In this paper, I described the teaching materials and how students have responded to them.

1. Characteristics of mathematics teaching materials at primary and secondary education in Japan

In Japan, in order to introduce new concepts, methods, or formulas, problems about applying mathematical theory to the real world are often used as teaching materials. Teachers organize cooperative problem solving activities at the first class of each chapter of textbooks in almost all mathematics classes in Japanese primary and secondary schools. However, after the first problem solving class, they tend to concentrate on just manipulating symbols, numbers, and formulas, explaining 'boring' proofs of theorems, and memorizing through the exercise of solving many problems.

2. Attitudes toward mathematics of Japanese prospective and in-service teachers

The results of the study of IEA (The International Association for the Evaluation of Educational Achievement) and OECD-PISA (Organisation for Economic Co-operation and Development) show the following attitudes of Japanese in-service teachers toward mathematics.

- Many Japanese in-service teachers see mathematics as having made little progress or few new discoveries,
- They think mathematics is just like a set of puzzles and that mathematics is not useful and has nothing to do with real world problems. The above negative images are also found among Japanese prospective teachers (Narita 1992).

3. The overall aim of my research including this paper

The overall aim of my research including this paper is to develop, evaluate, improve, and spread teaching materials that develop better images of mathematics for all people. I divide the notations of 'better' images of mathematics into the following two classes:

(1) interesting
    (i) entertaining, amusing
    (ii) wonder
    (iii) beautiful
(2) useful
    (i) help real world problem solving using mathematical thinking
    (ii) describing phenomena by modeling
    (iii) tools for simulation

I have been developing teaching materials aimed at the latter category. In order to change people's images of mathematics, it is very important to change school teachers' images of the subject, especially elementary school teachers' images, because if they have better images they try to teach mathematics in the most attractive way possible in their own classes.

4. Case study in mathematics class at Tsuru University

I have been teaching elementary college mathematics as a part-time lecturer for three years at Tsuru University (http://www.tsuru.ac.jp/index_eng.html), which is located about 50 km south-east of the University of Yamanashi and enrolls about 3,000 students. In this paper, I will describe my practice of teaching the mathematics class 'General Mathematics C'. Every Tsuru University student must take units from among the subjects 'General Mathematics A' - 'General Mathematics C'. Tsuru University has only one department, the Department of Literature. In addition, the department has five courses: Course of Elementary Education, Course of Japanese Literature, Course of English Literature, Course of Sociology, and Course of Comparative Culture.

Most students of this university generally are not good at mathematics and dislike it according to the journal writings of students in this class.

5. Questionnaire of mathematics subjects and teaching contents in high schools

The profile of the students who enroll 'General Mathematics C' is as follows:
(a) enrollment : 116 students
(b) taking the last examination : 103 students
(Freshman: 0, Sophomore: 64, Junior: 30, Senior: 9)

(Course of Elementary Education: 84, Course of Japanese Literature: 8, Course of English Literature: 5, Course of Sociology: 6, and Course of Comparative Culture: 0). Most students are in the teacher education course.

On October 12, 2004 (the second day of this class), I used a questionnaire (N = 91) to investigate the subjects studied, their teaching contents, and the self estimation of the extent of understanding of these areas in high schools.

In Japan, 'The Course of Study' of the Monbusho (MEXT:Ministry of Education, Culture, Sports, Science and Technology) has much influence on making the curriculum at each high school. The major subjects at high schools are described in 'The Course of Study'. They are the following six subjects.

(a) 'Mathematics I' (compulsory)
(b) 'Mathematics II' (not compulsory, but many students who want to enter departments of human or social sciences take this subject)
(c) 'Mathematics III' (not compulsory, but many students who want to enter departments of mathematics, natural sciences, or medicine take this subject)
(d) 'Mathematics A' (not compulsory, but many students take this subject)
(e) 'Mathematics B' (not compulsory, but many students who want to enter departments of human or social sciences take this subject)
(f) 'Mathematics C' (not compulsory, but many students who want to enter departments of mathematics, natural sciences, or medicine take this subject)

The results of the investigation show the following.

(a) The teaching contents of 'Mathematics II' include elementary differentiation and integration (drawing graphs using minimal and maximal values, integrals, integration and areas). Eighty students studied this subject, but only 24 (30%) of them responded that they understood the contents.
(b) The teaching contents of 'Mathematics III' include the notion of limits, intermediate differentiation and integration (trigonometry functions, power functions, and logarithm functions). Fifteen students studied this subject, but only 5 (33%) of them responded that they understood the contents.
(c) The teaching contents of 'Mathematics C' include the notions and calculation of matrices and simultaneous linear equations. Thirteen students studied this subject, but only 6 (45%) of them responded that they understood the contents.

6. Outline of the class 'General Mathematics C' at Tsuru University

The above results show that many students who enroll in 'General Mathematics C' generally studied differentiation and integration AND failed to understand, while only 12% of them studied the calculation of matrices and simultaneous linear equations, so many of the students have relatively few negative images of this field. Moreover, this field contains a variety of fun-like puzzles when solving simultaneous linear equations by Gauss-Jordan elimination, as well as many applications to real world applications. Thus, I developed teaching materials that have the following characteristics: (1) to minimize the emphasis on the skills of mathematical calculation, and (2) to introduce mathematical modeling using matrices and let students feel the usefulness of mathematical thinking in the real world, (3) to enable students to participate and understand without the help of technology, such as computers or LCD projectors. Also, I taught very slowly and did review in every class because many students have failed to understand from the 'high-speed' lectures at their high schools.

The following is the outline of the teaching contents of 'General Mathematics C'

(a) Gauss-Jordan elimination of simultaneous linear equations
(b) Addition, subtraction, and multiplication of matrices
(c) Application example (1): Describing and predicting using the theory of Markov chains without explicit expressions of probability
(d) Application example (2): Application of linear code (parity-check and Hamming code, error detecting/correcting code)
(e) How to write a report
(f) Examination on matrices and the calculation of Gauss-Jordan elimination.

6-1. Application example 1. Describing and predicting using the theory of Markov chains without explicit expression of probability

These materials are arranged from the example in Bradley, et al. (1986). However, there is no need to recall or to restudy the notion and calculation of probability in my teaching materials. The usual teaching materials of Markov chains use the notion of probability, but this seems too complicated for the students in the teacher education course of Tsuru University. Consequently, I modified the materials so that they do not need the notation and expressions of probability.

Supplement 1 shows a part of the teaching materials.

6-2. Application example 2. Error detecting/correcting code (Error correcting system of digital audio system such as audio-CD, CD-ROM, DVD, etc.)

Nowadays, everybody uses digital equipment, such as computers, cellular phones, audio-CD players, CD-ROM, DVD, IC audio recorders, and similar devices.

These teaching materials are aimed at letting students understand how the digital coding systems manage 'noise' effectively. Because of the limitation of abilities in the manipulations of symbols and the mathematical thinking of students, I only show how the systems use parity-check and Hamming code work, and I describe the outline about other code.

Supplement 2 shows a part of the teaching materials.

7. Excerpts from the journal writing of students

I request all students to reflect and write journal entries about the activities at the end of every class. The followings are examples of writing.

7-1. About application example 1. Describing and predicting using the theory of Markov chains without explicit expression of probability.

- It is interesting to analyze moving population problem using mathematics. I want to study by other books at my home town by similar method.
- It's very interesting. My guess was (d), but the correct answer was (e). I have never thought of that.
- This kind of mathematics and its applications are helpful when I enter a company. That idea is useful for decision making, for example, decision on where I should open a store.

- I understood the methods, but the result surprised me. I will read more books on this problem during the winter vacation.

7-2. About application example 2. Error detecting/correcting code (Error correcting system of digital audio systems such as audio-CD, CD-ROM, DVD, etc.)

- I enjoyed your explanation about the system of computers. The principles of parity check is especially interesting.
- I am interested in music, so it is easy to study and understand.
- I am impressed and interested in that some machines for daily use work in accordance with mathematics principles.

7-3. At the end of all classes.

- I feel I am beginning to like mathematics during the half year.
- I have a sense of fulfillment that I have been doing math well, and I enjoyed the classes.
- Your explanation is courteous and the pace of the classes is not too fast. I am very bad at mathematics but your lecture let me understand.
- I am very surprised to study absolutely different way of calculation from that I know. This method was difficult for me, but my brains were trained well.

The above descriptions show that the many students welcome the developed teaching materials.

8. Discussion for further research

I explained about the teaching materials on the calculation of matrices and its applications to the real world, and I described how students responded in their journal writing.

For further progress of the research, the following should be done.

(a) Development of teaching materials requiring less mathematical understanding and skills in other fields.

(b) Preparation of technology, such as laptop computers, graphing calculators, and LCD projectors.

(c) Similar education for in-service teachers

References

[1] Ian Bradley and Ronald L. Meek(1986). *Matrices and Society*: Matrix Algebra and Its Applications in the Social Sciences. , Princeton University Press

[2] Narita, Masahiro(1992). Images on Mathematics of Prospective Teachers in Department of Education at the University of Yamanashi. Research Reports of the Department of Education, University of Yamanashi. pp.127-130 (in Japanese)

Supplement 1: Modeling the movement of inhabitants between two districts (an application of Markov chains without using the notion of probability)

Assumptions:

(1) The number of inhabitants in the city and in the suburbs is one million people.
(2) The proportion of the inhabitants who move from the suburbs to the city next year is 12%, while the proportion of the inhabitants who move from the city to the suburbs next year is 8%.
(3) The moving proportions do not change.
(4) Each decision of the inhabitant in choosing the place of next year's residence is independent.

After sufficiently many years, 100 years for example, what will be populations of two districts? Which expectation do you think is true?

(a) All people concentrating in the city.
(b) All people concentrating in the suburbs.
(c) The numbers of inhabitants do NOT converge.
(d) The numbers of inhabitants converge in accordance with the first year's numbers.
(e) The numbers of inhabitants converge NOT in accordance with the first year's numbers.

Case1: $x_0 = 800, y_0 = 200$
Case2: $x_0 = 200, y_0 = 800$
Case 3: $x_0 = 600, y_0 = 400$

Consideration

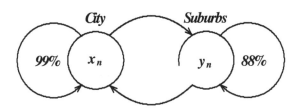

where x_n and y_n denote populations of the city and the suburbs, respectively, after n years.

Outline of writing on a blackboard

** Case1

$x_0 = 800$

$x_1 = 0.92x_0 + 0.12y_0 \approx 760$

$x_2 = 0.92x_1 + 0.12y_1 \approx 728$

$x_3 = 0.92x_2 + 0.12y_2 \approx 702$

$x_{n+1} = 0.92x_n + 0.12y_n$
......

$x_{10} \approx 622$

$x_{20} \approx 602$

$x_{50} \approx 600$

$x_{100} \approx 600$

$y_0 = 200$

$y_1 = 0.08x_0 + 0.88y_0 \approx 240$(using calculator)

$y_2 = 0.08x_1 + 0.88y_1 \approx 272$

$y_3 = 0.08x_2 + 0.88y_2 \approx 298$

$y_{n+1} = 0.08x_n + 0.88y_n$(generalized form)
......

$y_{10} \approx 378$

$y_{20} \approx 398$

$y_{50} \approx 400$

$y_{100} \approx 400$(convergence)

** Case2

$x_0 = 200$

$x_1 = 0.92x_0 + 0.12y_0 \approx 280$

$x_2 = 0.92x_1 + 0.12y_1 \approx 344$

$x_3 = 0.92x_2 + 0.12y_2 \approx 395$

$x_{n+1} = 0.92x_n + 0.12y_n$
......

$x_{10} \approx 557$

$x_{20} \approx 595$

$x_{50} \approx 600$

$x_{100} \approx 600$

$y_0 = 800$

$y_1 = 0.08x_0 + 0.88y_0 \approx 720$(using calculator)

$y_2 = 0.08x_1 + 0.88y_1 \approx 656$

$y_3 = 0.08x_2 + 0.88y_2 \approx 605$

$y_{n+1} = 0.08x_n + 0.88y_n$(generalized form)
......

$y_{10} \approx 443$

$y_{20} \approx 405$

$y_{50} \approx 400$

$y_{100} \approx 400$(convergence to same values)

** Let's try by other primary conditions.

** x_{100} will converge to 600 while y_{100} will converge to 400, even if you start from any initial values.

** Reason

Let $\mathbf{p}_n = (x_n y_n)$ and $A = (0.92 \quad 0.08 // 0.12 \quad 0.88)$

$\mathbf{p}_0 = (800 \quad 200)$

$\mathbf{p}_1 = \mathbf{p}_0 A$

$\mathbf{p}_2 = \mathbf{p}_1 A = (\mathbf{p}_0 A)A = \mathbf{p}_0 A^2$

$\mathbf{p}_3 = \mathbf{p}_2 A = (\mathbf{p}_0 A^2)A = \mathbf{p}_0 A^3$

......

$\mathbf{p}_{100} = \mathbf{p}_{99} A = (\mathbf{p}_0 A^{99})A = \mathbf{p}_0 A^{100}$

$\mathbf{p}_n = \mathbf{p}_0 A^n$(generalized form) $\cdots\cdots (*)$

$A = \begin{pmatrix} 0.92 & 0.08 \\ 0.12 & 0.88 \end{pmatrix}$

$$A^2 = \begin{pmatrix} 0.856 & 0.144 \\ 0.216 & 0.784 \end{pmatrix}$$

$$A^3 = \begin{pmatrix} 0.805 & 0.195 \\ 0.293 & 0.707 \\ \cdots\cdots \end{pmatrix}$$

$$A^{10} = \begin{pmatrix} 0.643 & 0.357 \\ 0.536 & 0.464 \\ \cdots\cdots \end{pmatrix}$$

$$A^{20} = \begin{pmatrix} 0.605 & 0.395 \\ 0.593 & 0.407 \\ \cdots\cdots \end{pmatrix}$$

$$A^{30} = \begin{pmatrix} 0.600 & 0.400 \\ 0.599 & 0.401 \\ \cdots\cdots \end{pmatrix}$$

$$A^{100} \approx \begin{pmatrix} 0.6 & 0.4 \\ 0.6 & 0.4 \end{pmatrix}$$

$$\mathbf{p}_{100}\mathbf{p}_0 A^{100} \approx (x_0 \; y_0) \begin{pmatrix} 0.6 & 0.4 \\ 0.6 & 0.4 \end{pmatrix} = (0.6(x_0 + y_0) \; 0.4(x_0 + y_0)) = (600 \; 400)$$

As a result $\mathbf{p}_{100}$ is not dependent on the initial value and constant.

Supplement 2: Error detecting/correcting code
(An error correcting system of digital audio system such as audio-CD, CD-ROM, DVD)

**Error correcting code
* multiple sending
If we send the same messages three times we can locate the message influenced by noise and correct it. For example, if the message is 1101, then, we send 110111011101 as a code word. If the error occurs one or fewer times, then we can correct the error.
* parity check
*Hamming Code((7, 4, 3)- Hamming Code)

$$H = \begin{pmatrix} 1 & 0 & 1 \\ 1 & 1 & 1 \\ 1 & 1 & 0 \\ 0 & 1 & 1 \\ 1 & 0 & 0 \\ 0 & 1 & 0 \\ 0 & 0 & 1 \end{pmatrix}$$

Let the message words as $\mathbf{x}$ that satisfy $\mathbf{x}H = \mathbf{0}$ (mod 2). Message words are as follows and total numbers of the messages is 16.

$\mathbf{x}_1 = (0\ 0\ 0\ 0\ 0\ 0\ 0)$

$\mathbf{x}_2 = (1\ 0\ 0\ 0\ 1\ 0\ 1)$

$$\mathbf{x}_3 = (0\ 1\ 0\ 0\ 1\ 1\ 1)$$
$$\mathbf{x}_4 = (0\ 0\ 1\ 0\ 1\ 1\ 0)$$
$$\mathbf{x}_5 = (0\ 0\ 0\ 1\ 0\ 1\ 1)$$

$$\mathbf{x}_6 = (1\ 1\ 0\ 0\ 0\ 1\ 0)$$
$$\mathbf{x}_7 = (1\ 0\ 1\ 0\ 0\ 1\ 1)$$
$$\mathbf{x}_8 = (1\ 0\ 0\ 1\ 1\ 1\ 0)$$
$$\mathbf{x}_9 = (0\ 1\ 1\ 0\ 0\ 0\ 1)$$
$$\mathbf{x}_{10} = (0\ 1\ 0\ 1\ 1\ 0\ 0)$$
$$\mathbf{x}_{11} = (0\ 0\ 1\ 1\ 1\ 0\ 1)$$

$$\mathbf{x}_{12} = (0\ 1\ 1\ 1\ 0\ 1\ 0)$$
$$\mathbf{x}_{13} = (1\ 0\ 1\ 1\ 0\ 0\ 0)$$
$$\mathbf{x}_{14} = (1\ 1\ 0\ 1\ 0\ 0\ 1)$$
$$\mathbf{x}_{15} = (1\ 1\ 1\ 0\ 1\ 0\ 0)$$

$$\mathbf{x}_{16} = (1\ 1\ 1\ 1\ 1\ 1\ 1)$$

* B.C.H.code (Bose-Chaudhuri-Hocquenghem Code)
* Reed-Solomon Code

FACULTY OF EDUCATION AND HUMAN SCIENCES, THE UNIVERSITY OF YAMANASHI, TAKEDA, KOFU, 400-8510, JAPAN

E-muil address: narita@yamanashi@ac.jp

CBMS Issues in Mathematics Education
Volume **14**, 2007

Workshop in Excel

Deane Arganbright, Erich Neuwirth, and Robert S. Smith

ABSTRACT. This hands-on computer workshop illustrates how spreadsheets can be use creatively in teaching mathematics to study a surprising range of significant mathematical concepts and models via *Microsoft Excel*, the principal mathematical tool of the workplace. Participants learn how to use Excel to create dynamic graphic displays that include animation.

1. Introduction

The electronic spreadsheet, of which *Microsoft Excel* is the leading version, is an excellent tool for the study of mathematics, mathematical modeling, and mathematical visualization. It can fit naturally into the university mathematics classroom for a wide variety of courses, providing both students and teachers with new conceptual insights, and giving students valuable experience in using the primary mathematical tool of the workplace. This workshop is a very brief introduction to some of the tools, techniques, and ideas that are particularly useful in the use of *Excel* in teaching mathematical topics. Because of time constraints we are only able to illustrate a few of these. Two Web sites that provide additional illustrations and discussions of educational uses of spreadsheets are [**2**], [**4**], and [**5**].

2. Euler's Method

Our first example illustrates Euler's method for approximating the solution to an initial value problem of the form $y' = f(x, y)$, $y(x_0) = y_0$. As an illustration we use the initial value problem: $y' = x + y$, $y(0) = 1$.

In Euler's method we start from an initial point (x_0, y_0) and repeatedly increase the x-value by a chosen step size, dx. We approximate the resulting change in y by traveling along the tangent line whose slope is given by $f(x_n, y_n)$, so that the change in y is given by $dy = y'dx$. Thus, at step n the new approximation is obtained from the old one as $y_{n+1} = y_n + y_n'dx$, or "new y" = "old y" + "change in y". We first enter headings for our output, the step size dx, and the initial values of x and y (Fig. 1).

We now will describe the subsequent steps by which we create the numerical output of Figure 2. We show the underlying formulas in Figure 3.

In the third column we compute the slope at the initial point as the sum of the x- and y-values. We do this by producing the formula =A4+B4 in Cell C4.

	A	B	C
1	dx		0.1
2			
3	x	y	y'
4		0	1
5			

FIGURE 1

	A	B	C
1	dx	0.1	
2			
3	x	y	y'
4	0	1	1
5	0.1	1.1	1.2
6	0.2	1.22	1.42
7	0.3	1.362	1.662
8	0.4	1.5282	1.9282
9	0.5	1.72102	2.22102

FIGURE 2

	A	B	C
1	dx	0.1	
2			
3	x	y	y'
4	0	1	=A4+B4
5	=A4+$B$1	=B4+$B$1*C4	=A5+B5
6	=A5+$B$1	=B5+$B$1*C5	=A6+B6
7	=A6+$B$1	=B6+$B$1*C6	=A7+B7
8	=A7+$B$1	=B7+$B$1*C7	=A8+B8
9	=A8+$B$1	=B8+$B$1*C8	=A9+B9

FIGURE 3

However, we want to emphasize that the best approach is <u>not</u> to type in formulas via cell locations. Rather, we create the formula by a "gesturing" method.

Thus, we first type in an = sign to indicate that we are entering a formula. We then use the mouse to click on the cell containing the value for x. We do not need to refer to the cell location. *Excel* does this for us. We then type the + sign and click on the y-value. Finally, we press the Enter key to complete the process for us.

Excel computes the value of our formula using the value of the cells that are referenced. This value appears in the cell. The underlying formula for the current cell appears in the formula bar. We have created the formula as the sum "two cells to the left" + "cell to the left".

We now enter formulas to compute the next iteration of our process. We begin by using the gesturing process to compute the new value of x by adding dx to the previous value of x (Fig. 5). However, in doing this we should think ahead. We will want to repeat this step in future replications, but while the previous value of x will change each time, the step size remains fixed. To ensure this will happen when we copy a formula, after we click in the cell for dx as we create the formula, we press the F4 key. This supplies $ signs to the column and row components of the cell reference that will serve to make the cell reference absolute. It will not be changed when we copy the formula.

Next, in the y -column we compute the new value of y as the sum of the previous value of y (cell above, relative) and the product of the step-size (absolute) and the previous value of y' (cell to the right and above, relative).

We have generated the approximation(x_1, y_1). We now want to evaluate y' at this point. We could enter the formula as we did above. Instead, since it is really the same expression as before, we will copy the previous formula for y'. We first click on the cell to be copied. There we see a small box, called a *fill handle*, in the lower right corner of the cell. To copy the formula, we use the mouse to place the pointer on the fill handle, where we see the large white cross turn into a thin black cross. We hold down on the left mouse button and drag it down into the next cell.

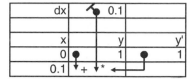

FIGURE 4   FIGURE 5

The copy command treats the locations for x and y as relative locations, or as "two cell to the left" + "cell to the left", that are updated as we copy.

Now that we have completed a second row, it expresses that way that all following rows are generated. We can just copy these expressions down their respective columns. To do this we use the mouse to click in the center of the left cell in the second row of output, hold down on the left mouse button and move to the right. This highlights, or selects, the cells in that row. We now release the mouse button, place the pointer on the fill handle in the lower right corner of the highlighted block, and drag it down as far as we wish to go.

We obtain the numerical output shown in Figure 2. The display of the underlying formulas in Figure 3 shows how the copy process treats relative and absolute references.

While we create spreadsheet formulas for algorithms and models in a very natural way, the standard display of formulas provides a rather inadequate way to describe the creation process. In [2] Neuwirth and Arganbright have developed an alternate way of describing formulas that corresponds to our gesturing approach to model creation. Thus, the new x (Fig. 4) is the sum of the previous x (cell above, relative) and the value of dx (absolute). The new y (Fig. 5) is the sum of previous y (cell above, relative) and the product of dx (absolute) and the previous y' (cell above and to the right, relative). A similar diagram can be created to show the computation for the derivative as the sum of the two cells to the left. We can indicate the copy process by using heavy shading for the cells that are copied and light shading for the cells into which they are copied. These arrow diagrams are not part of *Excel*.

Once our spreadsheet model is created, we can vary the value of initial condition or the step size and see the ensuing results as the spreadsheet is immediately recomputed. We can change the differential equation by entering a new formula into the initial cell of the y' column and copying it.

We now illustrate the algorithm by creating an interactive graphic display within the worksheet. To show the steps of the algorithm we use the mouse to highlight the block of (x, y)-values and then click on the chart wizard button. In *Excel* graphs are called charts. This produces a series of four dialog boxes. In the first we choose the xy (scatter) chart. It plots the (x, y) Cartesian coordinates and connects consecutively listed points by straight line segments. We choose the option in the lower left corner that will show both the markers and the connecting line segments.

After we finish with the first dialog box we click on the Next button to go to Step 2. When we are finished there, we again click the Next button and go to Step 3. There we can adjust gridlines, legends, and other features

After completing the process, we click on the Finish button of Step 4 and obtain a graph like the one in Figure 6. Our chart will be updated as we change

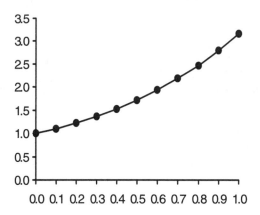

FIGURE 6

	A	B	C	D	E
1	dx	0.1			
2					
3	x	y	y'	x	y
4	0	1	1	0	1
5	0.1	1.1	1.2	0.01	1.0101
6	0.2	1.22	1.42	0.02	1.020403
7	0.3	1.362	1.662	0.03	1.030909
8	0.4	1.5282	1.9282	0.04	1.041622
9	0.5	1.72102	2.22102	0.05	1.052542

FIGURE 7

any of the parameters or other aspects of our model. In teaching, this allows us to demonstrate aspects of an algorithm by varying parameters and seeing the results visually. The graph can be resized and reformatted to adjust many features to improve its appearance.

To show how Euler's approximation relates to the actual solution, it is helpful to display the true solution in the same chart. To do this we first obtain the analytical solution, $y = 2e^x - x - 1$. To graph this we generate x-values in steps of size 0.01 in one column, use our gesturing technique to enter a formula for y at the top of the column to the right (Fig. 7), and copy it down the right column. Figures 7 and 8 show the output and the generating formulas.

Next we use the mouse to click in the center of the first cell in the x-column, hold down on the left mouse button, and drag the mouse to select the entire block of the (x, y) values. Then we position the mouse pointer on an edge of the selected block, hold down on the left mouse button, drag the block into the chart, and release the mouse button. When the Paste Special dialog box appears, we click in the New Series and the Y values in Columns circles, and tick the Categories (X values) in First Column box.

Since we are plotting both (x, y) point markers and connecting line segments, the resulting display is not ideal. To adjust this aspect, we right click on the new

	D	E
1		
2		
3	x	y
4	0	=2*EXP(D4)-D4-1
5	=0.01+D4	=2*EXP(D5)-D5-1
6	=0.01+D5	=2*EXP(D6)-D6-1
7	=0.01+D6	=2*EXP(D7)-D7-1
8	=0.01+D7	=2*EXP(D8)-D8-1
9	=0.01+D8	=2*EXP(D9)-D9-1

FIGURE 8

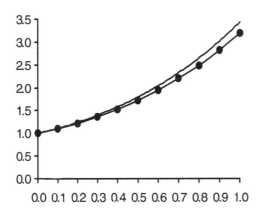

FIGURE 9

curve in the chart. In the resulting option box, we click on the option: Format Data Series.

In the resulting dialog box we click on the Patterns tab, change the Line color to red and increase its thickness. We also click on the option, None, for Marker. The resulting display is shown in Figure 9.

Now we can see what is happening. The approximation diverges further and further from the true solution in each step. Using this model in teaching, we can study the effect of changing the step size, dx. In Figure 9 we show the result for $dx = 0.1$. We will get a better approximation with $dx = 0.01$, but to do this we need ten times as many points to obtain the approximate solution over the same interval. At this stage in the classroom we can discuss the strengths and weakness of this approach and consider more sophisticated algorithms, which we then can implement in *Excel*.

Our model will be even more effective in our teaching if we can change the value of dx continuously. Surprisingly *Excel* gives us ways to do essentially this. We will connect the value of dx to a scroll bar or slider. In *Excel* these can only take on non-negative integer values. So in Cell C1 we enter an integer (here 10) and obtain the value of dx by dividing this value by 100 (Figures 10-11). Then as the value of C1 varies from 0 to 50 in steps of size 1, dx varies from 0 to 0.5 in

	A	B	C
1	dx	0.1	10

	A	B	C
1	dx	=C1/100	10

FIGURE 10   FIGURE 11

	A	B	C	D	E	F
1	n	2			N		3
2						
3	deg	t	r	x	y	Y
4	0	0	1	1	0	0
5	1	0.017453	0.999391	0.999239	0.017442	0.017442
6	2	0.034907	0.997564	0.996956	0.034814	0.034814
7	3	0.05236	0.994522	0.993159	0.052049	#N/A
8	4	0.069813	0.990268	0.987856	0.069078	#N/A

FIGURE 12

steps of 0.01. To create the toolbar, we click on the command menu View and tick Control Toolbox.

In the toolbar that is produced we first ensure that the Design Mode button (upper left) is selected. Then we click on the scroll bar button. We move the mouse to where we want the scroll bar located, hold down on the left mouse button, drag out the outline of a scroll bar, and release the button.

To create a link between the scroll bar and our model, we right click inside the scroll bar that is generated and choose the option Properties. There we click in the box to the right of Linked Cell and type in C1. We also set the maximum size for the linked cell to 50. We then click on the upper left button of the Control Toolbox toolbar to exit the design mode.

Now the scroll bar is linked to the value of dx. When we move the slider on the scroll bar we see the effect of continuous changes in dx.

3. Graphs of Polar and Parametric Equations

For a second example we will create an animated graph of a polar equation. Both the process and the resulting model closely follow the traditional classroom approach to the study of these equations, but provide much more versatility in what teachers and students can do in graphing. We create the graph by computing polar coordinates (r, t) and converting them to Cartesian coordinates by the equations $x = r\cos(t)$ and $y = r\sin(t)$. Here we produce a graph for $r = \cos(nt)$, where n is a parameter of our spreadsheet model set in Cell B2.

Following the model in Figures 12 and 13, we begin by generating degrees in steps of size 1 down the first column. In adjacent columns we will generate values of t (in radians), r, x, and y. We discuss the use of an additional column, Y, later.

To convert from degrees to radians, we type =radians(, click on the cell to the left, type), and press the Enter key. Another way is to use the Insert, Functions commands. This keeps us from needing to memorize function names and leads us through the steps required to create the function. We generate the value of r as $\cos(nt)$ in a similar way, pressing the F4 key when we click on the cell containing n to ensure that it becomes an absolute reference.

In the next two columns we compute $r\cos(t)$ and $r\sin(t)$ with all references relative (Fig. 43-44).

	A	B	C	D	E	F
1	n	2			N	3
2						
3	deg	t	r	x	y	Y
4	0	=RADIANS(A4)	=COS($B$1*B4)	=C4*COS(B4)	=C4*SIN(B4)	=IF(A4<$F$1,E4,NA())
5	=1+A4	=RADIANS(A5)	=COS($B$1*B5)	=C5*COS(B5)	=C5*SIN(B5)	=IF(A5<$F$1,E5,NA())
6	=1+A5	=RADIANS(A6)	=COS($B$1*B6)	=C6*COS(B6)	=C6*SIN(B6)	=IF(A6<$F$1,E6,NA())
7	=1+A6	=RADIANS(A7)	=COS($B$1*B7)	=C7*COS(B7)	=C7*SIN(B7)	=IF(A7<$F$1,E7,NA())
8	=1+A7	=RADIANS(A8)	=COS($B$1*B8)	=C8*COS(B8)	=C8*SIN(B8)	=IF(A8<$F$1,E8,NA())

FIGURE 13

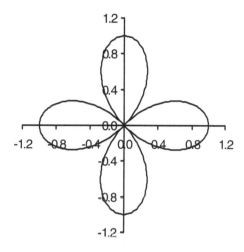

FIGURE 14

All that remains is to copy the formulas down through 360 rows. We do this using the drag technique. However, since we have already generated values of n through 360, we can highlight the cells in the top row and double-click on the fill button and all of the values will be generated.

Next, we highlight the columns of x- and y-values and create an xy-chart just as before, except this time we choose only to plot the connecting lines and not the point markers. In Figure 14 we see the resulting curve, and experiment with changes in the value of n.

We conclude this example by demonstrating one more effective use of a scroll bar. Before doing this we first use *Excel*'s built-in IF function to generate y-values only for those points whose degree measure is less than a value N that we enter in Cell F1. The formula shown is interpreted as "IF degrees is less than N, THEN reproduce the y-value, ELSE generate the "not available", NA(), value. We then copy to generate the output. We next drag the new column into the chart as another y-series, after which we delete the original curve. The curve in Figure 15 uses $N = 250$. Notice that only the points for degrees less than the value of N are plotted.

We now create a scroll bar linked to the cell containing N and set its largest value to 360. As the scroll bar is moved we see the curve traced out continuously. The display can be even more effective if we remove the original curve to see only the heavy red one that is being produced. The use of the scroll bar enables students

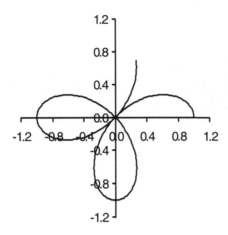

FIGURE 15

to examine the process of drawing the curve, in addition to seeing the completed drawing. Additional curve sketching ideas are found in [1], [2], and [3].

We also can explain the steps in our construction via arrow diagrams (Fig. 16-18).

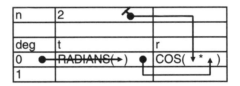

FIGURE 16

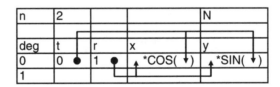

FIGURE 17

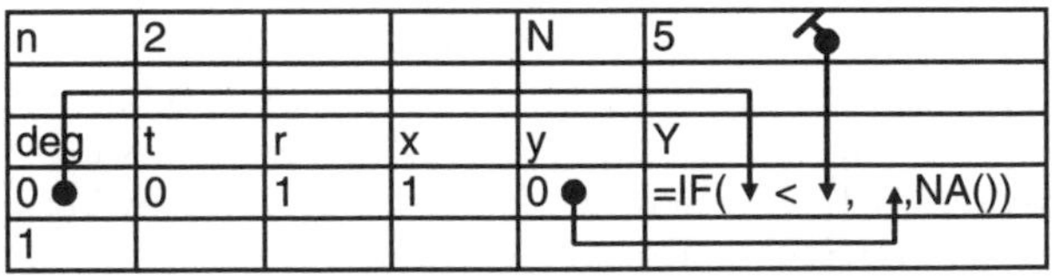

n	2			N	5	
deg	t	r	x	y	Y	
0	0	1	1	0	=IF(▼ < ▼, ▲NA())	
1						

FIGURE 18

The two examples in this workshop where chosen to provide workshop participants with some fundamental skills for using spreadsheets in teaching mathematics. Further discussions of the wide range of other possibilities and applications may be found in the references. Animation techniques are discussed in more depth in [2] and [3].

References

[1] D. Arganbright, *Practical Handbook of Spreadsheet Curves and Geometric Constructions*, CRC Press, 1993.

[2] D. Arganbright, Deane. *Enhancing Mathematical Graphical Displays in Excel through Animation*, Spreadsheets in Education, Vol. 2, No. 1, Nov. 2005, http://www.sie.bond.edu.au/.

[3] E. Neuwirth and D. Arganbright, *The Active Modeler: Mathematical Modeling with Microsoft Excel*, Brooks-Cole, 2004.

[4] E. Neuwirth, *Web site on educational applications of spreadsheets*, http://sunsite.univie.ac.at/Spreadsite/.

[5] S. Sugden, *Spreadsheets in Education*, Bond University (Australia) Web site on educational uses of spreadsheets: http://www.sie.bond.edu.au/.

DEPARTMENT OF MATHEMATICS, KOREA ADVANCED INSTITUTE OF SCIENCE AND TECHNOLOGY, DAEJEON 305-701, KOREA
E-mail address: arganbright@math.kaist.ac.kr

FACULTY OF COMPUTER SCIENCE, UNIVERSITY OF VIENNA, VIENNA, A-1010, AUSTRIA
E-mail address: erich.neuwirth@univie.ac.at

DEPARTMENT OF MATHEMATICS AND STATISTICS, MIAMI UNIVERSITY, OXFORD, OH 45056-3414, USA
E-mail address: smithrs@muohio.edu

Titles in This Series